Dedicated to the countless souls lost at the bottom of the Mediterranean Sea.

CHAPTER 1

I'm winning, blasting my enemies into vapour as I stride through the wilderness, the taste of victory on my tongue. The sound of rustling to the left alerts me to the presence of an enemy, and I lower the little finger of my left hand; my field of vision descends as my character responds to the stimuli, bending its knees, my knees. I raise my arms together to my left, the slight bridge in my middle fingers indicating a firm grip on the virtual firearm, taking aim in the direction of the noise. It only takes a few moments to hone in on my target, hidden as best as possible inside an overturned barrel, but with the tips of the feet protruding conspicuously from its base. Bullets pass through wood. I move my index to trigger the shot without hesitation and the subsequent grunt and moan I immediately hear indicate that the barrel provided little protection.

The smooth feminine voice confirms this. "Enemy down, kill count 17, two minutes 14 seconds remaining." The number inside the little blue rectangle in the corner of my field of vision flickers from 16 to 17.

A slight opening in the spread of the fingers on my right hand indicates forward movement, I open them further and proceed into a sprint, trying to reach the final barrier. If I pass through it in the next two minutes the clock will be extended by a further 10. Another rustle to my right, and in my haste to reach the barrier I have been less than prudent in surveying my surroundings, when I turn my head, I find myself staring down the barrel of a gun. The bang rings out in my ears, and a red liquid starts to drip slowly into my field of vision, obscuring my view of the assailant, the words "game over," flashing neon-green, greet my eyes- followed by:

"17 kills, taken down by player 72: TimWeiber47." I breathe in sharply.

Down after only 17 kills. This will surely affect my ratings, and to be beaten by a 12-year-old kid only rubs salt in the wound. Well, 12 or 13, born in 2047 either way, unless there have been 46 Tim Weibers who had set up accounts before him and TimWeiber47 was the first username that wasn't taken. I remove the sensor gloves from my hands, drop them on my desk, and then finger the back of my headset, locating the release clip and loosening it before lifting the device off my head and placing it on top of the gloves. Free from the drama of the game, my hands are free to pursue their other central purpose. I place a hand on each pushrim, the circular, metal rings that jut out parallel to each wheel, but with a slightly smaller perimeter so as not to touch the floor and pick up dirt, and wheel myself into the corridor of the house. It's been four years since the accident, and in that time I have learned to do many things that once seemed impossible, but I have not learned to walk again, another barrier I haven't managed to reach. The games have become an escape, once I put on the headset they are so realistic that I forget about my disability.

Have you ever seen a cortical homunculus? It's not a monster from ancient Greece or the character in some myth. But it does look like one. It's that model that you might have seen online of an alien-like humanoid creature, with massive hands and lips, a monstrous tongue, protruding eyes that seem like globes, and a tiny shrivelled body besides. It's basically a model of the human body based on motor or sensory processing, based on how many sensory nerves lead from that part of the body to the brain. Take a look on Google images, type in "3D cortical homunculus." You'll see them.

I have to admit that I was at first repelled by them because they had spindly legs, a bit like mine since the accident. When I found out why the legs were spindly, I started to see them in a different light. Their legs are weak and spindly because, at the end of the day, our legs don't really receive that much sensory information. We order them to walk, to run, to jog, to sit cross-legged or on a chair, but it really doesn't take that many neurons to do so. The hands of the cortical homunculus, in contrast, are so huge because they are so sensitive, because we use them for so many varied, differing and diverse tasks; because playing an instrument or writing a novel or handling tools requires such dexterity, such sensitivity in the slightest of movements. With my sensors, my hands are sensitive enough to control a whole body. In the world of games, with my headset and gloves on, I'm transported to a world where I can walk again.

"Dinner!" my mum's voice comes from the kitchen, just in time, two doors down the corridor. My bedroom is- of course- on the ground floor, for reasons that I hope are obvious. As the smell of stew drifts towards me, I find myself happy that the cortical homunculus also has a large tongue, as the extensive sensory nerves in my mouth will soon be enjoying Mama's cooking. As I roll through the kitchen door, the buzz in my pocket tells me that mum has texted me too, well aware that had I still been in the world of the game her call would have fallen on deaf ears, blocked out by the headset and the sound of gunfire. Many a time, the vibration in my pocket has acted as my call to the kitchen table.

My mother turns around and looks at me in surprise. "Here already? I thought you'd have to finish off blowing up a zombie or something. You're usually not here for a couple of minutes. Always so engaged in your games." I feel a hint of reproach in her voice, but only a hint. She doesn't approve of me spending so many hours locked away in a virtual world. But the accident had been her fault. She had been driving under the influence. The court had said as much. And now I'm in a wheelchair. And she knows. She knows she has no right to tell me in which way I should try to escape my predicament.

"I made your favourite," she says, "C-food stew." And don't I know it? The smell in the kitchen is stronger than in the corridor, and I can't wait to get tucked in. It's called C-food stew, rather than seafood stew, because all of the ingredients are synthesised in a laboratory, so they don't really come from the sea. In reality, there are barely any shellfish, prawns or tuna left in the ocean, they were overfished to near extinction. But thankfully we found ways to grow them in the lab, as evidenced by the bubbling plate my mother sets down on the table before me. My brother appears at the door, my little sister's hand in his. When Mummy's seafood stew is on offer, no one is late for dinner. My siblings sit down at the table and I wheel my chair towards it, already seated. Eternally seated. For the first few minutes, as usual, we're all too busy eating to engage in conversation, sipping at our stew, and nibbling on the bread that accompanies it. Dad works late, so he'll eat his stew on his own when he gets back, but Mum sits with us. Once she has allowed a few minutes of hungry wolfing, she starts with her questions.

I feel as though she feels that dinner time is the only time she can get us together as a family, before I drift off into my games and my brother disappears into his books. She still has plenty of time with my little sister, but she must know that, as her only daughter grows into a teenager, she too will see that time after school, those weekends, her few weeks of holiday, as her own. She too will become possessive of her time, and designate less and less to spend with her parents. And so, once our bellies have received their initial portion of sustenance, dinner time is the time for conversation.

"So how is your latest book, Toby?" my mother asks my little brother, "What have you been reading?"

"It's an alternate history," my brother replies.

"Alternative history?" asks my mum. "What does that mean?"

"Well," says my brother, "it means that you go to some event that happened in the past and you imagine if it had happened differently, if the outcome had been different. And you think about what the repercussions of that would be, what the world would be like today if we had taken a different path."

"Well, that's very interesting, isn't it?" smiles my mum, turning to me and then to my sister, who both are nodding in agreement but saying nothing as our mouths are still full of bread and soup. Mum probably started with my brother because she saw he was the one with an empty mouth at the time.

"So, in this book, what happens differently?" She asks him.

"Well, the book starts at the end of the Second Cold War, with China coming out on top. But I've only just started reading it, so I can't really tell you what the repercussions of that are yet." replies Toby.

"Well, very interesting," says my mum, still smiling, but seemingly reluctant to talk about war in front of my little sister. My sister is now taking more time between spoonfuls, as she knows she may be called upon at any time to speak. Sure enough...

"And what have you got up to today June?" my mother asks her, sweetly.

"I make ickle biccle!" she replies.

"Very good, how lovely!" says my mum. "And are you a big girl on your bike?"

"Yes, I ride round and round," she giggles. No one else around the table knows what ickle biccle is, but apparently she's been making it for the past three weeks.

"Soon you'll be big enough to go cycling beyond the garden, on the roads, your brother can take you!"

"No question which brother..." the words almost escape my lips, but I catch myself at the last second and manage to give a mild cough instead. My mother seems to read my mind, however, and her eyes flicker to me in a way that is almost panicked, her smile flickers. I feel guilty. This is not her fault. Well, in a rather large way it is her fault, but I still feel guilty looking at her panicked eyes. To defuse the tension, I enter the conversation.

"Toby will be a wonderful teacher." I tell my sister, smiling. Then, turning to my mother, I ask her how her day had been.

"Excitement, excitement, excitement." she replies, a hint of sarcasm in her soft voice. "While you're out in the wilderness hunting zombies and saving maidens, I'm taking work calls. But I still found time for a bit of TV and a bath. So I really shouldn't complain."

I look right into her eyes and she looks back. The panic has gone. Good. My guilt subsides. "And your guitar?" I ask her "Did you find any time to practise?"

"I might knock out a few chords after dinner." she replies. "If you take off your headset for long enough to listen and come along to the living room after dinner, you may even hear me singing."

Her tone now is cheeky, without the hint of reproach that her first comment about my gaming held, the comment she made when I first rolled into the kitchen, but the hint is still there. I do like listening to her playing, however, and I've been gaming all evening without cease. She never drinks, not since the accident, and she had to find something else to fill her evenings with. She played guitar as a young girl, so she's taken it up again. And I think it's true that these things never really leave you. All the melodies learnt in her youth have come back to her, and brighten up our living room many an evening. But if I pass by the living room it will have to be brief. My ranking will have taken a hit after losing to Mr Tim Weibers the 47th, and I need to play a few more games today if I'm going to put that right.

In fact, that should be the priority this evening. Mum's guitar can wait until tomorrow, or whenever the next time she plays happens to be.

"Next time." I tell her. "This evening I have an appointment with my zombies."

"Well," she replies softly. "If the undead stand you up, the offer remains open. You know where I'll be."

The truth is that very few of the games I play have anything to do with zombies. Arideth is a fantasy game in which I become an ancient warrior-mage, wandering the netherworlds in search of meaning, choosing between harnessing the power of weaponry or of spells, and whether to use my powers for the benefit of the peasantry, or to ingratiate myself into the high society of the pre mediaeval nobility. Final Facedown III is a multiplayer first person shooter, your opponents are real people who are also plugged into the VirtuWorld. Getting kills is key, but it must be balanced with the ever pressing need to beat the clock. The Evolution of Wildness is one of my favourites.

Most of the animals it features are now extinct; the tiger, the rhino, the snow wolf. Many of its other creatures never truly existed, but are actually idealised versions of how particular animals may have eventually evolved, as determined by complex artificial intelligence simulations that plot random mutations over millions of generations. The animals in the game form packs, they hunt, they flee from other predators, they fight over the right to mate.

When I am a wolf, I have four legs, as an octopus I have eight, each one a finger, my interlocked thumbs guiding them.

But I know my mum doesn't approve of me spending so much time playing these games, so I don't describe them to her like my brother does with his books. And there's something about that that I find... not comforting, but appropriate. The world I share with my mother is the world in which I am a cripple. Restricted in my potential. Bound to my chair. When I enter the VirtuWorld, I become someone different. And that different person... enjoys a degree of privacy. But this person - the one who lives in the physical world - still exists, and still has to make conversation with his mother. After all, it's dinner time.

"And the work calls?" my voice lifts at the end to indicate the question. "Any interesting discussions?"

The question hangs in the air. No one really wants to talk about my mother's work. Not me, not my brother, not my sister, not her.

"Nothing of note." she says wistfully. "Some office gossip. But you guys really don't know my colleagues well enough for it to be interesting. And it's probably a bit too saucy for your sister's young ears."

My mother smirks. Not in a conceited way, but in a way that speaks of some complicity. A private joke between me, my brother, and her, designed to fly over my sister's innocent head. A smirk that says she knows that we have grown beyond some of our youthful innocence. I catch my brother's eye, finding my mild astonishment mirrored back at me. My mother, her gaze flickering between our identical expressions, bursts into a fit of giggles. Despite the implied lewdness behind the joke, the moment seems so innocent, as innocent as my sister's questioning face, her cheeks once again full of soup. Once she succeeds in swallowing it, she too starts to giggle, purely from the joy of seeing her mother's laughter. And when I catch my brother's eye again, our faces are still mirrored - but this time, the mirror reflects a smile. The rest of dinner passes quite quietly. Perhaps because none of us wants to taint the purity of that moment. I roll myself back into my room with a warm feeling in my chest, and yet my face falls into lines of focused concentration. I lift my headset from the desk and clip it into place over my eyes, before pulling on each glove in turn.

For a moment, all I see is darkness, before a sparkling array of stars start to glitter before me, and the words "Welcome to the VirtuWorld" appear in italics, letter after letter materialising on the panorama before me. I should really get back to Final Facedown III and start gaining some of the ground I lost when taken out by TimWeiber47, but I find myself instead saying the words "Open Game. The Evolution of Wildness." Within a minute, I am a leopard, hunting the undergrowth for prey...

CHAPTER 2

Hello, my name is Hakeem Abu Bakar. I am Hausa. My people constitute one of the largest tribes in West Africa. I was born in Northern Nigeria, close to the border of Niger. The border is not heavily policed, and technically, there is free movement between the countries. When my father lived, I occasionally accompanied him to trade with merchants from across the border, so I have spent some time in Niger and picked up a tiny bit of French. Apart from Hausa, English is the language I am confident in, though I can recognise Fulani and Zarma and quote a few Quranic verses in Arabic. My father had two wives, but he has now died. My mother was the second wife, and the first wife has taken the very small inheritance for her children. And so, my mother and my two younger sisters have fallen into difficult times.

The population of Nigeria is not rising like it used to. So many have died from the heat, and so many have fled. The Sahara has spread its tentacles deeper into Niger, now encroaching on Nigeria, and its heats now surpass even the durability of the Tuareg. Sandstorms are regular and the desert is spreading like wildfire. Everybody is thinning. The weather is so hot that crops just die, and livestock too. Hunger reigns and drives people from this land. Hunger and heat. But the journey is not easy, and is not cheap.

Fleeing southward, further into western and central Africa, would provide a respite from the worst of the heat. But temperatures are still hot and rising. Resource wars are commonplace. Real safety lies in Europe, where temperatures are rising, but not apocalyptic. But getting to Europe involves passing through the Sahara Desert, and no man can fathom doing such a thing without help. And help requires money. And so even to be given the opportunity to try to make the crossing; to risk it all in the desert and pass through North Africa to the promised lands of temperate coolness beyond is beyond my reach. And so I sweat, boiling from the heat and from my helplessness.

My younger sister, Fatima, has contracted malaria once again, and we have no medicine for her. Every year there are more mosquitoes. They thrive in heat. My mother, I and my two sisters live together in the same small hut. We have a small solar panel and a battery which provides us with a little electricity, which we use to power the small fan, provide some light to a flickering freestanding bulb in the evenings and charge the one rudimentary mobile phone we share between us. Though I mentioned we live in a hut, don't go imagining that we are rural dwellers with ample space and a collection of goats and chickens, passing out our lives in the midst of a small village in the African bush. This could not be further from the truth. We live in the city of Sokoto, which is large, urban and still densely populated, given the impotence of so many of its residents to flee. Our hut has no garden, and there is no room for us to cultivate our own crops. Within this small parcel of land, there are 30 such huts, each as small as ours, with roofs of corrugated iron or, for those who cannot even afford that, roofs of thatched straw.

Between all 30 huts, which house a total of over a hundred residents, there is only one tap, and the water that comes from it is not guaranteed to be suitable for drinking. There are informal rules about how many five-litre jerry cans each family can take from the tap each week, and this amount fluctuates depending on how much water the tap itself can provide at any given time. It is not a consistently reliable resource. However, given that this is an urban area with no open rivers, streams or lakes in walking distance, it remains our only source. Small plastic packets of water that can be bitten and sucked are sold by the young homeless almajiris that fill the streets. Boys as young as five and six, spending their days running between cars, hoping to hawk a bit of water for less than pennies, sweltering, their ragged stained clothes testament to their desperation. But I don't trust these packets either. Since the recent droughts, the manufacturers have been getting more unscrupulous and friends of mine who drink only from packets have fallen just as ill as others. We drink the water that comes from our communal tap, but boil it first in our small hut, over the small portable stove that fills our living space daily with the smell of kerosene.

Without medication, the symptoms of malaria are brutal, and my sister is currently suffering. The disease causes her to have a high fever, vomit and experience severe shaking chills. She is weak and exhausted, and her body aches all over. She has no appetite and has lost a lot of weight. The disease is especially hard on children, and my sister is only eight years old. We are doing our best to care for her, but we are limited in what we can do. We have no money for medication, and the nearest clinic is miles away. We can only hope that she recovers soon. To comfort her, I tell her stories. The same stories my father told me when I was her age.

"There was once a rich man," I tell her. "He lived in a large house, and was so rich that he ate meat every day."

Despite her tremors and her fever, my sister's eyes grow wide.

"Every day?" she asks incredulously.

"Every day," I confirm. "Every day, this rich man would eat two whole legs of buffalo. His servants would go to the market and ask for 'Two hind legs. Two hind buffalo legs!' " I put on a high-pitched voice and Kano accent to imitate the servant and my sister gives a squeal of pleasure, she loves my voices when I storytell.

"And the servants would cook it and the rich man would eat it." I continue, "But this man could not eat the bones, and so he would walk to the window that overlooked the street below and throw them to the ground. They would fall out of the window and land with a clatter."

"And did he eat the buffalo legs properly?" my sister interrupts me. "Was there any meat left upon them when he threw them from the window?"

"No," I respond. "The man was rich and wasteful, but he really liked buffalo meat and was greedy. He also didn't like the idea of the poor beggars who lived on the streets eating any scraps of meat from the bone. When he threw the bones from the window, all the meat was gone. Now this rich man wanted everyone in the area to know how rich he was. And that meant not only that he lived in the big house and wore fancy clothes, brightly coloured fabric, inlaid with jewels and the finest gold from Timbuktu. But also, that his servants were forbidden to clear up the bones until the end of the week, so that over the course of the week everyone could see the pile of bones grow bigger, knowing that the rich man could afford to eat meat every day. Not only one buffalo leg, but two legs of buffalo."

"He sounds like a strange man," my other sister, Karima, says to me from the corner.

"He was a strange man." I reply. "Now one day, the man heard laughing from his window. High-pitched laughing. But it was night time and he was in bed. And he did not want to rise because he had been in the land of dreaming, and waking to go to the window and look out beneath to find the cause of laughing would make it difficult for him to go back to sleep. And so, he told himself that the laughs had been part of his dream, that he had somehow imagined them. When he woke up in the morning, he was surprised to see... he decided to peek out of his window and investigate... and he was surprised to see that the pile of six buffalo bones... for it was the fourth day of the week... had gone. He called his servant immediately to ask if the bones had been cleared by any of his staff, and the servant told him, 'No'."

I put on the servant's voice again for this single word, and get another giggle.

"So, the man went about his day, hoping that no one would take the absence of bones on the street outside his window as an indication of a reduction in his wealth. He ate his buffalo legs as usual and threw them from the window, and there was no laughter that evening. And three days later, the pile of bones had grown to eight, and the rich man was smiling to himself, happy in the knowledge that those walking by on the street below would know that he was wealthy. But in the early hours of the morning, again he heard laughter from the window. This time, he did not stay in bed, but threw himself out of his comfortable duvets and made his way quickly to the window, looking down onto the street below. He saw a hyena eating his pile of bones. 'Hey!' The man shouted at the hyena, 'Who gave you permission to eat my bones?' "

The voice I fabricate for the rich man *mai arziki* is thick and guttural, formal with a supercilious tone.

"The hyena paused for a moment and a crunching sound echoed through the street as he finished his mouthful.

"He looked up at the rich man. 'Your bones?' he asked incredulously, and laughed, a high-pitched, rapid laugh that also echoed through the street. 'These bones are on the streets, as though they have been discarded.'

"The hyena laughed again. 'Yes,' said the man, increasingly angry, 'and I threw them there after I bought them with my money. You have not asked my permission to eat my bones.

Please leave them. And I will have them cleared at the end of the week. They are not your bones to scavenge.'

"The hyena laughed louder this time, and said, 'I have a proposition for you. We hyenas have a bad reputation. We do not like being seen as thieves. If you come down these stairs and are able to eat this tiny splinter, then I will accept that the bones are yours and will not come again. If you do not, then I see no use you have for them. And so, I will continue enjoying my dinner.' As he said this, the hyena patted a small splinter of bone with his paw.

The man thought over the proposition. Like many rich men, he had a very high opinion of himself, and when challenged to do something, felt the need to prove that he could. He put on his finest spotted robe, so as to outdo the hyena with its elegant polka dots spattered across its fur, and made his way down to the street below. The hyena pushed the splinter that he had indicated towards the man. It was small and white. The rich man saw that the hyena had already completely devoured two of the eight bones, and felt a surge of superiority rush through his body. If this unwashed, vagrant, scavenging creature could crunch through two whole bones without issue, surely he could eat this splinter. But when the rich man tried to swallow the splinter, he began to choke, and soon enough, he lay dead upon the floor."

The topic of death does not scare my sister. Despite her young age, she has seen more than her share of death.

"The hyena continued his dinner as promised, and ate the remaining six buffalo legs. However, he did not eat the body of the rich man immediately. He waited until the morning and talked to the servants of the house, who had always been mistreated, and to the poor beggars on the street, who the rich man had always looked down on. They agreed that his body should be left for all the street to see for seven days, as a reminder that riches are not everything, and on the seventh day - despite the servants having bought no buffalo legs that week- the hyena came back to feast again."

Karima is frowning from the corner.

"And so, the moral of the story is to not be rich?" she asks me, sounding unimpressed. "If we were rich, we could afford medicine for Fatima."

"No," I respond. "The moral of the story is to not be conceited and selfish and proud if you are given wealth. The man in the story had no use for the bones, but he didn't want to share them. If we had the money for medicine, it would be very useful. And if we had medicine that could not cure malaria, but could cure a neighbour's sickness, I hope we would share it with them."

"I loved the story," Fatima tells me in her soft, almost falsetto voice. "I always love your stories," she tells me before she descends into a fit of coughing.

I pour her a small glass of water and bring it to her lips, and the coughing subsides. The wooden door of the hut swings inwards, and my mother stoops and enters the room, a small, very thin cluster of 100 Naira banknotes clutched in one hand, a plastic bag containing a loaf of bread in the other. She looks exhausted. Her feet are dusty and her cheekbones stand out on her face in a way they never had when my father lived, and could provide a little more sustenance. She has been out for the past three and a half hours, and has left the hut in this way multiple times over the past week, always returning with small amounts of money. Small amounts, but still too large to have been gathered by a few hours of begging. When I asked her yesterday where the money came from, she evaded my gaze and told me that Allah provides. I have my own suspicions, which horrify me, but I do not raise them - for my little sister's life hangs in the balance.

"When your father first told me that story, before any of you were born, I also thought mostly about the rich man and his conceitedness." It is obvious that she has been listening at the door. "Hearing it back now. I think more of the hyena's challenge, and all the dead livestock since the latest drought, with their skeletal frames. I wonder if there is a way we can eat their bones without choking."

CHAPTER 3

I sit astride my steed, a muscular horse that trots beneath me, following my direction on its reins. The cobbled road curves off sharply to the right, inclining slightly, and thickets of trees and bushes line either side of the road, concealing any passers-by from visibility. A small bird, perched atop one of the trees, watches me as I ride, but it does not make a sound.

The silence is eerie.

I ride for a while, but there is no sign of anyone else on the road. The only sound is the occasional snap of a twig, or the rustle of leaves in the breeze. I begin to feel as though I am being watched, but every time I look around, there is nothing to be seen but trees and bushes. An expansion of greenery. A questionable labyrinth in which anything could be hidden. The road is boring me. I know I can reach my destination quicker through the foliage. I make my decision and turn off the road, pulling sharply to the left and into the trees. The horse is hesitant at first, but soon follows.

The going is slower through the undergrowth, but I don't mind. I am more alert now, senses heightened, looking for any sign of movement. The horse seems to sense my tension, we move together as one, pushing through the foliage. There are more obstacles to step over or move around. Trees in particular form barriers, with low hanging branches obstructing corridors through the woods as though they were outstretched arms. I begin to question my hastiness. Yes, cutting through the woods means for a shorter distance to travel, but at this speed the journey may well take the same amount of time. But I have committed. I do not turn back, but continue on my course.

A sound. A substantive rustling in the trees, too loud to be made by a bird. I stop abruptly, peering intently in the direction of the noise, and it does not take too long for me to ascertain its source. From behind one of the trees steps a bandit; stained, rusting armour covering his torso, but not his arms and legs, stubby blade in hand. His lip upturned in a snarl, he is eyeing my horse greedily, and drops his knife, his hand flying to the bow on his back. He pulls an arrow from the quiver and nocks the bow in a single, swift movement.

"I mean no harm, fellow traveller," I say cautiously. "I am Arideth. I seek the melancholy fountain; the maiden of mystery awaits me there. Her joyful tears are needed in my potions."

"Your potions will remain unmade," the bandit responds. His voice is gravelly, thin. "The fountain is too far to walk on foot, and you seem to have lost your horse. You could always have paid a fellow traveller to grant you voyage. But it seems you have lost your gold as well. The only question that remains, and only you can answer it, is have you lost your life?"

He pauses for effect and shows some teeth.

"Dismount your steed, drop anything of value, and you may wander to the path again without disturbance. Any other course of action means your death."

"You are most merciful, " I tell him. "I believe your first instruction was to dismount, and I shall do so right away."

'Yes,' I tell myself. Casting the spells takes intricate hand movements that must be executed flawlessly, they rely on muscle memory more than anything. Releasing the reins and maintaining balance on a horse whilst casting them is not to be advised, though sometimes inevitable. Dismounting works to my advantage. I release the reins and make to dismount the horse, but as my feet touch the ground, I bring my fists together and quickly release them, splaying all the fingers, putting myself in spell mode. I quickly, serendipitously, hands still lowered and in the periphery of his vision, twist my wrists, the fingers still splayed, such that my two hands are parallel with one another. I bend the second and third fingers of my right hand and the first and fourth of my left, before flexing my left wrist down as though moving to stroke something and my right wrist up, as though about to push open a door. With my hands in these positions I whisper, "Lentiempo."

Immediately, everything slows, even the sound around me. A falling leaf seems almost static, creeping through the air almost imperceptibly. Though I have sped up my thoughts, and correspondingly slowed the world around me, the restraints of my body remain unchanged. I too move as slowly as the leaf and as the bandit. But I am able to react much more quickly. And the spell has given me some moments in which to think. A quick finish is possible. A simple fire charm will burn the bandit thoroughly and can be cast quicker than the arrow would be released. The initial shock and pain of the charm will surely invoke some bodily reaction, and hopefully that movement will throw the arrow off course. There isn't really time to risk throwing up a shield charm before casting an offensive spell, but if the arrow is thrown off course, my fast reactions will assist me in dodging it.

However, the bandit did offer the option of walking away. I'm not entirely joking when I call him merciful. There are many bandits, probably the majority, who would not have made that offer, and just released the arrow. It may well be the case that he was lying and just wanted me to dismount my horse immediately so as to not scare the steed into running away. Maybe he meant to take me prisoner and finish off the job once his assets were secure. All of this is speculation unless I make efforts to read his mind, and there is no time for that at this moment. He said he would be merciful, not to offer him the same mercy too seems dubious. My magic draws from the bright spirits, the spirits who advocate mercy and love, not the spirits who advocate darkness. Furthermore, he may well have information that could be useful, he may inform me of a larger band of thieves, hidden throughout the forest or awaiting travellers along the path. His earlier response indicated that he knew the location of the fountain, so he must have some further information about these parts. Some of it may be useful.

I decide to immobilise him, interlocking my fingers at the knuckle joints and clapping my hands together in his direction, whispering 'pielgaga'. A faint clunk rings through the undergrowth and, from the toes of his worn leather boots to the tip of his head, he is enveloped in a very thin, but very solid, layer of stone. The arrow and bow do not change, but two stone fingers now curl around the elastic of the bow, maintaining the tension. I perform the hand movement necessary to lift the spell that slows down time, and my surroundings resume their usual pace. I step away from my horse and towards the bandit, trusting my steed to stay in position. From behind the stone lips comes the muffling of a man who is suffocating. I join the index, middle and ring fingers of my right hand together and place them on his lips, stroking them lengthwise, and a thin layer of stone melts away. The bandit gasps in the surrounding air greedily.

"I can't see. I can't move!" he exclaims, his voice panicked and nasally, his nostrils still having no access to air, he sounds like a man with a bad cold in a lot of fear. "What have you done to me?"

Unlike the characters in Final Facedown III, the opponents in Arideth are not real people that exist in the physical world, but are in-game characters that have been granted extensively human-like artificial intelligence. In first-person shooters like Final Facedown III, the dialogue is not central. Thus, the multiplayer format works. In Arideth, you are supposedly immersed in a pre-mediaeval world, and so your interactions, conversations, and the motivations of those you engage with must be based on approximated understandings of the mannerisms and motivations of people in those times, in order to be authentic. This bandit is not another player, wearing a headset and gloves, sitting somewhere else in the VirtuWorld, but is an embedded and integral part of the game. Yet his fear is so realistic, his panic was indistinguishable from real panic.

"Do not worry," I tell him. "I will be merciful. For the moment, you seem to have lost your ability to move. But as long as you answer my questions, I will tap the rock that surrounds you, such that a small crack will appear. The crack will spread through the rock slowly, over the course of an hour or two, and eventually it will crumble, leaving you free to continue your endeavours. The bow will be destroyed and the knife I will take on my travels. I will not leave you instruments with which to steal from others. But I will grant you your life if you answer my questions."

The whimpering bandit makes a soft noise of assent. In the thin slit in the stone that surrounds his mouth, a bead of sweat appears from in between the skin and stone, dribbling down along the crease between his lips and settling in the corner of his mouth.

"Are there others?" I ask him, "Yes or no?"

"No," he responds, almost too quickly. Given that he is encased from head to toe, I cannot scan his features for any indications of dishonesty. He does not look away from me or bite his lip or hunch his shoulders. But in the lift of his voice, I hear that he is lying.

"How many?" I ask him sharply. This time, his response is longer in coming.

"Two." He responds finally. Almost flatly. "Further along the path. Like me. Hiding. On the edge of the forest. Close to the path. Waiting for travellers. If you continue on your current route through the forest, you are unlikely to encounter them."

"Good," I respond. "And is there anything else on the way to the fountain of which I should be aware? Dangerous creatures? Swamps?"

"A small swamp a few hours along," he replies. "When you reach it, follow it round to the left. Taking it to the right will lengthen your journey."

"I will return along this path," I tell him. "And if your information is inaccurate, on my return, I will not show mercy."

"What reason do I have to lie to you?" he asks me. "My life is in your hands. I am a bandit. Once you have gone from here, your fate has little impact on my fortunes. I do not lie."

A small buzzing on the upper section of my thigh, my real thigh, not the thighs that I control with small movements of my wrist in the VirtuWorld. I still have feeling in my thighs, though I cannot move them. Someone is texting me. "Pause VirtuWorld," I say. The scene around me dissolves, replaced by twinkling stars. A menu bordered in blue.

"Connect to mobile phone. Open texts," I order.

A list of messages appears before me, the most recent coming from my mother.

"Play latest unread message," I demand.

A woman's voice, not my mother's, but very realistic, echoes her words. The accent is American.

"There are two men at the door to see you," it says, "They say they're from the Government. Could you pause your game and come along, ASAP?"

"Two men from the Government?" I think to myself. "Two men

from the Government at the door to see me. What on earth can this be about?"

I can't think of myself as having done anything illegal and, even if I had, I'm a 15-year-old boy, still at school. If I had been caught smoking weed or hidden a machete in my wheelchair, they would send policemen, not members of the Government. I pull the gloves off my hand, still perplexed, and they are soon joined by the headset on my desk. I wheel my chair towards the door, open it, and push myself into the corridor. The wheelchair bumps slightly as it lands on the corridor floor, which is a few millimetres deeper than the floor of my bedroom. I turn the wheelchair, pulling and pushing on the left pushrim and the right, until the wheelchair is parallel with, rather than at right angles to, the corridor. Then I move the wheelchair along the corridor and towards the front door.

My mother calls from the living room as I pass it.

"We're in here," she says.

I stop my chair outside of the living room and make the same 90-degree turn. I see my mother sitting on the small rocking chair in which she plays guitar. The two men are facing her with their backs to me, and above the edge of the sofa, I see the shoulders of their suits. The white collars fold into perfectly ironed lines, uniformly peaking above the border of the midnight black suits. I'm certain that when I see them from the front, their ties will not be undone. Even their haircuts are official. Neat. In line with regulation. I wheel into the room and they turn on the sofa, craning their heads leftwards towards me. I am surprised to see them smile.

"Hello Elijah," the one to the left says to me. "You are Elijah Walker. EW565 in the VirtuWorld, are you not?"

"I am," I reply, before the absurdity of his question reaches me.

My VirtuWorld username. Why on Earth is a Government

official in my living room? Why on Earth is a Government official in my living room, referring to me by my VirtuWorld username?

"We have a proposition for you, Elijah," says the man on the right, his left arm perched on the edge of the sofa, his head twisted over it. A broad smile curves his lips. He has pinched eyes and a rather large nose. His cheeks have no stubble, clean shaved. His tie is on, and his top button done. He looks to be about 50.

"A proposition where you could serve your country, make money, and become a very wealthy boy. All by playing games."

CHAPTER 4

"I'm going," he tells me. "Two weeks from now I'll be gone."

"But what about your family?" I ask him. "Your siblings. What about your parents?"

He turns to me. His features are clustered in incomprehension.

"You think I can provide for them here?" he asks incredulously. "There is no work to be had. The only hope is escape. If I can make it to Europe, I will find a way to bring them to me. Before they die of thirst or hunger. Abdoulaye is two years younger than me, yes, but he is just as capable. He can provide for the others in my absence as well as I would be able to. I have spoken to a smuggler who is ready to take me next week. This time I am for real. I am going," he tells me.

"Going where?" I ask him. "You do not have the money for the whole journey. How far has this smuggler agreed to take you?"

Mustafa exhales sharply from his nose, obviously troubled.

"Through the Sahara," he tells me. "Into Libya or Algeria. But I will not be the first to do this thing leg by leg."

No, he certainly won't. Those few who can afford it will pay a lump fee to a single smuggler to guide them through their voyage from start to finish. Some smugglers claim that, for the right price, you can be in Munich or Barcelona within two weeks. But many hopefuls set off on their journey without the funds to make their way to Europe, paying for each leg of the journey independently. They search for work in Algeria or Morocco or

Libya, often even working for the smugglers themselves for a period, in the logistics and day to day business of moving human cargo. Scratching and saving when the cash runs dry, hustling the funds to continue on their odyssey. Mustafa will certainly not be the first to take the journey leg by leg. And the point he makes is valid. What can he provide his family here? What can I provide my family? My sister. My mother, who I am convinced is selling her own body. Taking the journey leg by leg is risky. But staying here is risky too. Familiar, but risky.

"What about my sister?" I ask myself silently. "What about my sister and her intermittent bouts of malaria? What can I do for her whilst I am hustling my way across the Sahara?"

"What can you do for her here?" another voice in my head insistently responds. If I stay here I remain impotent. If I go, there is a chance I may reach a place from which I will have some power to help. I could even start to help sooner. If I find steady work in Libya or Algeria, I can put some money aside to save, in order to make the journey across the Mediterranean, and I can start to send some home before I even cross the sea. The heat will be worse in those countries. True. However, it will be temporary, only to be endured as I raise the money to continue my journey. And it will be me that is bearing it, not my sisters or mother. Surely I could make more money in Libya than here.

I open my mouth, half intending to continue to challenge my old friend, to talk him out of what will surely be a reckless, dangerous journey for which he will be ill-prepared. Instead, I hear myself say, "Who was the smuggler?"

"A friend of Muhammad," he responds. "Muhammad says that, three years ago, this smuggler helped his uncle reach Italy. He does not know him well, but a successful journey speaks for itself. Muhammad even showed me the photographs of his uncle in Rome."

"What is Rome?" I ask.

"A city in Italy," he responds.

"And did this uncle pay for the journey leg by leg?" I question.

"I do not know," he responds. For a moment, we are silent.

Mustafa is in a state of semi-reclination. His legs lie out to his left, his torso bends sideways at a 45-degree angle with his elbow touching the surface of the rug and the right side of his face supported by his hand. I am sitting up, hands clenched together, thoughts whirring furiously. Thoughts of money, as always. Even were I to join my friend in this madness, where would I even find the money for the first leg? Every penny brought into my household goes either to food, of which there is always too little, or rent for our small hut. If we were to suddenly come into an extra source of funding, the priority would be to pay for Fatima's medicine. Why am I entertaining thoughts of joining Mustafa when such a journey remains beyond reach?

Another voice starts up in the back of my head and slowly works its way forward. "There is money," it says. "Money that is rightfully yours by the law of God and of man. Money that was stolen from you. Money that your father meant for you to have."

"Money that is out of my reach," I respond to the voice. "Money that is behind locked doors. Money that is tied up in a small property to which we no longer have access."

The first wife, upon my father's death, produced a document which she claimed expressed his will. It left her and her children almost everything. Even the small, secondary house in which I grew up with my mother and sisters (for Islamic law mandates that a man with multiple wives must house them separately) was claimed by this woman as hers once she produced this document. It is now occupied by her oldest son and his wife. Her youngest son still lives in the main house with her, whilst her daughters have all been married off and moved out of the compound. I do not know whether my father produced a second will taking us into account once he married my mother, which this first wife has hidden.

I don't know whether he had not yet gotten round to updating his will, as his death was not expected and he was not yet at the age when death's sceptre becomes a constant concern and companion. I do not know whether he produced no will at all, meaning for his inheritance to be dealt with according to the traditions of the law - perhaps this document that the first wife produced is a complete fabrication. I do know that my father loved me and my mother and he would not wish for his youngest daughter to be on the brink of death, suffering destitution, whilst that woman enjoys all the fruits of his labour.

A plan starts to form in my head, and I find myself once again speaking almost automatically.

"How much is passage?" My mouth says independently of my brain.

Mustafa seems to have been lost in thoughts as deep as mine. He starts at the question, turning to me and asking, "What?"

"How much is passage?" I repeat. "Passage through the Sahara?"

"300 US dollars," he responds.

"What is that in Naira?" I ask him.

"130k," he tells me.

I wince. 130k is a lot. I think again about my plan.

The woman may well have 130k squirrelled away somewhere in the house, but I don't know exactly where and so I would need time to find it, or to take some objects of value that can be sold to fund the journey. I would go directly for the big house. Her son is unlikely to have anything of value squirrelled away in the smaller house, and breaking into two buildings just doubles my chances of getting caught. Her youngest son will be the main concern once I have entered the building. As long as she is sleeping at the time, I have nothing to worry about from her. She is not a huge woman, there is not enough food around for anyone to be huge. She is, however, a prodigious snorer, and when she sleeps it is almost impossible to wake her.

When I was six or seven years old, I was playing on the hard, baked, umber earth that lay between the two buildings. As she sat sleeping in a white plastic chair outside the larger house, I slipped and my knee landed on a stone, drawing blood. The pain was fresh and, in my youth, I had not yet learned to harden myself to it. And so I began to cry. Not silently, but loudly so as to solicit help, emitting the sort of oscillating police siren noise a young child will make when crying. For four or five minutes I simply sat there with my knee bleeding, wailing my head off, waiting for my mum to come back from the market. And this woman, the first wife, continued to snore, her snores blocking out my cries. Dead to the world.

For many years, I secretly believed that she had been woken by my cries, but had not had the compassion nor the motivation to get up from her chair and help me, and so had pretended to continue to sleep. I cradled this belief for seven years until, at the age of 13, I was woken by the sound of a woman screaming obscenities. I got up from my bed and moved to the window of the smaller house, peering through to identify the source of the unfamiliar voice. A young lady was screaming at the first wife's eldest son, who stood outside the building with another young lady cowering behind him. The first girl was showering abuse upon both of the others in rapid Hausa, accusing him of being a cheat and a lousy liar, a rogue dog who could not be satisfied with the woman he had.

"*Kai munafiki,*" she was shouting, '*you hypocrite*'.

This whole scene unfolded only a few metres from the same plastic white chair in which my father's first wife once again sat, snoring loudly, dead to the world. Her son did not even seem to be concerned about the possibility of waking her. He responded to the girl's accusations in an equally loud voice, defending himself and telling her that it was over between them. Having grown up in the same house as his mother, he was obviously more familiar with her inability to be woken by sound.

Whether this inability is something shared by her youngest son, who still lives in the same building, I am unsure. However, it is very unlikely that anything of value or any cash will be hidden in his room. If I can avoid him, and take care to move as quietly as possible, I stand a good chance of remaining undetected.

I suddenly find that my heart is beating more quickly than usual. If I am to leave, it must be with Mustafa. It is well known that those who take such a treacherous journey alone are less likely to succeed. Mustafa is my good friend. If I leave, I must leave with Mustafa, and Mustafa is leaving in two weeks or less. I am suddenly faced with the prospect of uprooting my existence, of attempting to leave the place I have spent all 15 years of my life, of travelling to unknown lands and facing unknown challenges, in the search of something better for me and my family. My heart beats in my ribcage like a wild animal that is trapped, seeking to escape, seeking refuge. Mustafa has now drifted back into his own thoughts. His eyes are softly closed, but the fact that his head still remains propped up on his rigid arm eliminates the possibility that he is sleeping.

"Is there room for two?" I ask him.

His eyes flicker open and he looks at me with a trepidatious mix of curiosity and confusion. He raises one eyebrow slightly, before his gaze flickers to the floor and then resettles upwards to meet mine once again. Until this moment, he has seen my questions as questions of curiosity, perhaps as a sign that I was collecting information so as to better dissuade him from his resolution. For the first time he realises that I am considering undertaking the journey alongside him.

"There could be," he replies, watching me intently.

CHAPTER 5

My chair is now positioned between the sofa and the rocking chair, between my mother and these two men from the Government who are smiling at me in a way that seems solicitous. My mum seems relatively calm, though by the way her foot is tapping up and down at the end of one of her tightly crossed legs, I am aware she is subject to some agitation.

"Have I thought about my future?" I try to take in the significance of the question one of the men has just asked me.

"The future? I guess so. Sometimes," I say. "I'm still only 15..."

"Is 15 old enough to serve your country?" The man on the left asks me in reply.

He himself looks to be about 50. He has large ears and a strangely sloping nose that looks almost like an inverted beak. Two deep creases run from each corner of the nose to each corner of the mouth, forming a perfect triangle. Three further wrinkles are gouged across his forehead in perfect parallel. His hairline is only slightly receding, and the exceedingly neat parting which runs from it to the nape of his neck is easily visible from his front. He cocks his head to one side, whilst examining me, and says, "I hear you're a very talented boy, Elijah, and your Government rewards talent."

"Have you ever heard of the Home Office?" asks the second man, who is much thinner than his partner and who has rested a Fedora hat upon his knees. The man has a strange smile, which seems to involve lifting both his lips upwards and showing the top layer of teeth, whilst entirely obscuring the bottom layer, somewhat inhibiting the ability of the corners of the lips to turn upwards. He seems to compensate for this by tilting his head forward ever so slightly, giving the illusion of an upward tilt at each side of his lips. But doing so casts shadows under his eyes. Or perhaps he is simply sleep-deprived. I've seen such shadows under my eyes, both after marathon gaming sessions and in the hospital, and in both cases it had nothing to do with the lighting.

My mother's foot begins tapping more quickly, but when I look at her she just smiles at me politely and nods back towards the men, indicating that I should give them a response.

"No?" I say. "What's the home office?"

"The Home Office," replies the man on the left, "is a very important part of our Government. It's essential to maintaining order and cultural integrity. The role of the Home Office is to protect our borders. There are lots of people who are jealous of what we have in this country and who want to come here to leech off of our systems illegally. The Home Office makes sure that those who come into this country are those who have been given permission to do so, and in doing so it keeps you safe."

"So, you guys deal with immigration? Is that it?" I ask them.

"Exactly," says the man on the right, showing his teeth and tilting his head forward even more. The shadows around his eyes grow deeper as he does so. But his smile gives the illusion of growing wider.

"Did you know that immigration was the number one issue that voters in this country allowed to influence their choice of candidate in the recent election. The numbers are astounding if you look at them. People from all over the world are trying to come here. And Britain just isn't big enough for them all. Not this little island. Not Europe, really. We do work with other countries too. To keep Europe..." his voice trails off for a second.

"To keep Europe's cultural integrity," he finishes.

"Yes," the man on the left drawls. His voice is upper class and official. "You could even end up on one of the programmes we have got going on in partnership with Spain's and Italy's immigration services at the moment if we're successful in recruiting you." At this point, I am more than confused. What qualifications do I have to work in a Government office, especially a Government office that focuses on immigration? And what on earth is the connection between their desire to recruit me and them referring to me by my VirtuWorld username? This whole situation makes no sense! Perhaps if they were from the Ministry of Technology or something, they might have wanted me to engage in some kind of Artificial Intelligence product testing, but even that seems far-fetched. At this point in the conversation, I have nothing to say, and so I say nothing, politely waiting for them to explain themselves.

"You must be very confused," says the thin man on the right. "Most of our fresh recruits are when we first approach them. The skills we refer to are your motor skills, your fine motor skills, to be precise. Your recent rankings and scores on Arideth, Final Facedown III and The Evolution of Wildness indicate to us that you will be particularly adept at remote robot piloting. There would usually be an internship, but at your level of performance, that really isn't necessary. If you choose to take us up on our offer, you will of course be excellently compensated."

My mother's leg stops bobbing up and down and for the first time she enters the conversation.

"Isn't he a little young to be starting a job with such responsibilities and commitments? He hasn't yet done his A-Levels. And we were hoping he would make it to university. Isn't this something he could look at in a few years, once he's graduated?" She asks all these questions very quickly, as though she's been holding them in, and also as though she's nervous about turning these men down.

Both men turn their heads towards my mother as she speaks. The man on the left pulls out a small brochure from his pocket, hands it to her and addresses her directly when he says, "Of course, the education of children, especially gifted children like Elijah, is a top priority for the Government. Elijah will be provided time to work with the best private tutors, and if he cannot complete his A-levels in two years due to time constraints, exceptions will be made in order to allow him to complete them in three. Furthermore, if Elijah decides to go on to university, there is every opportunity for him to take a break from his job with us, or for him to take an online course which will be fully accredited. Either option has the full backing of the Government, and in either case his fees will be covered by the Home Office, on top of his nominal salary."

After a moment, the significance of his words hits me. If I join this program, not only will I be getting paid a salary at the age of 15, I would have no fees to pay at university if I chose to go. And if they have chosen me for this job based on my ability to play the games I love, then surely this job cannot be so different from playing them. I might be offered a career where I work in something like the VirtuWorld, where my everyday job might involve walking or flying. Intricate movement through real places, controlling robots and drones. Since the accident, I have always been worried about what jobs I might be able to get with my disability. Nothing manual. Nothing active. Since the accident, a part of me has always believed I will be resigned to sitting at a desk, doing something unspeakably boring. This might just be a way to escape that. And disabled life is expensive. You have to pay for wheelchairs and other equipment, not to mention all the adaptations to your house. If I could get a job that could cover the cost of all that when I eventually leave home, it would be amazing.

My grades aren't as good as my brother's, who spends all his time buried in books. Video games don't make you the most academic student in the school. And if the academic route might not be the route to riches, maybe this job will be. It's not just the salary, it's the security. It's the chance to have a career doing something I love.

I open my mouth to say something, I'm not quite sure what yet, but my mum gets in there before me. "Let's not rush to any conclusions," she says. "That all sounds very, very generous, especially covering his university fees. But I think Elijah would like to know a little bit more about the programme and what it involves before he commits himself to anything. Right, Elijah?"

She turns to me, and I nod back at her. "Right," I reply, half-heartedly.

"That's no problem at all." says the man on the right, his voice silky, and deeper than his partner's, though his accent is completely identical. "No problem at all. How about Elijah coming to visit us in the control room. He can take a look at some of the equipment, speak to some of the current employees and really understand what it is that we do, and what it is we would be hiring him to help us with. That way he'll be able to make an entirely informed opinion. Does that sound suitable, Mrs Walker?"

There are a few seconds of silence whilst my mum seems to consider the offer. It hits me that I am still a legal minor, and that I almost definitely need her consent to agree to this.

After a second or two, the man on the left chimes in. "The control room is of course completely wheelchair accessible, and we will organise all transport ourselves. He'll be picked up here by a chauffeur in the early morning and back in time for dinner. You're free to accompany him if you wish. And if Elijah concludes that working for the Home Office is not for him, we will of course be disappointed, but there will be no hard feelings".

"I want to go, Mum," I say firmly, loud enough for both men to hear. "I at least want to see what this is all about."

Her brow furrows as her eyes flicker between the three of us. After a few moments more, she assents. "Ok, we'll visit, his brother can babysit after all. When is suitable? When are office hours?"

"Anytime," replies the man on the left, a faint ripple of relief spreading across his bureaucratic features. "Literally anytime. The control room is open 365 days a year, 24 hours a day. The immigrants don't stop, so nor do we."

"Not," hastens to add the man on the right "that you will be required to work those hours."

"Not in the slightest," recommences the man on the left. "We have a rota system which works like clockwork and, as a minor, your son will be given the option to work less hours if he so wishes. If, of course, he takes the job." He pulls out a business card from the inside pocket of his jacket and stretches it out to my mother. "Just reach out to me with a time and date on the number or email on this card and I'll ensure that a car is here waiting to pick you both up an hour before."

"I'll make sure I do," replies my mother.

"Well, that settles it then," says the man on the right. "We won't take any more of your time."

Both of the men stand up and shake my hand before turning to my mother and doing the same.

"I don't believe I caught your names?" I say to them.

"Of course," says the man on the left. "I am Thomas Rutchers, Head of Recruitment for the Home Office. My partner is Joe Gradle, Head of the Remote Immigration Surveillance and Management Department. We'll introduce you to more of the team when you come for your visit, but I'm sure you will fit right in. The boys in the control room are generally much younger and less official than the two of us."

His partner, Joe, chuckles appreciatively and says, "Well, that's certainly true. To be young again, eh?" Looking up at him from my seat, I see his mouth from below and, even with the forward tilt of his head, there is no way to hide the incompleteness of his smile. He seems to genuinely enjoy this joke, however, as at least his laugh sounds real enough.

They make their way over to the front door, but I do not follow. When you're in a wheelchair, it's not really seen as rude to neglect to accompany your guests as they leave the house. My mother goes with them, and I hear them exchange pleasantries before a click tells me the door has closed again. I picture the taller man, Joe, re-doffing his fedora hat as they stride side by side towards the company car. Correction, Government vehicle.

After a few moments, my mum re-enters the room and sits down in her rocking chair. She rocks backwards and forwards for a few moments, glancing at me every couple of seconds, before stopping her rocking and picking up her guitar. She strums out a few chords, biting her lip, and then stops that as abruptly as she had stopped her rocking. Her eyes fix on me again, this time holding my gaze.

"Something seemed off about those men," she tells me. "I don't really know much about what goes on at our borders, but I don't know why they would need video gamers."

I frown.

"They seemed okay to me, Mum," I respond, neglecting to mention my reservations about Joe's smile. "Let's go and check out what they have to offer. Like the man said, we can always turn it down."

My mum bites her lip and continues to look at me with a

furrowed brow, but in the end, I know she will take me. I know she won't turn me down. The accident was her fault. If she tries to renege on her promise to take me, I'll give her all the reasons I have thought up for why this job was perfect for a boy, soon to be a man, who cannot walk. Her guilt will work in my favour, but that's a path that both of us would rather not go down. And she knows that too, so she nods, and says we can visit next weekend.

"Thanks, Mum," I say, smiling. "And since I'm down here, why not play me a few songs."

CHAPTER 6

The sky above covers me, dimly lit by a fattening crescent moon, as I make my way through the streets of Sokoto. My feet patter on the unpaved roads. Somewhere in the distance, a dog can be heard howling. I am moving towards the home of my youth, and the closer I get, the more effort I make to deaden the sounds of my footsteps and of my beating heart. Before long, I arrive at the fence, or rather at the gate. I see the bent bar in the metal, and remember how I used to slip out in the night through this slightly wider gap in the gate and play with the Almajiri children on the streets in the dead of night. I remember my mother's fury when she caught me, and the beating I received from my father when she told him. The gap looks smaller than I remember, but I try to push my way through regardless, and soon come to the conclusion that it is not the gap which has shrunk, but my body which has grown. My shoulders are broader and my head larger. Pushing myself through is, unfortunately, a losing battle. Bending the bar further to widen the gap could work. However, this could be a noisy and time-consuming alternative, unsuited to the secretive mission I am undertaking, which should be completed as quickly as possible.

I grip the spikes at the top of the fence and pull myself up, instead trying to lift my leg up so that my foot can be placed on the small rung of straight metal between two of the spiked tips that run the length of the fence. Once I have succeeded in placing my right foot on the metal, I tug with my arms, balancing precariously on the one foot as I manage to wedge my left foot in a narrow point between two bars. I pause to catch my breath. The next step is to swing my right leg over the top of the fence. I grip the spikes with my hands and lean over to the side, stretching my leg out over the top. The tips of the spikes scrape against the skin of my leg as I swing it over. I wince, but manage to avoid impaling myself. Soon my body is over, on the other side of the fence, and the drop is not far. I land with a thud on the ground, and then scamper away, slipping into the shadows.

It has been over a year since I was last inside this compound and, even in the dim light of crepuscule, I pause for a moment as a barrage of memories hits me. To my left, the smaller house where I grew up. Not much bigger than the hut in which I now live, but with a better roof, thicker walls, more privacy and relatively consistent power. Further forward and slightly to my right, the other house, where my father's first wife lives. Though it's slightly larger, it's still not what could be called luxurious. There's the plastic white chair, sat outside in exactly the same spot. I turn my head from left to right and remember mornings playing with my siblings, conversations with my father in the evenings, the stories he would tell me. Right there, I remember, by the thorn bush, was where he had told me the story of the hyena and the buffalo bones. So, the first step has been taken. I am officially committing a crime. I have broken into my childhood home.

There is a sleeping goat tied to a pole, a few metres from the larger house, but apart from that, I have seen no signs of life so far. No one seems to have been woken by my grunts and thuds whilst hopping the fence. So far, things are going to plan. I resist the pull of nostalgia and ignore the smaller house, making my way over to the larger one. Sure enough, as I approach, I hear the faint rumbles that indicate that she is sleeping. 'Good,' I tell myself. 'Another box ticked.' I tiptoe over to the small window of her younger son, Ibrahim's, bedroom. The curtains are undrawn and I am able to peek inside. There are no panes to the window, but instead a mesh-like material designed to keep out mosquitoes. The small holes in the material make it relatively transparent, and I am pleased to see that the room is empty. It seems that Ibrahim is not currently at home. To be safe, I wait for a few moments to ensure that I am not mistaken, and that he doesn't return from a trip to the bathroom just as I am climbing through his window. After a minute, having only heard the volcanic snoring of his mother, I take a small knife from my pocket and slice through the mosquito mesh with its serrated blade, pulling and pushing on the knife so as to cut through the tough material. Once this has been done, I climb in through the window.

By this point, I'm sweating. I feel as though I have gone past the point of no return, and a mixture of adrenaline, fear, and excitement courses through my veins. I give the room a cursory glance. It is small and basic, with a little cabinet and a mattress on the floor. I don't expect to find much of value in here. I make my way into the corridor. The house is unfamiliar to me; despite growing up in this compound I rarely entered this house... it is not huge, and has a total of three rooms and only one floor. It is the sound of snores which tells me in which room I will find her. I open the door, turning the handle as quietly as possible, just in case. For a second, I wonder whether she really had been faking her snores on the day when I had tripped and hurt my knee. I consider whether she had been faking her snores when one of her son's girlfriends came to denounce him, too. I half expect her eyes to flicker open as I enter the room and catch me in my crime. My face is covered fully by a pillowcase with holes cut out for the eyes and mouth, but were she to call for her older son and a fight to break out, it would not be hard for me to be unmasked.

As I enter the room, the rumbling snores seem to grow even louder. She does not wake from her sleep. I quickly avert my eyes from her nakedness, she lies on the bed with her top half exposed. A surge of embarrassment passes through me, but I shake it off, reminding myself of the task at hand. My eyes scan the room, looking for anything of value, debating where she may keep her cash. After a few seconds, they land on a heap of clothes on the floor at the foot of her bed. I make my way over, hoping to find something of worth in the pockets, but as I bend down, I am distracted by something else. Something that I have not seen in a long time. I reach out and touch it, and as I do, a memory comes flooding back, a memory of my father in his traditional Hausa thobe, the same thobe he is wearing in this photo on her bedside cabinet. I have no photos of him myself, and seeing this one brings back a flood of memories, just as jumping over the fence to look once again at my childhood home had done. The photo reminds me of his smile, the way it was slightly mischievous and always accompanied by a chuckle. It reminds me of his fair sternness, it reminds me of his stories. I pick it up and place it in the small bag slung over my shoulder, before returning to the pile of clothes.

I rummage through a few pockets without much luck, but I soon get to a pair of trousers which has some notes and coins inside a purse in its back pocket. I quickly count through the money. Around 90,000 Naira. Not quite enough, but more than half of what I need. The purse goes in the bag as well. The snores continue. I open the drawers of the bedside cabinet, and find a small jewellery box with a few sets of earrings and a watch inside, along with a further 12,500 Naira and a smartphone. These go in the bag too, I know that I can sell the jewellery to a local hawker, and once I've done so, I should have the 130,000 Naira needed for the first leg of my trip, and perhaps a little extra to give my mother for Fatima's medicine. I will take the smartphone for my trip, as I cannot take the family phone with me and still be able to contact my mother and sisters. Or perhaps I will leave the smart phone with them, and take the family phone with me. I quickly check that it is not password protected, and I'm not disappointed. I decide to quit while I'm ahead, and turn towards the door, making my way out into the corridor and closing it softly behind me, but as I get back to Ibrahim's room, I am struck by a realisation.

What kind of thief would steal a picture of the burglary victim's dead husband? Certainly not a stranger. It would have to be someone with some kind of sentimental connection to the dead man. A friend or relative, a son, a daughter, a second wife. In taking my father's photograph, I am incriminating myself and pointing the finger of blame at me and my family. As I make my way towards Europe, my father will have to live in my memory, just as he has for the past few years. I cannot take the photo with me. I turn back and let myself into her room again. She continues to snore, dead to the world, as I take the photograph out of my bag and place it back on the bedside cabinet, positioning it exactly where it had been when I first entered the room. I make my way back out into the corridor, into the bedroom, and scamper through the window once again to find myself back in the courtyard.

The goat has woken up and is staring right at me. My first reaction is one of panic and fear of being caught in the act, but I quickly remind myself that goats do not understand concepts such as property and theft, and are generally docile creatures. Even were the goat to make some noise, and bleat, that would not in itself be suspicious. It definitely wouldn't wake my father's first wife, her oldest son, who now lives in the smaller house and is probably sleeping in there at this very moment, may well be used to the goat bleating at night, and would be unlikely to rise from his bed because of it. I pause for a few moments, another idea forming in my head. This goat, if I can find the right buyer and hide it somewhere in the meantime, is worth a significant sum. It's a little on the skinny side, but compared to most of the animals that have survived the recent drought, it is fairly healthy. It can provide milk and cheese, and at the end of its life will provide meat. Its skinniness may actually prove an advantage, meaning that it can fit through the gap in the gate that is now too narrow for me to squeeze through. Instead of quietly backing away, I find myself untying it from its post and guiding it towards the gate.

For a brief few minutes, everything goes smoothly. The goat remains quiet and follows my guidance. I push it through the gap in the gate, and once it is safely settled on the main road, I tie the rope with which it was attached to the pole to one of the gate's bars. I climb over the gate again myself easily enough, with no injuries and only a slight rip in my trousers. I untie the rope from the gate, ready to walk off into the night with my prizes. When I finish untying the knot and look up, I see Ibrahim, whose room I just used as an entrance to the larger house. He is staring at me, his face displaying a mix of astonishment and fury. Everything seems to pause, and thoughts run through my head at rapid speed. He must have been coming back from wherever his midnight stroll had taken him just as I was guiding the goat to the gate. I have to remind myself that my face is still covered. He cannot currently recognize me, but I see his hand moving towards my head and know that he intends to rip off the pillowcase and unmask the thief. I kick the goat hard in its rump. It squeals and begins to run down the road as fast as its legs will take it. Ibrahim pauses for a moment, his hand freezing in mid-air. After a second's hesitation, he turns to chase after his family's valuable goat before it disappears into the streets of Sokoto. I turn on my heels and sprint in the other direction, without looking back for a second.

CHAPTER 7

The dream in which I'm flying comes to an abrupt end as the generic jingle of my alarm pierces it. The familiar melody which tells me to begin the day. I take a few moments to recalibrate myself, shifting between fiction and reality, but my eyes flicker open at once when I remember that this morning we will be going to visit the control room. Snooze for five minutes, I tell my phone, having, as always, budgeted myself an extra pocket of time to slither between the hinterlands of waking and dreaming. By the time the second alarm rings, I am ready to prop myself up on my elbows, place my hands below the small of my back and push myself to a sitting position. I push myself backwards so as to rest against the backboard of the bed before grabbing each leg with a hand and pulling them physically over the side of the bed so that my feet rest on the floor.

I place my left hand on the handle of my wheelchair, which is turned towards the bed at a 45-degree angle, and keep my right hand on the bed before pushing myself upwards and to the left and landing with a small exhalation of air. I roll myself over to the far end of the room, opening the door and letting myself into the ensuite bathroom. I grab my towel from its hook and drape it over the side of the wheelchair, before transferring myself over to the bath board, a horizontal plank of wood which sits across the rim of the bath, allowing me to sit with my legs hanging outside the tub. I use my hands to bring my legs inside and then lower my naked body gently into the bathtub, letting my back rest against the bath board.

Before turning on the shower, I run the tap and hold my hand underneath it to check the temperature. If I was to start with the shower, and if the water was scalding hot, my legs would tell me so, but I would have no knee jerk reaction with which to move them out of its path. Once I'm satisfied that the temperature is safe, but not freezing cold, I pull a little lever and the flow of water shifts from the steady stream of the tap to the light drizzle of the shower head. As the water falls upon my body like warm rain, I practise my hand movements. I curl and splay my fingers. I gyrate and twist my wrists, closing my eyes and imagining that I am wearing my headset, casting spells and running through the forest as a lynx. After a few moments, however, I open my eyes and grab the shower gel, giving myself a good squirt. I take a large sponge on a stick from the side of the tub and use it to scrub my body.

Once I am happy with my cleanliness, I push myself back onto the bath board and pull my legs outside of the tub, spreading the towel over the wheelchair so that my soggy bottom does not drip onto the seat. A damp wheelchair can ruin a perfectly good morning. I transfer myself back onto the wheelchair and make my way back into the bedroom, pausing at the sink to scrub at my teeth quickly with some Colgate. Once I get into the bedroom, I go through the equally complex process of dressing myself. I choose a green turtleneck and jeans before making my way into the kitchen. I prepare myself some toast. Once I have almost finished eating, my mum sticks her head into the room.

"The car should be here in ten minutes," she tells me. "They booked it to arrive at 9am."

"Great," I respond "I'm almost ready to go." I pop the remaining quarter of a slice in my mouth in one, giving myself a little bit too much to chew on. I then wiggle my fingers as if to say, 'all finished with breakfast'. Mum nods at me, and her head disappears back into the corridor. I leave my plate on the table.

The toaster and bread are on a low shelf, which allows me to prepare my own toast, but the kitchen sink is fitted at standing height, so washing up is a job that is not too easy to do whilst seated. Either Mum or my brother will handle the dishes, Dad is away on work again.

I start to make my way back to my room, intending to pick up my headset and gloves so as to have something to do on the journey, but I pause halfway down the corridor. Keeping Mum happy today is key. Keeping her happy and showing her that, if I take this job, I'm not going to disappear forever into an artificial world. Not taking my headset with me in the car, but instead using the journey as an opportunity to speak to her and sweeten her up seems like the more sensible course of action. I wheel myself round and wait in the corridor instead, and at nine o'clock on the dot, the doorbell rings.

There's a man at the door with South Asian features. A light caramel tone to the skin, thick eyebrows and dark eyes. His facial hair is meticulously trimmed, with sideburns that draw the letter L across his cheekbones. A pencil beard encases his lips and chin in a perfect square, and a downward facing triangle sits below his lip and points towards his neat bow tie like an arrowhead. He's wearing spectacles and a funny black hat that seems like a mix between a baseball cap and a chef's toque.

"Good morning," he drawls in affected upper class tones. "I believe you are expecting a vehicle. My name is Jeffrey. I will be your chauffeur for this morning. Are you ready to depart? Or would you rather I give you a little more time?"

"Oh no, we're ready," says my mother as she makes her way down the hallway towards us. My previous conversation with her had been a conversation with a floating head that peeked itself around the corner of the kitchen door. Only now do I see that she is dressed rather smartly, with neatly ironed light grey suit trousers that start at her ankles and end at her waist in a thin but elegant brown belt. The only two creases in the trousers are very deliberate, and draw vertical lines down her legs that can only be the result of meticulous ironing. An elegant blue shirt and white jacket are accompanied by black heels. My mum works from home, and we rarely go out together. I am used to seeing her in a dressing gown or tracksuit bottoms, and so I'm quite startled by the sight of her looking rather elegant.

"Wonderful," Jeffrey replies, stepping back from the doorway to allow us to exit the house. "Would you like assistance pushing the wheelchair?"

"No," I respond with a slight edge to my voice. "I'm able to push myself thanks." I roll myself down the small ramp at our front door into the driveway. I notice the unfamiliar vehicle immediately. It is a sleek minibus with chrome wheels and a lift for wheelchairs. I can't help but be impressed. The morning sun glints off its glossy exterior and an array of solar panels splay out like petals from its roof, presumably ready to retract when the vehicle departs on a journey.

"Part of our executive fleet." Jeffrey tells me with a smile. "The CFO of VirtuWorld has the same model in his collection, without the accessibility modifications."

I roll myself over to the lift and press a button which raises the platform to the level of the van's interior. Once I am inside, Jeffrey steps in and points towards a bracket in the middle of the van. "We have a wheelchair tie down system in place here, so you can go ahead and secure yourself before we take off. I can assist here if you please, or you may prefer your mother to help."

This time, I accept his assistance, and Jeffrey quickly and expertly secures my chair to the bracket and climbs into the front seat of the van. My mother joins me in the back, sitting on a fold down seat opposite my wheelchair and smiling. Seeing her more closely, I notice that she is also wearing tasteful makeup. Eyeliner brings out the contours of her eyes, and her lips are delicately tinted with a rosy blush.

"Ready?" Jeffrey asks, and I respond in the affirmative. He starts the engine, and we set off through the streets of London, my wheelchair moving only slightly as the van weaves and turns through the road.

For half an hour, nothing of any real substance is said, but eventually, my mother tells me something that makes me look at her questioningly.

"The problem I had before your accident," she says, "was that I was looking for a way to escape. And I found that escape..." She lowers her voice almost conspiratorially so as to block Jeffrey, who is separated from us by a metal partition with a small glass window and audio interface embedded into it, out of the conversation. "I found that escape in the bottle." As she proceeds, she keeps her voice low, not quite whispering, but projecting as little as possible.

"I think you've been escaping too," she tells me, "And I only have your best interests at heart. Let's see what they have to offer today. But let's not rush into anything. And if you do take this job, ease yourself into it. Keep some time for you. I know that in your spare time you'll still want to play your games, but we can find you another hobby too. My guitar has replaced the bottle as my escape. I don't think you need to replace your games, but maybe we can buy you an instrument to learn, a violin or a trumpet, so that between this job... if you take it... and your games, you'll have some other form of expression and creativity. Maybe we can even play music together on the weekends. Let's go today and check out what they have to offer. But all I ask you is not to rush into anything." She smiles and raises her voice again to its normal speaking level. "How long left until we arrive, Jeffrey?" she calls out towards the interface.

I acknowledge her advice with a double thumbs up and a nod, and Jeffrey replies from the front. "Not too far at all. The traffic is being very kind. Perhaps another 25 minutes." The traffic is even kinder than expected and, within 20 minutes, we are entering the carpark of a skyscraper in a central London street.

We park up and my mother unstraps me, helping me out of the car. Jeffery takes us over to an elevator, which he informs us will take us directly from the car park, which is underground, to the lobby of the Government building which houses the Home Office. He tells us that we should ask at reception for either Joe or Thomas, the two men who previously arrived at my house in the hopes of recruiting me. He doffs his weird hat and makes his way back to the swanky vehicle, leaving my mother and I to enter the elevator alone. My mother presses the button 'ground floor', and the lift ascends in silence. Just before it arrives and the doors open, I turn to my mum and tell her, "I'm not looking to escape, Mum, I'm looking to live authentically. When I play my games, I feel alive. This job might give me a way to earn money and to provide for myself and my future family. But who knows, it might not. As you say, let's check out what they have to offer." I say this all very quickly, at the very moment that I say the word 'offer,' a ding rings out and the elevator doors slide open, revealing the lobby of the building.

As I wheel myself in, I am greeted by marble floors, plush furniture, large metal pillars that seemed polished to the point of being almost reflective. An array of huge windows floods the room with natural light. An elegant spiral staircase, which I will never have the pleasure to use, ropes its way from floor to ceiling, and I can make out a few people bustling about the lobby in suits, looking extremely busy and important. The reception desk is in the middle of the room, and at the far end of the room are turnstile barriers which seem to require keycard access. I take a deep breath and make my way towards the reception desk, accompanied by my mother.

The receptionist is a young woman between the age of 20 and 30. Her hair is tied up in an extraordinarily neat bun, and both her smile and voice have that artificial sweetness of someone who is paid to be sweet, even to the people she despises. Not to say that she despises me. Though her voice is almost robotic in its pleasantness, there is something in the sparkle of her eyes which tells me she's probably a kind person.

"Hello." she says to me. "Welcome to Marsham Street, the home of the Home Office. How may I help you today?"

"We're here to see Thomas Rutchers or Joe Gradle." replies my mother. "We have an appointment to visit the control room."

"Ah, so you're a potential recruit. How lovely. I'll issue you with visitors' badges and then you can make your way over to security. They'll let you through the barriers. And you can take a separate elevator up to the fourth floor, where you'll find Mr. Gradle."

My eyes automatically turn again to the turnstiles, and they settle on a detail that I missed before. A security scanner, not unlike the kind you find at airports, where one man is removing his shoes and belt and placing them in a little box to go through the scanner. My stomach sinks a little in annoyance. Going through security in a wheelchair is never simple. The metal rods in my hips always set off the hand-held detectors and, on more than one occasion, an overly zealous security guard has seemed convinced that the chair itself could be a repository of hiding places for contraband. The receptionist quickly takes our names and prints off our visitor badges, handing them to us each in turn. However, just as I prepare to wheel my chair towards the security section, a voice calls out from behind me, a silky deep voice that I have heard only once before. I turn, and I'm greeted by the false smile of Joe Gradle coming towards me. There is so much light streaming into the lobby from the huge windows that today his eyes have no shadows.

"Mrs Walker! Elijah!" he exclaims jovially, before turning to the receptionist. "There'll be no need for them to pass through security. It will just be a hassle for Elijah. I'll give him clearance on my own authority." He turns back to my mother and me. "How wonderful to see you." he continues. "Let's make our way over to the control room. The team is eager to meet you."

CHAPTER 8

A bead of sweat trickles down my forehead as if fleeing from my thoughts and settles in the corner of my eye. It rests there for a moment before, compelled by gravity to continue its descent, it finds its way to my nose, from which it drips - landing with a hiss upon the baking gravel below. I am standing outside our hut, awaiting my mother's return. My younger sisters are inside, but I don't want them overhearing this conversation.

There has been no suspicion about the robbery. Two days have passed and no one has come knocking on the door to ask about that. The goat was my salvation. However, today is the day that Mustafa and I will go to meet the smuggler, and I know that I can no longer put off informing my mother of my intentions. It is at least 50 degrees Celsius, and the cloudless sky is centred by an orange sphere of fire, a sweltering circle which makes the air that surrounds it shimmer. At this temperature, I feel as if I'm melting, as if the beads of sweat which pepper my skin are actually the skin itself, melted from solid to liquid. Washing away my body into the cracks of the baked earth below, transforming me from something fixed to something fluid.

But I am not melting. I am waiting. Waiting to have a conversation with my mother. Wondering how she will react. I am her eldest child, and even if my mission is successful, the likelihood is that I will not see her again in person for years, perhaps decades, perhaps ever. If I make it to Europe, there is no guarantee that I will be able to bring them along after me. After I have arrived, having some livelihood that would enable me to send them some funds will still be a success, but even then there will be an ocean between us. Then there is the possibility of failure, of death in the Sahara or the sea.

She will doubtlessly know women, or know of women, who have lost children on the journey, who have given their consent to their sons and daughters to leave; perhaps even scraped together what little money the family had to finance the trip; perhaps even encouraged their children to go in the hopes of a future of financial security, and ultimately... lost them. She will probably also know women who have done the same and whose children have survived the journey, but she will know there is a risk. And she will know that, even in the case of success, she will be losing a son to a different continent. She will be assenting to a future where our only communication will be conducted over phone, and dependent on Sokoto's famously unreliable internet data connection.

Perhaps that is why she has never really discussed the prospect of me leaving. Maybe she didn't want to give me ideas, to sow the seed of travel in my head. The seed, however, has now been sown. I have the funds to make it through the first leg of the trip, and a little extra to give her for Fatima's medication. That at least may soften the blow for Mother. I notice her turn the corner, here she comes, walking towards me with a questioning look on her face, not understanding why I am standing outside in the sweltering heat, waiting to greet her, rather than sheltering from the sun inside the hut. I walk towards her, intending to greet her far enough from the hut for my sisters not to hear me, not wanting to draw them out in curiosity. Once I reach her, I do not speak, but beckon her imploringly with a movement of the head. She follows me around the corner, where we both take refuge under the shade of a large and inviting tree. It is an acacia tree, wider than it is tall, with six seemingly independent trunks emerging from the same spot in the ground, all in slightly different directions, ending in tufty green afros whose strands of hair are a heavy, deep, dull green - leaves symmetrically stretching to the left and right of each stem like the legs of a centipede.

My dad once told me a story about why so many acacia trees were surviving the persistent droughts. For the sake of the story, let us break the fourth wall. A scientist may tell you that there are several interlinked reasons why droughts can lead to trees dying, up to a year or more later. Thirst will starve the tissues that transport water and permanently damage them. They could tell you that thirsty trees become more vulnerable to pests and diseases, such as bark beetles and funguses, that can weaken and kill them. They might mention that the lack of water can also reduce photosynthesis, which is essential for the growth of new leaves and branches, or that - during a drought - the water in the soil often evaporates and is unable to reach the tree's roots, causing them to dry out, become brittle, and rot. A scientist would tell you that the reason the acacia tree in particular has always been able to survive in these desert-like temperatures is because of the tree's deep root systems, which can reach underground water reserves, and its ability to store water in its leaves and stem, a dewy afro which helps to keep it hydrated even during periods of drought.

But I am not a scientist. I am a 15-year-old boy from Sokoto in Nigeria, who can no longer afford the luxury of school since my father died, and I can tell you none of this. And so my explanation for why so many trees have died, and why the acacia trees have generally survived, comes in the shape of another of my father's stories. He told me that, though trees seem to be the most idle of living beings, with spirits that simply sit inside their trunks all day, growing and shedding their leaves, in reality the spirits of the trees live in their roots. He told me that it is below the ground where they talk, trade, fight and discuss their future- away from the prying eyes of humans. And thus, unknown to man, all the tree spirits of Sokoto, and Birnin Kebbi, and Birnin

Konni and Gunmi and Zaria and all of Northern Nigeria pushed out their roots one day to meet in Gusau, to discuss what was to be done about the issue of humanity, to whom they had given so much and and from whom they had received so little. For tree spirits are very proud and believe in reciprocity. They both take and give, and are central to the cycle of life, and they cannot understand a creature that only knows how to take.

My father told me that, as humans moved to cities en masse, abandoning the countryside, cutting down many trees to construct buildings and roads of concrete, the spirits of these trees, living in the roots, had survived, but had been angered that they could no longer rise above the surface from time to time. Because the spirits that inhabited these roots could no longer come above the surface, they pushed deeper into the earth, where they established a new community, far away from mankind and its troubles. They sent a delegation to the meeting in Gusai, and convinced many of the spirits that were still connected to living trees to come and join them in this new community. Over the years, more and more spirits decided to descend into the earth and join the new community, no longer impressed by the surface, which they found to be increasingly dull, hot and barren. A spirit might sit inside a tree for days with no one to talk to, whereas deep below the ground it always had company. Without the spirits close enough to the surface to give them life, many of the trees began to die.

However, the spirits that inhabited the acacia trees had a love of sand and empty space and solitude, and found the new dry and barren landscape inviting. They could never be convinced to leave and join the new community, and so to this day the acacia tree stands strong. A scientist would tell you this is a silly story because the very reason the acacia tree stands strong is because its roots are the deepest of them all. But that scientist would be missing the point and purpose of such a story, which is there to entertain and give some sort of explanation of an earthly phenomenon to a child to whom science is a distant and inaccessible world.

"So what is so important that you have to ambush me?" my mother asks me. "What secrets do we have that must be hidden from your sisters?"

"It is no secret," I respond to her in Hausa. "*Ba asiri ba ne*, but I think it is something that should be broken to them gently. Something we should tell them together."

My mother's face shows concern. If something must be 'broken' to my sisters, then she assumes it can be nothing positive. She has had so much hardship in these recent years, and I rush to reassure her that I am not bringing news of some additional hardship of which she is not aware, but instead bringing my choice to the table. A choice that I hope will help pull us from hardship and brighten our future. Waiting will not make it any easier. I look her directly in the eyes and say,

"I am making the trip to Europe."

A few seconds of silence follow before she seems to deflate, the concern not quite disappearing, but diminishing in her features and being replaced by a deep and unnerving weariness and resignation. She looks towards the ground, breaking our connected gaze.

Her response somewhat surprises me.

"I cannot say I have not expected it," she responds in Hausa. "And I cannot say the idea does not have its merits. Were you my only child, I would tell you not to go. I would forbid it. But your sisters suffer too. And I know you would not abandon us. Ayesha's son has travelled north. He has made it as far as Morocco, and he sends money home. I saw all the remaining children only yesterday and they seem better fed than I have ever seen them before."

She looks up again at me, suddenly, her eyes first widening in question and then narrowing, not in suspicion, but in incomprehension. She continues, " Ayesha funded her son's trip. You know we do not have the money to pay for you to travel even as far as Niamey or Zinder. Travelling north without the funds to even begin your journey is a death sentence. Why discuss something that we do not have the money to consider?"

I put my hand in my pocket and pull out my reclaimed inheritance in response. I sold the jewellery yesterday, and received slightly more than I had expected for one of the watches from the local hawker. He told me it was a fake, but a better fake than most, which he could probably pass off as real to the right buyer. I immediately hand my mother 15,000 Naira.

"For Fatima's medicine," I say "and so Allah does not have to 'provide' for a few weeks. The rest of this..." I lift the wad of notes to eye height and wave it back and forth so that it flops over the top of my fingers, "Will get me through the Sahara."

Her look of incomprehension deepens and then her eyes narrow further. This time, the suspicion is clear. "Where did you get that kind of money?" she asks me. "Has my only son become a thief?"

There is reproach in her voice, but there is steel in my answer. "I only took what was stolen from us, and only a part of that. I wish I could have taken it all."

Her eyes narrow further, but then widen again, this time not in a way that is questioning, but in understanding. They flicker from side to side and her mouth opens slightly, before she closes it and purses her lips, her brow furrowed. It seems that two sentiments are battling within her for approval. After a few moments, the shadow of a smile plays at the corners of her lips.

"Hmm," her chuckle affords me great relief. "Hmm. It can't have been too difficult, the way the woman snores. The nights your father spent with me were his only respite, the only time he got any rest. You are not wrong. This money should be ours." Her bony hand closes into a fist around the 15,000 Naira I have given her, accepting it.

"It is ours," I respond. "And once I am in Libya, I will send more. I plan to work to support you, Fatima and Karima, and also to save until I have enough to make the trip to Europe. One day, once I am settled, I hope to bring you with me. The heat is only getting worse. But if I can send you money, that will help for now." A moment passes before I smile at her and say, "I almost had their goat, but it got away. I did, however, manage to get my hands on this."

I pull the mobile phone that I took during the robbery from my pocket and hold it up for my mother to see. It is less basic than the one that we as a family currently share, with a larger screen and a sleeker, thinner design.

"You guys will keep this phone, and I will take the cheap one on my travels. Where I am going, I know full well there will be many thieves. I do not wish to tempt them. But we will stay in contact. I will let you know before I make any decisions, and I will not rush. I will do this thing as safely as I can. Mother, do I have your blessing?"

She looks at me, a long, deep look in which I see that, once again, two conflicting sentiments fight for her heart. Finally, she says, "This is a dangerous journey, and you are my only son. I cannot say you have my blessing, but you have my consent. When will you be leaving?"

"Within a week," I respond. "I will now go to the mosque to pray, and afterwards Mustafa and I have a meeting with the smuggler."

"A week?" she replies despondently. I can tell she had hoped it would be longer. "Well," she continues, "hurry to your meeting and hurry back home then. We must make the most of the time we have together."

At that very moment comes the call to prayer. A deep yet grainy voice, somewhat muffled by the loudspeakers which project it through the streets of Sokoto, filters through the branches of the acacia tree that covers us.

"Allaaaaahu Akbar. Allaaaaaahu Akbar. Allaaaaahu Akbar. " A sound as familiar to Sokoto as the honking of sirens or the voices of bartering customers and salesmen at the *kasuwanci* market stalls.

My mother gives me a final nod and heads towards the hut where she will pray with my sisters. Only men will go to mosque for prayer, and I wander out into the streets of Sokoto, making my way towards the local mosque. I arrive there in a matter of minutes. It is not a grand building, but is rather a long, rectangular structure with a large open-air courtyard.

A large crowd of men approach the building from all directions, dressed in their thobes, ankle-length robes with long sleeves, and their Kufi hats, round brimless caps of patterned cloth. We all remove our shoes at the entrance to the mosque. We use the small plastic teapots of lukewarm water that are dotted around to perform ablution, or Wudu, washing our faces and our arms, rinsing behind our ears and in our mouths, wiping the head and feet with water in ritualistic order. We are economical with the water, not wanting to waste it, for drought is an ever-present threat; but the feel of it on our skin provides those of us who will pray outside some respite from the beating rays of red and gold that fall on us relentlessly. We arrange ourselves inside the building, outside the building, everywhere there is space, in horizontal rows of prayer mats, facing the direction of Mecca.

The muezzin continues the call to prayer and the serenity of the moment consumes me. The stillness around me is broken only by the occasional rustle of a prayer mat or the silent hum of devotion. The prayer itself has a number of steps, different movements and words, and I follow the Imam as he leads us in the recitation. We raise our hands to our ears, palms facing forward, we bow our heads, standing erect, hands folded in front of us, repeating the words of the prayer. We kneel and touch our foreheads to the ground. I have done these movements and said these words so many times before that they unravel like clockwork, and my mind wanders not to the contemplation of the divine, but instead to the meeting that lies very close in my future, the meeting with the smuggler who I am to trust with my life.

Once the prayer has finished, my eyes are scanning the crowd, searching for Mustafa. It isn't long until I see him, four rows down from me, facing in the other direction, but with his head moving from side to side in a way that tells me he is also scanning the crowd for me. Mustafa is tall for his age, and even at 16 stands at around 6 foot 2, so it is not difficult for me to spot him through the crowd. I make my way through the cluster of bodies and tap him on the shoulder. He turns to me expectantly, a purposeful look on his face.

"Are you ready?" he asks me, with no preamble.

"I am ready," I respond.

"He will meet us in the back of an electronics shop, about a 15-minute walk from here. He is a character, but don't let that put you off. Remember, he has a track record of success." Mustafa glances at his watch. "We should leave now in order to be on time," he continues.

"Then let's go," I reply, sounding a lot more confident than I feel.

CHAPTER 9

The elevator doors slide open.

"Fifth floor, the control room." says its disembodied voice, as we are greeted by a neat corridor, about six metres across, with a high ceiling and polished oak floors. Joe Gradle steps out into the corridor, beckoning us forward.

"Follow me," he says. "We're almost there." He walks, Mum walks, I roll down the corridor, towards a thick panel of glass which partitions it from some sort of room. The glass is translucent, and though I can see indistinct figures moving behind it, I cannot make them out in detail; they appear blurred. Joe Gradle lifts his left hand and places it against the glass. Another disembodied voice, equivalent in pitch and in timbre to the voice in the elevator, greets him.

"Good morning, Mr. Gradle," it says. "Welcome to the control room. Would these two individuals be your visitors?"

"Yes," Joe replies. "They can enter on my clearance."

The voice replies. "Understood. Security clearance granted. Welcome to the control room."

There is a soft note of hissing, which is almost serpentine in character. Two parallel, uniform fissures extend vertically along the glass, connected by a third horizontal fissure of about a metre and a half in length, two and half metres above the ground. This smaller segment of glass, which appears to have cut itself from the larger pane, pulls itself backwards about an inch before sliding off to the left and revealing a large opening for us to pass through. On the other side of the opening is what must be the control room, but it does not resemble a room so much as an entire floor. As we enter, I see rows and rows of desks, with their occupants sitting in front of large, circular, bowl-like screens which portray a variety of scenarios.

The screens resemble satellite dishes. They are not flat, but rather heavily curved, seemingly intended to portray as large a field of vision as possible in a realistic fashion, allowing the viewer to look above and below, as well as left and right. A few of the people sitting at the desk, generally dressed in comfortable clothes of their own choosing, rather than tailored suits like Joe Gradle, are looking at these screens intently - but most are wearing headsets instead. The principal purpose of the screens seems to be to allow people to see what their colleagues are doing. Joe leads us over to a desk on the third row.

"I've lined up a number of employees that work in a few different areas for you to speak to so you can get an idea of the scope of different roles available. We'll meet with Becky first. She works in reconnaissance."

We arrive at the desk and I meet Becky, who is there waiting for us. Becky makes an immediate impression. She has fiery red hair which seems almost artificial in its flame-like vibrancy. Extremely white makeup foundation makes the red stains painted around her chin and cheeks, surrounding her lips, even more blood-like in quality - and contrasts heavily with the dark brown, almost black, eyeliner and mascara - intentionally smudged to give the impression of tears. The reference is immediately obvious to me, and instead of greeting her as Becky, I find myself saying, "Hello, Delilah," while stretching out my hand.

Delilah, the maiden of mystery, the one whose tears have healing qualities and, if purchased, can be utilised for potent and lucrative potions in the world of Arideth. The face is not quite the same, obviously, but the outfit, the pale skin, the flaming red hair, which I now realise is probably a wig... I am standing before Delilah, the maiden of mysteries.

"Not quite the real Delilah, Becky, but I'm impressed you got the outfit right in one!" she replies, shaking my hand gently, "not that impressed though, there's lots of gamers in the control room after all and I'm sure a fair few have taken the mage route in Arideth. If you can guess correctly the next three or four times we meet, that's when you'll really impress me, Elijah."

"Becky," Joe Gradle chips in, "is one of our more eclectically dressed employees. The first day of her internship, she showed up wearing blue dungarees, a red jumper, white gloves and a red hat with an M on it. The dress code was supposed to be smart casual. No one on the floor could tell who she was supposed to be except Dale. He's into his retro games that were popular 50 or 60 years ago, before glove controllers, when people used things like joysticks. He figured out she was supposed to be some guy called Martin."

"Not Martin," Becky replies exasperatedly. "Mario." She puts on an Italian accent and pinches her fingers together whilst moving her wrists. "It's-a me, Mario!" She gesticulates, but the reference goes over my head. She looks at me hopefully, but seeing that I do not recognize the phrase, she smiles ruefully. "We'll let that one slide, since I'm not wearing it at the moment. You get the next four, and you've impressed me."

"We are not here for him to impress you." Joe Gradle interjects, wagging his finger. "We're here for you to impress him. Tell him a bit about what you do here, Becky. And do we have a working Falcon to hand so we can give him a live demonstration?"

"Sure we do," she replies. She turns her head and shouts down the rows of desks. "Hey, Toby! Toby? He's got his bloody headset on. It's just on Toby's desk. I'll go and grab it."

"No," replies Joe. "Don't worry about that. I'll go and grab it. You tell Elijah a little bit about your role."

Her dark lips curl into a smile as Joe walks off to Toby's desk. "Recon," she says. "I work at the coast. Well, at a number of coasts, depending on where it's needed. I control what's called a Falcon, an artificial bird which from a distance, to the naked eye, is indistinguishable from a real one, but which is in fact a complex drone which lets me see for miles around. If there's a ship heading towards waters or a beach it should not be approaching, filled with people who are not legally supposed to be on board, I am the first to see it. Have you ever played Bird of Prey?"

No, I haven't actually, but I know the game. It's a direct competitor to The Evolution of Wildness, but it focuses only on birds, whereas The Evolution of Wildness has a whole range of animals. And only three of them are birds. The owl, the hummingbird, and the eagle. Bird of Prey has a much wider selection of airborne creatures. There was even a spin-off which focused on flying dinosaurs. I tell her I have not.

She follows up the question, "What about The Evolution of Wildness?"

"That, I have played plenty," I respond. "So, you're telling me this falcon is a bit like Eagle Mode, but controlling a real eagle?"

"A robotic eagle," she corrects me, "but yeah, the concept is similar. The controls are slightly different, more akin to those in Bird of Prey. But it's really not too hard to adjust. Just a few different hand movements and signals. Our Falcons, of course, have the ability to shift between different modes. It looks like I can give you a demonstration," she says, and with a jerk of her head she alerts me to the sight of Joe Gradle making his way back down the row, with a large robotic bird perched on his forearm.

At close range, it is obvious that the bird is not a real animal of flesh and bone. There are small metal pistons which connect the wings, which are more sharply angled than real wings but still covered in brown and white markings that resemble dappled feathers. The eyes have no pupils, but are instead glassy black orbs that I immediately recognize as cameras. As if to confirm my suspicion, a small, bright light blinks in the left eye in a way that makes me think of the words 'standby mode'. The beak and the face are painted convincingly, with yellow markings around the eyes and a sharp curvature to the beak itself, also yellow in colour. I notice that each wing is adorned with two tiny helicopter blades, painted in with the artificial feathers to be as inconspicuous as possible. Joe Gradle is also carrying two medium sized gloves in his hand, which he throws in my direction, I catch them from the air.

"So that you can give it a go once you've had your demonstration. I'm sure you'll be eager to try it out," he says.

I turn back to Becky, who is pulling on her own gloves and headset, and then I turn to my mother, smiling at her excitedly. She still has a slight air of scepticism about her, but also seems curious. She is looking at the bird appraisingly when she notices me trying to catch her eye, and seems to try to rapidly rearrange her features so as to not seem too engrossed in the imminent demonstration. I turn back to Becky and notice that she has purposefully cut out small holes at the ends of the fingers of her gloves in order to allow two-inch fluorescent red nails to jut out of the ends. The nails are the one thing about her outfit which are not faithful to Delilah, the maiden of mystery. I guess changing nails every time she changes an outfit would be prohibitively time consuming.

"Connect to Falcon number 357B12," she says silkily, placing her hands side by side, with her thumbs touching. She raises her fingers and stretches them, and a soft whirr to my right makes me turn my head. The Falcon is still perched on Joe's forearm, but it is now stretching out its wings, and they are extended at an impressive wingspan of around a full metre and a half.

"Big wings," I comment simply.

"Not even," replies Becky. "This is slotted wing mode. These wings are ideal for picking up heavy things or setting off from the ground quickly. If you want to see big wings, let's put it into albatross mode. Falcon, engage albatross mode."

The effect is immediate. The wings immediately start to reform, with metal feathers retracting and pushing out on themselves until the wingspan is closer to about 10 feet, with the wings somewhat thinner.

"Albatross mode is better for efficiency." Becky continues. "The large wingspan allows for a more efficient use of the wind current and less strain on the motor and batteries. It's ideal for when you're spending days over the ocean and need to maintain the bird in the sky for an extended period of time. They are streamlined. They catch lots of air without letting drag or turbulence slow them down. Good for catching rising air currents too. The downside is that manoeuvrability suffers. Stopping or turning quickly isn't easy in albatross mode. So, it's not ideal for a demonstration in the office. Falcon, engage swift mode." Again, the effect is immediate. The wings start to retract, until they are much shorter than they were. Becky curls her fingers and starts to move her hands in a soft flapping motion, and the bird starts to move its wings. A few moments later, it takes off.

I am certainly impressed. My eyes flicker between Becky's fingers and the robotic bird as she makes it spiral into the air, then drop swiftly and suddenly towards my wheelchair in a sharp vertical line before turning out of the free fall just before impact. I try very hard not to flinch at this point. She weaves the bird around with such dexterity that I find it hard to follow its progress at times, and at one point the bird drops out of sight, ducking in and out between the desks, re-emerging underneath Becky's own desk. At the last minute, she opens her legs and the bird appears from between them, spiralling upwards again before flickering down back onto Joe Gradle's arm.

Becky takes off her headset and passes it to me.

"Your turn," she says, gesturing towards the gloves that lie on my lap.

"But don't try all that fancy stuff," interjects Joe Gradle again. "Not on your first fly. We don't need an insurance claim from an employee who's been hit by a Falcon. Just try to fly a few times around the room, above the desks. If you find you're losing control, say 'engage autopilot'."

"Alright," I reply eagerly. I put the gloves on, and touch them to each side of the headset, connecting them together, simultaneously disconnecting Becky's gloves.

"Remember," Becky tells me, "There are minor differences between the flying controls here and the controls on The Evolution of Wildness. It's the curvature of the fingers which indicates the rate of flaps per minute, rather than the extent to which they're splayed. And you ascend and descend using the wrist more than the palm. You'll pick it up soon enough."

With the headset on, I see the room from the bird's perspective rather than my own, and find myself looking directly at a boy in a wheelchair with VR goggles on, biting his lip in anticipation. I see my mother standing at the back of my wheelchair, no longer feeling the need to hide her curiosity as, from her perspective, it is the bird watching her, rather than me. I take off, and just as Becky predicted, it does take me 30 seconds or so to acclimate myself to the slightly different controls. But once I do, I am spinning and weaving in the air, ducking and diving, barrel rolling, dropping a few feet and doing flips. I know, without having to see the bird from my own perspective, that to those watching from the ground below, it will look like excellent flying.

I remind myself that this is an interview of sorts. They are trying to place me in the right department. Despite what Joe Gradle says, it is important that I should be impressing them as much as they are impressing me. But I resist the temptation to get cocky and dive to the level of the desks. I must also show that I am able to follow orders. After a few minutes of losing myself in the Falcon, I descend shakily back onto Joe Gradle's outstretched arm. When I take off the headset, a young boy is standing next to Becky's chair with an impressed look on his face. He looks like he may not even have reached his teenage years.

"Impressive," he says. "That was your first time flying a Falcon? Impressive." He stretches out his hand. "Tim Weibers," he introduces himself. "Combat and Control. I shoot things, and sometimes people."

"TimWeiber47?" I ask him questioningly, outstretching my arm to shake his small hand.

"In the VirtuWorld, yes." he says, his brow slightly furrowed. "How did you...?"

"You shot me," I tell him. "In Final Facedown III. A few weeks ago. I'm still recovering my ranking."

"Ah, well," he replies bashfully. "Don't feel too bad. I'm one of the top-rated Final Facedown players in the country."

"You're not special here, Tim." Becky responds sharply. "This room is full of the best of the best. I'm sure that's only a little bit of what Elijah can do, which is why they're recruiting him. Don't get big headed."

"No fighting," Joe Gradle's voice says sharply. "We're supposed to be impressing our guest and showing him how great a team we are."

"No fighting," repeats Becky with a dry chuckle. "Just some

sisterly advice."

"Sisterly advice from a woman who's not my sister," says Tim snarkily. "But I'll take it on board. Elijah? Is it? Drop by my desk if you want to see some remote-controlled weaponry that will blow your mind!" He saunters off with just about all the arrogant swagger a 12-year-old can muster. I do, in fact, visit Tim's desk eventually, but first Joe takes me to a number of employees working in different areas. One is a middle-aged man named Jim who says he has been gaming almost every waking hour from his teenage years. My mother winces at this. He points to one of the glass doors that adorn the outer edges of the room and tells me that it leads to his pod. Pods are small bedrooms utilised by employees who want to sleep at the office. For Jim, between his work and his gaming, he finds that commuting to-and-fro takes too much time. I can tell my mum is uncomfortable with the idea of someone living in the control room, alternating between sleep, the VirtuWorld, and working monitoring robots that run the length of the border walls thrown up on the Moroccan coast. I am quick to move on from that desk, to find someone with a better work-life balance to parade in front of her.

We visit five or six desks before I make it over to Tim Weibers. As he already mentioned, he works in Combat and Control, remotely controlling a robot designed to subdue, repel and intimidate large crowds of migrants on land, decked out with weaponry - pepper spray, rubber bullets, real bullets and tasers.

He explains that the robot he controls is designed to be a nonviolent, nonlethal tool for border security. It provides a physical barrier between border agents and migrants, allowing agents to remain safely out of harm's way. The robot is equipped with audio and video capabilities to allow agents to control the situation remotely. Whatever Tim says, the robot does sound fairly violent and fairly lethal in the wrong hands. This is the official spiel, the stuff he is supposed to say to new recruits. But I don't forget the first words he told me as he introduced himself.

"Combat and Control. I shoot things, and sometimes people."

CHAPTER 10

As soon as we enter the store, the look on the face of the man behind the counter tells me he knows we are not here to purchase electronics. The outfit is your typical Nigerian phone shop, with Tecno phones on display alongside Samsungs and other well-known brands, a laptop which is in the process of being deconstructed sitting on the countertop without its screen, an old computer in the corner with a tattered sign that says "An hour of internet time: 1,000 Naira," and a few dusty chairs. Nothing about the place gives any indication that a very different type of business is sharing these premises.

The man behind the counter is tall and wears an ill-fitting suit, flecks of dandruff sit on its shoulders. He looks to be about 40. He raises his head towards the ceiling, pointing upwards with his eyes and says,

"He is waiting for you upstairs. Follow through the corridor."

He lifts the desktop barrier that separates those in front of the counter from those behind it, and we traverse the threshold, subsequently making our way into the corridor beyond. A narrow set of stairs curves off to the left and Mustafa takes the lead. Once we reach the top of the stairs, a wooden door in black peeling paint stands before us. Mustafa knocks three times, and we wait side by side.

For a few seconds there is silence, and then a thick Yoruba accent emerges from behind the door. "Hey, Mustafa!" it says. "Come on in. I have been waiting for you ohh." Mustafa opens the door, and I follow him through it into the room. It is relatively bare.

Storage boxes line the outside perimeter, filled with old dusty electronic material, computers and cables. I wonder whether this is actual stock for the store below or a ruse to make the room seem less suspicious if the authorities were ever to visit.

There is a very basic folding table in the centre of the room, behind which sits a short man wearing several gold and silver chains, a basketball jersey with matching shorts, and expensive looking sandals. He has a pair of stylish sunglasses on, even though the light in the room is dim. He is puffing on a large shisha pipe, which sits on the left side of the table, and blowing ringlets into the air in quick succession. He holds up a finger as if to tell us to give him a moment. We wait for at least 20 seconds as he attempts to pass a small ring of smoke through a slightly larger one in the air. He succeeds on his third attempt, and then beckons us forward to sit on the two plastic chairs on the opposite side of the desk. I notice they are the same type of plastic chairs as those in my childhood home. Mustafa shuts the door behind us and we seat ourselves opposite him.

"And you even brought a friend as promised," he says to Mustafa. "Well done. My name is Olusola," he says to me. "So, you know the name of the game."

His deep voice suddenly takes on a sing-song quality.

"Take the journey sea, right to Germany.
Make your new home in Paris or Rome.
Hire a fleet to take you to Greece.
As long as you pay, you'll get to UK!"

We both nod. We know what he is talking about. He is offering us a way to illegally travel to Europe. He is a smuggler.

He leans back in his chair, takes another long drag from his shisha pipe and exhales, "But first," he continues, "I must not forget my hospitality." He extends the flexible hose of the shisha pipe towards Mustafa. Mustafa catches my eye. I can tell we're both asking ourselves the same question. Is this shisha haram? We both know the answer, but Mustafa takes the pipe anyway and takes a small puff, exhaling a smoke that smells like blueberries. Mustafa seems to enjoy both the sensation and the taste and takes another, slightly longer, drag on the pipe. As he does this, the smuggler reaches into his pocket and pulls out a pack of cigarettes. He takes one out of the pack and puts it between his lips, moving his head towards the burning carbon squares that sit on top of the foil at the summit of the shisha pipe, using them to light his cigarette. "Cigarette smoke is much thinner," he says. "Not as easy to do tricks with, but I'll smoke this and you guys can enjoy the shisha."

Mustafa passes me the pipe and I take a small drag. The blueberry taste is pleasant, but the smoke makes me cough, and the smuggler gives a small chuckle before reaching out and taking the pipe back himself.

"All right then, you're not used to the stuff. For now I can handle both."

He places the hose of the pipe in his mouth, next to the cigarette, and takes a deep drag of both - exhaling the mixture of fumes through the corners of his mouth without removing either. He takes the pipe out afterwards, but leaves the cigarette in his mouth between his teeth, so that when he talks his voice is slightly muffled.

"Now, let's get down to business," he begins. We both nod, eager to hear what he has to say. The smuggler leans forward and begins to outline the details of his plan.

"Mustafa tells me that he only has enough for the first leg of his journey to Libya. Now, there's no pun intended in what I'm about to say because probably you will tell me you don't have enough money to get to that stage of the journey. But are you in the same dinghy? Are you in the same boat?"

"Yes," I reply, "I only have enough to get me to Libya. 130,000 Naira."

"Or 300 US dollars," he confirms. "That is fine. As long as we know where we stand. Mustafa, you pay 270 dollars. 10% discount for having brought a friend."

"We will split the discount," Mustafa says in response. "5% each."

I turn to my friend with a look of surprise. Five percent of 130,000 Naira is not an amount to be sniffed at. "Thank you," I tell him.

"You have a good friend there," the smuggler's voice comes across from the other side of the table, again with a plume of smoke. "Keep hold of him in Libya. One of the most important things you can have on a voyage like this is a good friend. Logistics. We leave on Friday. You pay me 50% today in cash. The other 50% on departure. We set off from here. It's a two-hour drive from here across the border to Birnin Konni, and a ten-hour drive all the way to Zinder. I take you as far as Zinder and then you will get on a big truck with lots of people that will take you to Agadez overnight. In Agadez, you can have a small break, because the next stage of the journey is the most difficult and the most dangerous. The desert, and the border with Libya.

Between here and Niger, Nigerian citizens can move freely, but technically, you aren't supposed to go into Libya without papers. So the driver will have to evade the authorities for that leg of the journey. The main things to remember are to stay alert, trust no one who is not endorsed by yours truly, listen to instructions, and stick together. Bring a small bag with your possessions, but not two, if you bring too much stuff then things will be stolen. Space on these vehicles is money and once you make it to the next leg, space on a dingy is gold. You're paying me to smuggle you, not your childhood teddy bear. That's it. Any questions?"

I am too overwhelmed to form any questions. Mustafa and I look at each other and shake our heads.

"Right then," the smuggler says, standing up. "Looks like you are all set. Almost. Dame la pasta!"

"What?" Mustafa and I ask in unison.

"Dame la pasta," Olusola repeats. "It means, 'Give me the money' in Spanish. Fun mi ni owo. Ka ba ni kudi. Nye m ego" Olusola repeats the phrase in Yoruba, Hausa, and even Igbo, the three largest languages of Nigeria; the Yoruba phrase, I barely understand; the Igbo, I only understand because he has just repeated the phrase in three other languages. He holds out his hand expectantly and then taps the desk.

Mustafa reaches into his pocket and pulls out a wad of cash. He counts out the money, taking care to make sure that Olusola has the right amount, 50% in advance, and then hands it over. I do the same for my share, and Olusola takes it all and puts it into the desk drawer. This feels like the act where my decision becomes final - I am leaving for Libya. He then looks at us both and says, "Good luck on your journey. And remember, stay together, trust no one, and obey instructions. I will see you at 10am on Friday, downstairs."

Olusola continues puffing on his cigarette and his shisha pipe and Mustafa and I let ourselves out, descending the stairs in silence. Once we enter into the electronics shop, an idea comes to mind, and I turn to the tall shopkeeper in his dandruff sprinkled suit and ask him if he could sell me a SIM card.

"Yes," he replies. "But if you are a customer of mine, and not a customer of the man upstairs, then you have to get on the right side of the counter before I will do business with you."

"Sure thing." I reply, and make my way back through the barrier so that I face him over the countertop.

"I'm guessing you don't want a local SIM card?" he asks me

with a smirk. "I'm guessing you want a SIM card you can use internationally in Algeria or Libya or even Europe. Is that correct?"

"Something like that," I respond. "Yes. Can you help me?"

"I have just the thing," he replies, turning around and dancing his fingers across the various products before landing on one with a tap. He clutches between his fingers a thin piece of cardboard with an item taped to it. He pulls back the tape from the cardboard and underneath it is a SIM card.

"This one is international." He says "Easy to top up in different countries and a reasonable rate for international calls."

He hands it to me. I have no grounds on which to distrust him, especially as I haven't understood some of what he's said. I nod. Then this one I will take.

"How much is it?" I ask.

"5000 Naira," he says.

"Ah!" says Mustafa as if deeply offended, slipping into Pidgin English.

"5,000 be too much oh. You dey give him 2,500 and the deal is sealed."

The man behind the counter sucks his teeth. "2,500?" He questions, scandalised. "Dis one na premium SIM card. I know say you don spend plenty money upstairs so I go do 4,000. 4,000 na my best price."

Mustafa immediately takes a conciliatory tone. "My friend, my friend oh," he replies. "Make am 3,500 and di deal go sweet."

"Okay" replies the man behind the counter. "But the 3,500 only be for this SIM card, and I dey assume say you go want at least 1,000 credits. 4500, I'm giving you a deal."

"Make that 1,500 credits. An even 5,000." I come into the conversation.

"Done," replies the man behind the counter, handing over the SIM card. I take out the money and pay for the item. He taps away at his computer and asks me the number written on the SIM card. I read it out to him, and he adds the 1,500 to the account.

"So where are you guys headed then?" He asks us. "Germany? Morocco? France? Sweden?"

"Europe," I reply, realising that I have not thought of which specific country in Europe I would like to find myself in; that I do not even really know the differences between them.

"Italy to start with," Mustafa replies, "That's where we'll land. I go love reach somewhere for Scandinavia. I heard that it's only just starting to get warm, and that very rarely in Scandinavia you even experience truly cold weather. Some people don say that Scandinavia will be habitable the longest. If I reach there, find some stable work, and somehow carry my family come follow me, ee go be dream."

Mustafa has certainly done his research. I remember that he was the initiator, the one who brought me into this. He must have been planning in advance, seeking out the smuggler. Of course it's something he has thought about more deeply. But I listen to his words, trying to commit the syllables to memory - skan da nei vi ya - hoping I will remember the name of that place.

The man behind the counter shakes his head wistfully and I can't help but notice a few more flakes of dandruff settling on his suit.

"It dey hard journey, it dey dangerous journey," he says "You do know that? Everybody know about Sahara and di heat and di thirst and di cars wey full of young men wey dey smothered for sandstorm for night. And everybody don hear about di big water. Di dangerous wahala. But sometimes I dey hear stories wey no quite natural. Strange. Crazy birds wey dey dive from sky and use dia beak puncture boat and even tear life jacket. Giant eight-leg octopus wey dey rise from down to sink ships and, sometimes, bullets wey dey fall from sky. No every traveller go reach their destination."

"Indeed," replies Mustafa dryly, "Every day go be battle to survive. Struggle to continue against di odds, see people around you die. Basically the same as if we were to stay..."

To know is one thing, and to be reminded is another. I am reminded of the risks at hand, the possibility of death by thirst, by heat, by drowning, by murder. But Mustafa is right. The same weight hangs over me here at home. I smile at the man behind the bar and tell him we will do our best to be careful.

He smiles back, gives another rueful shake of his head. "I hope so," he says. "I hope so."

"Does Olusola know that you're down here talking down his business to his new customers?" Mustafa asks the man behind the counter.

"His business?!" replies the man disdainfully, "Olusola no get sense to run business like this. E dey smoke too much. Is my business. Olusola is my son, my pikin. But because I dey work for carry people, I dey work for traffic human being, dat one mean say I dey dishonest? Di SIM card wey I sell you. If you go travel and find that I have lied to you and that it is not international, you go call me liar. Fraudster businessman. You go call me 419. I no be any of dem things. I no go take your money without warn you about di danger of di journey. I dey smuggle, but I no be criminal. I dey provide service wey dem dey demand for. I provide service for which there is a market."

The man behind the counter looks at me quizzically for a moment and sighs. "Good luck on your journey," he tells me.

"Thank you." I reply.

We leave.

CHAPTER 11

I'm sitting in the living room in my chair, waiting for my father to come home. I have decided to take the job with the Home Office, but I still need to confirm my decision with my parents. I still need to allay my mother's fears, and to explain my new ambitions and the benefits they hold to my father, a stern man, who is rarely home and yet who I'm sure still takes deep interest in the prospects of his children. I need to give my pitch. Mum has agreed with me that, once Dad gets home this evening, we will discuss it as a family - minus the other children.

I'm rehearsing my reasons in my head. The fact that the job is entirely wheelchair friendly, yet still allows me to be in some way stimulated by the external world. Not trapped on Excel and Microsoft Word all day, but plugged into nature, seeing different parts of the world - all from the comfort and safety of my chair. The fact that I will be guaranteeing myself some security, some financial independence, removing myself of the burden of student debt, whilst keeping open the option of continuing my studies alongside. Tim Weibers is 12 or 13. I distinctly remember that his username was TimWeiber47. That shocked me. Being born in 2047 means he is 12 or 13 years old, and he is working for them. Legally he must be in school. They have found some way to make that work, and I am three years older. Taking the job will allow me freedom to feel secure in pursuing my education, not hinder it. That is what I must tell my parents.

I will accept my mother's suggestion of taking up an instrument. Put her at ease. Spend some time detached from work and the VirtuWorld and learn to play some music. After all, I do so love when she plays guitar, and how I have seen her improve since the accident. It would be good for us to play together. It would allow us another way to bond. My train of thought is sharply interrupted by my brother, who slips into the room, hands in pockets, still dressed in his pyjamas. His skin is slightly more tanned than mine, and his features have much more of the Caribbean tone of my mum's parents. He looks less European than I, and kids at school sometimes ask us if we're full brothers or only half brothers, unable to do the maths in their heads.

"We're full brothers," I usually reply. "You just didn't realise I had so much Rasta in me." A few of the kids act weird when they realise I'm half Jamaican, but most of the kids are cool about it. I've never really asked my brother if his experience is different, but I guess it probably is.

"I'm locked out of Fixflix. Can I use your account?" He asks me, not quite descending to the level of puppy dog eyes, but pouting slightly.

"Sure thing," I say.

"What's the password then?" he asks, taking out his phone.

"It's the same password I use for everything, so bring it here and I'll type it in," I respond.

"What, you don't trust me?" he asks.

"If you can lose your own password so easily, why should I trust you with mine?" I respond, raising my eyebrows. "Bring the phone, I'll type it in." He smirks, walks over, and hands me the phone. It's already on the Fixflix login page, and I type in my account details and password, purposefully leaning the screen of the phone away from my brother as if hiding it from him. Hamming up the joke.

"Yeah, yeah, yeah, very funny," he says as I hand it back to him. "Nice one. I'll see you later, yeah?" He turns and exits the room.

I try to recalibrate upon his exit. I know that him entering the room blocked off some train of thought, but I'm not immediately able to remember where that train of thought was headed. Why am I in the living room? To see my parents. About what? The Home Office. Yes, Home Office job. Rehearsing reasons as to why they should let me take it. That's the train of thought. Wheelchair friendly. Education. Learn instrument... I hear the front door of the house open down the corridor and the distinctive rhythmic shuffle of the feet on the doormat, and know it's him. Okay, the conversation's imminent. I hear him make his way down the hall and he pokes his head inside. 45 years old with hair that melts between copper and brown, green eyes and a greying beard. A hairline that's receding at the sides more than the middle. A slightly crooked nose. There is definitely no Rasta in my father.

"So," he says matter-of-factly, "Elijah, what's all this I'm hearing about you getting a job? Wait..." He holds up his finger to me and turns his head into the corridor, shouting, "Darling, I'm in the living room with Elijah."

"I'll be there in a minute." My mum's voice comes back down the hall. He turns his head back to me and it is followed by the rest of his body into the room. He comes and sits close to my chair on the arm of the sofa.

"So," he repeats matter-of-factly, "Elijah, what's all this I'm hearing about you getting a job?"

"The Home Office approached me," I say very quickly, trying not to stammer. "Because of my scores in my video games, they think I will be a good fit for one of their teams that works in migration control. Everything would be done remotely, controlled with gloves and a headset, just like when I play my games. I'd be able to do it from my wheelchair. I wouldn't have to pay for university. They'll pay for that. And I'll be earning a salary. Building myself a nest egg. We went to visit the offices and..."

"Hold on, hold on, hold on. You're going too fast. Let's start from the top. Do you like this job? Having seen what you've seen, do you think it will make you happy?"

"Yes," I say to him. "I do. And if it doesn't, I can always get out of it."

"Okay," he says. "And what do you know about migrant control? What makes you passionate about that in particular?"

I don't really know what to say, but I try to say something. "It's not that I'm that passionate about migrant control. It's that I'm passionate about using the technology. I'm passionate about being able to spend my days, in some way, out in the world. I didn't think such a job would be possible for me."

"Okay," my dad pauses, his eyes fixed somewhere over my shoulder, and strokes his moustache with his pinky finger as he always does when in thought. "It's a respectable career," he says. "In a way, I guess, since you're working for the Home Office, you could be called a civil servant. And it is important for us to control our borders. Legal immigration, like your great, great grandparents, is one thing. But illegal immigration without documents, quite another. You'll be serving your country and helping to stamp it out."

I've never really thought much about immigration, whether it's legal, whether it's illegal, or how important it is, but my dad seems to approve, so I nod enthusiastically and say, "yes, it would be a pleasure."

My dad resumes the stroking of his moustache, his eyes becoming even more pensive, and he begins to nod his head slowly up and down, my mum surprises us both by appearing as if out of thin air in the rocking chair opposite us. She must have entered the room silently, and who knows how much of the conversation she has been privy to. She doesn't waste time.

"We need to look at this thing from every angle," she says diplomatically, as if negotiating the hardest bargain of the century, "Elijah, I can see that you want to take the job, and Jeremy, I can see that you are inclined to grant your permission. Okay. There are plenty of benefits to him taking it, I accept that. And who am I to tell him that he can't? But I think we should take them up on the offer of you starting out part-time, on as little hours as possible to begin with, to give you some sort of trial period, and we should have another conversation with them about exactly how you can balance this with studying."

I smile at her gleefully, and I'm sure I see the shadow of a smile play on her lips in reply.

CHAPTER 12

There are six of us, including Olusola, the smuggler. Six of us stood around a small blue four-seater. The car appears to be in a state of semi-disrepair, but still functional. Its paint is chipped, its rims are a bit rusty, and it is riddled with several dents and scratches. I'm relieved that at a first glance I see no trace of bullet holes.

One of the strangers pipes up. A small man with large pupils framed within eyes that do not have whites but yellows. His hair is so closely cut that he appears almost bald, a thin layer of stubble that would be more at home on his chin than his scalp. Tribal scars extend his smile, carefully traced symmetrical gouges that run from the corners of his mouth towards his ears like whiskers. Indentations, a darker, woodier, nuttier brown than the rest of his skin. He wears a shirt that must once have been colourful. Geometric zigzags and stripes of pink, blue, and orange peek through vertical lines of what can still be distinguished as white, but dust and grime have long muddied both the colours and the whiteness, dulling its vibrancy.

"How do we fit?" he interjects.

He does not ask the question incredulously. We have all seen overloaded cars before, with passengers clinging to the upper edges of open windows and standing on side rails, mothers with babies attached to wrappers on their backs, sitting on the rooftops of moving vehicles, passengers sitting on each other's laps. All of this is common in Sokoto. The question is not one of incredulity, but one of logistics. It is a 10-hour drive to Zinder, and 10 hours is a long time to sit on a roof, exposed to the elements, if the vehicle is moving quickly.

"I drive," Olusola says. He is smoking again, although, by the smell of the smoke, I do not think it contains tobacco this time. "One passenger in the front passenger seat. Three passengers share the back. The smallest person goes in the boot. Halfway through, we'll swap them out with the second smallest."

I glance around the group surreptitiously. The man with the tribal scars is clearly the smallest in the group. Mustafa is one of the taller migrants, although one giant who stands at about six foot four stands taller than him. I assume that he will take the front seat, where there will be room for his giraffe legs. Another quick review of the group and I am resigned to the fact that I am indeed the second smallest. At 16 I have not quite finished growing, and stand at only about five foot seven. Halfway through the journey, I will be relegated to travelling in the boot.

"Don't worry," Olusola says to the man with the tribal scars. "There are holes in the boot for ventilation. You will not suffocate. It's dark in there, but a good place to catch a nap." For some reason, I don't quite believe him about the nap. I move closer to take a look at the supposed ventilation holes, and they are visible at the top corners of the boot, uniform and fairly large. Again, I'm relieved that they appear to have been made with a drill rather than a bullet. We load into the vehicle with our backpacks of belongings. I am squashed into the back with Mustafa and a spectacled man with a pencil moustache who sniffs regularly.

As predicted, the giant takes the front seat. We give him the nickname Dogo, which means long, high, or tall. Our journey begins smoothly. We head north on Abdulah Fodio Road towards Niger, passing the regular sights, donkey drawn carts carrying young men and their cargo, women with large baskets of fruits teetering on their heads, children playing and begging on the sides of the roads, the occasional police officer or soldier, endless stretches of mudbrick buildings and straw huts melting into the roadside alongside buildings of concrete and steel.

When we begin to approach the border with Niger, Olusola asks the wider group, "Who has Ecowas passport?" I have my own passport from the days in which I used to traverse the border with my father, picking up and dropping off merchandise to trade: fabrics and trinkets, jewellery and blunt ceremonial swords. The bespectacled man in the back with us also has a passport, and I doubt that the man in the boot will need one, unless for some reason they decide to check it. However, both the giant and Mustafa tell Olusola that they do not have any documents. Olusola pulls up the car, opens the glove compartment and pulls out a thick wad of passports attached to each other with a large elastic band.

He starts with the giant, going through the passports one by one and lifting them to eye level, scrutinising first the passport and then the giant's face, eyes flickering between the two. He goes through four or five passports before deciding that the resemblance is strong enough and handing over one of the documents.

"What's your name?" he asks the giant. "I am Abdulai," responds the giant, without looking at the document he has just been handed. Good, I can now stop referring to him as the giant and call him Abdulai moving forward. But Olusola is not satisfied with his response.

"No," he shouts, making those of us in the back of the vehicle jump, our limbs - already squashed together - clatter against each other like bones in a bag. "What is your name?" Olusola repeats.

Abdulai looks fleetingly towards those of us in the back of the vehicle as if asking for help. "Abdulai Kareem.." He responds to Olusola with a hint of confusion in his voice.

"No!" shouts Olusola again, following his second outburst with a deep disappointed sigh before taking a long toke on the joint between his fingers. He grabs Abdulai's hand, which still contains the passport, and lifts it to Abdulai's eye level, manipulating Abdulai's fingers in such a way that they open the pages of the little green book.

"What is your name?" he repeats for the third time.

'Oh!' says Abdulai. His voice and expression filling with realisation. "My name is Muhammad. My name is Muhammad Hasan."

"Correct," responds Olusola. "For the next half hour, your name is Muhammad Hasan. Do not forget it."

He repeats the process with Mustafa, who ironically receives a passport which also holds the name Mustafa, so that he only needs to memorise a new surname. Olusola sets off again on the road, and before long we reach the checkpoint, where we are waved through by an extremely bored looking customs officer who takes only the most cursory of glances at the documents.

"If only every border was so easy to cross," says Mustafa, once we have crossed it.

"Do you want to put me out of a job?" Olusola responds.

For the first time, the car is filled with laughter, I even think I hear some chuckles coming from the boot.

The bespectacled man who is squashed on the other side of the back seats, against the opposite window to mine, turns to me and Mustafa.

"So, where are you guys headed?" he asks.

"For now we only have the money to take us to Libya," Mustafa responds. "But we hope to work there for a while and then eventually head for Europe."

"Ah, that's a shame," replies the bespectacled man. "I am hoping to go to Germany. I have paid up front for as far as Libya, but my parents have more money, which they will send once I arrive in Libya, for me to go straight to Europe."

"I'm making the journey straightaway too." says Abdulai from the front. "I have a brother who made it to Greece and will send the money to me. Once I arrive in Libya I want to go and join him there so we can help our family. The one in the boot, however, Hasan, I spoke to him this morning. He is like you. Heading for Libya and hoping for the best."

At this we all fall silent for a minute, lost in our own thoughts. We continue to Birnin Konni, a small town not far from the border, before turning onto the national highway of Niger, where the landscape becomes even more barren. As the day moves into afternoon and the sun comes out in full force, the heat of our squashed bodies mingles in the car, such that my skin under my clothes becomes sticky with perspiration. Opening the windows does help, but the strong gusts of breeze that buffet the left side of my face when the window is fully opened come with their own degree of uncomfortableness, so we open and close them at regular intervals. As the clock ticks on, more and more do I find myself dreading my time in the boot. We have two and a half five-litre bottles of water in the vehicle and we gulp at them periodically, but we do not go overboard, as they have the last us the whole journey.

At this point, the landscape is barren and the trees are scarce, although the occasional acacia tree stands - its spirit having refused to descend into the earth. Olusola pulls over outside a petrol station after a few more hours, but after exiting the vehicle and having a short discussion out of earshot with the owner, he comes back to the car, swearing under his breath. "They have no diesel," he announces to the vehicle. "They have been robbed. And we're running low. We'll have to try to get to the next station, or risk buying from a hawker."

There are plenty of hawkers around, of course. Men who sit by the side of the road with jerry cans full of questionable liquid, collecting money to pour it into the fuel tanks of passing cars. The liquid that the hawkers sell is usually the same stuff that the bandits have stolen, but sometimes it is cut with cheap kerosene or stale diesel which has long gone off. By the time the vehicle breaks down, it has travelled far enough from the hawker for him to face no repercussions. It may well break down in the middle of the Sahara, full of thirsty, hungry, tired migrants, without a petrol station or a hawker in sight.

Abdulai the giant pitches in. "Don't worry, I'm an engineer. Not officially but that's all I've ever done; work with cars. At times I have hawked petrol myself. Go to a hawker and I will taste the diesel and make sure we do not get stung."

Olusola squints at him suspiciously, but seems to conclude that we have little choice. We continue on the road, and after five minutes or so come across one of the hawkers, sitting on the roadside in ripped trousers and a torn stained t-shirt next to five or six jerry cans. Olusola pulls up beside him and winds down his window. "Petrol or diesel?" He shouts out of the window.

"I get petrol. I get diesel. I get both," responds the hawker. Even his rudimentary Pidgin English is accented with French, as we have passed the border into Niger, a Francophone African country, where English is rarely spoken. But we are still close enough to the border for some of the hawkers to know a few basic words.

"How much?" responds Olusola.

"10 litres, 10,000 Naira," replies the hawker. Olusola revs his engine as if about to set off again.

"Wait, wait," says the hawker. "Okay,... nine thousand. Dubu tara. Neuf mille."

"Eight." replies Olusola.

"Eight thousand five hundred, ten litres, 20 litres - 15,000," replies the hawker

"20 for 15,000 sound fine, c'est bon," replies Olusola. "But we no go dey trust una blindly. *Mon ami va tester le diesel.*" I think I understand what he's saying. The trips I made with my dad across the border when I was younger have given me a slight ear for French. He's indicating that we will test the diesel. Olusola indicates for Abdulai to get out of the car. Abdulai turns back towards us in the back seats and points towards our feet at an empty transparent five-litre plastic bottle.

"Pass me that, please," he says. Mustafa does so. Abdulai exits the vehicle and walks around towards the Hawker. "Pour diesel inside this bottle, please," he says to the hawker, who looks like he does not quite understand. Abdulai repeats himself in Hausa whilst miming the action of pouring.

"Wait," replies the hawker. He bends down and scoops up a funnel from behind the jerry cans, placing it into the top of the water bottle. Abdulai secures the bottle in place with one hand and the funnel with another, whilst the hawker pours diesel from one of the jerry cans into the bottle itself. A few bubbles rise towards the top. At this point, I am craning my neck across Mustafa so as to see what is going on out of Olusola's door, which is open, allowing us to view the scene. The diesel itself is a blue colour, but a clearer liquid, which has a slight orange tint, seems to settle at the bottom of the bottle beneath the diesel.

"Water contamination" declares Abdulai, "And a little rust, no emulsion, we will have to let it settle and then decant it in, diesel sits on top of water so that should work. If we had put this straight into the tank, we would have been screwed." He dips his little finger into the diesel at the top of the bottle and licks it. "The diesel itself is good though."

"Did you hear? You almost screwed us! 20 litres, 10,000 Naira - I want discount for am!" Olusola exclaims.

The hawker seems to understand and begins to protest, but Olusola opens the glove compartment and takes out a small pistol, and the hawker quickly shuts up. Decanting the watery diesel into the fuel tank is simple enough, just requiring Abdulai to pour the diesel into the plastic bottle first, five litres at a time, allow it to settle, and then pour the diesel into the tank without allowing the clear but slightly orange tinted water at the bottom of the bottle to pass its mouth. The hawker takes his 10,000 Naira quietly and goes back to sit next to his jerry cans.

"We're about halfway through the journey," says Olusola, after the tank has been topped up. "We may as well do the swap now. Hakeem, it's your turn in the boot."

CHAPTER 13

These are the terms. To start with, two days a week. Friday and Saturday. Remember, the control room is open 24 hours, seven days a week. Immigration does not stop and nor do they. So working weekends is perfectly normal, and this arrangement allows me to still go into school four days out of five. That was the most my mother would allow. And I think it is good. I still have Sunday to spend in the VirtuWorld, and I am able to explore this new avenue, to begin in the work that might take me through the next few decades.

For the next four weeks, I will spend two days each with four different teams. Usually, when someone comes in through the internship program, they spend more time on each rotation. But because of my scores in the VirtuWorld, and possibly because of my performance with the Falcon, they don't deem a full internship necessary, and I want to find out which team I will be best suited for as quickly as possible. Four weeks, four teams, four different applications of my skills. I will try reconnaissance, utilising a real robotic Falcon at the Italian border, where many migrants from Africa are trying to penetrate Europe across the Mediterranean Sea. That rotation will be with Becky, the cosplaying pretty young employee from the reconnaissance team who wears a different outfit each day, meticulously put together to resemble a well known gaming character.

I will do a rotation with Tim Weibers, the 12-year-old member of the combat and control team who is far more cocky than any 12-year-old has the right to be, and defeated me in Final Facedown III a few weeks ago. His robots are placed at the Calais border in France, where many migrants try to make the crossing over the Channel to the white cliffs of Dover. Intense and frequent storms have worn away at the cliff face and beach erosion has led to damage at the base of the cliffs, but people still make the passage. Many of the migrants who come from sub-Saharan Africa and the Middle East come from countries where English is either their first language or their second. And when they find themselves in Europe, in continental or southern Europe, they find themselves in countries where they do not understand the language, and so they try to breach our borders. When large crowds of them gather, or get too close to the coast, or try to storm the tunnels for the Eurostar, Tim Weibers' robot acts as crowd control, dispersing and controlling large groups of people.

I'm most nervous about this rotation because I fear it might involve enacting violence. I've played plenty of violent games. Final Facedown III and Arideth can both be intensely violent, the first focusing on modern warfare and the second involving sword fights, mace fights and sorcerers' spells. But even though the characters in those games can sometimes seem like real people, even though the artificial intelligence is convincing, the people I might have to enact violence on in this rotation will be real people. People who are breaking the law and trying to make their way illegally into an already overcrowded Britain, but still real people. And something about Tim gets on my nerves too. At the moment, I'm leaning more towards reconnaissance and Becky.

The third rotation is with Jim in Ceuta, controlling the monkey robots that construct, maintain, monitor and defend the Great Wall. Ceuta is at the northernmost tip of Morocco, but it's recognised as Spanish territory, and those who manage to get over the Great Wall find themselves in a position to attempt to cross into mainland Spain. The boundaries of Ceuta have shrunk in the past few decades as sea level rise has put some of it underwater, and it is expected that soon the Great Wall might actually have to be reconstructed further back, to keep it as far from the coastline as possible, reducing the chances of migrants who manage to pass it then making it on to Europe.

I am quite interested in this job because there's something mechanical about it. Maintaining and reconstructing a wall. It's almost like a jigsaw puzzle. It would allow me to use my brain. I'd be doing the rotation with Jim, who spends all his time in the office. He even sleeps there. He's also a big fan of Arideth, but he focuses on the warrior route rather than the mage route, and I'm more of a mage warrior, focusing on aspects of magic and archery, along with a little sword work too. He's recommended me a number of quests which he says are particularly rewarding. I like Jim and I get along well with him, but there's still something about reconnaissance with Becky that is making me lean towards it. And I must admit, perhaps it's not just the reconnaissance.

My fourth rotation is quite exciting, but also rather scary. It will be underwater. I will not be underwater, of course, I'll just be sitting at my desk. But the robot itself will be underwater. Apparently, it has all sorts of adaptations to accommodate this. Shaped like an octopus, covered in watertight silicone, it even has adhesive suckers and can spew a thick oily 'ink'. The robots are massive, and are used to patrol the waters for illegal migrants making the sea crossing in boats across the Aegean Sea, from Turkey to Greece, and coerce them into heading back. Ironically, it seems the need for it to be watertight and the use of silicon has made the robot appear even more lifelike. The OctoBot team is headed by a 50-year-old woman called Jill. She apparently comes from a science background. I haven't met her yet, but Becky tells me she's nice.

I am quite pleased with myself, because I managed to guess Becky's outfit for a second time, and she told me last time I saw her that if I guessed it four consecutive times she would be impressed. Today she is dressed as Shimako, the main character of the Japanese samurai game, "The Swords of Samurai." I have not played the game much, but it was very heavily advertised a few years ago, and the way Becky is dressed today is a mirror image of the way Shimako was dressed in the adverts. Traditional Japanese attire, such as sandals, tabi socks, a kimono and a hakama. Her hair is also done in a traditional samurai style, with two long braids, held together with a red ribbon. A wooden katana is sheathed in the woollen sash she wears around her waist. I doubt she could have gotten a metal one through security. Her makeup is the makeup of traditional Japanese opera, with a deeply white foundation, but heavily red lipstick and eyeliner. Even the eyebrows, seemingly dyed red.

"Got it in one," she had said when I had identified her. "Got it in one again," and she smiled at me cheekily. Yes, I think reconnaissance with Becky might be the rotation for me.

She swivels her chair and turns to me, her virtual reality headset pulled up to her forehead like swimming goggles when the swimmer is not in the pool, ocean blue fingernails protruding from the tips of her gloves. The fingernails are just Becky, not Shimako. I remember being able to swim.

"Okay," she tells me. "We're going flying together. I'm going to take you on a tour of the Italian coast; show you the areas I monitor. There are two Falcons on autopilot in the same approximate area. So we will commandeer those. And then I'll take you on a tour."

She gives me that cheeky smile again. "Sounds like a plan to me," I reply.

"You are Falcon 357C4, go ahead and connect and I'll do the same," she continues, "I've paired our devices so my voice will come to you through the headset. So you'll be able to hear both me and what the bird hears at the same time." Without further ado, she pulls her headset down onto her eyes and says, "Connect to Falcon number 357C8." I also put my goggles on and connect to my Falcon, and suddenly we are in the sky.

"Okay, I see you," she says. "You're about 20 metres to my left, but 50 metres below me." This is the real magic in flying, of course, that there is an added dimension. That your hands do not only bring you forwards and backwards and side to side, but can be used to make you rise and fall. That you can be meeting with someone who is above you, and fly upwards towards them. And that is what I do. I turn the Falcon upwards, tilting my hands back so my fingers face skywards, rising swiftly. I also drift slightly to the right.

"Much closer," she says. "You're only about 15 metres away from me now. Slow down and let me overtake. Today you will be following me, not vice versa."

I oblige and slow my Falcon down. Another robotic bird drifts into the upper boundaries of my field of vision and overtakes me, drifting gracefully through the evening sky. Below I see water, an endless stretch of it. We are flying above the Mediterranean Sea.

"Put yourself in albatross mode," Becky tells me. "You couldn't do it when you were flying about in the office, but here we have all the space we need. Give it a go."

"Falcon, engage albatross mode," I say, and I hear a very slight metallic whirring as my wings expand. I glance to my left and right and see them extending. With longer wings, my flight feels different; manoeuvrability is much different. I don't have to flap my wings much, as the large surface area allows me to pick up on currents of air and use them to move me. But the ability to turn sharp corners and make quick movements is sacrificed. Honestly, there is no need for me to make quick, sharp movements here in the open sky. I find myself drifting lazily, following the direction of Becky's falcon but not religiously emulating her path, using currents of air to my advantage, continuing to learn how to fly.

"Okay, let's descend. Let's get closer to the water," Becky tells me, and I see her Falcon start to drift downwards at a uniform pace. I tilt my hands forward and follow her. We drop maybe a hundred and fifty metres until we are almost touching the waves. I see no fish jumping on the surface of the water, and think back to my mother's C-food stew, how all its ingredients are grown in a laboratory, because most of the fish have died.

"In albatross mode we can utilise dynamic soaring, which is a particular pattern of flight which suits these birds. In dynamic soaring, you fly up and down in a series of broad sinusoidal movements with the waves, each curve taking you closer to where you intend to go, wind speed is minimal directly above water surface, but increases during the windward climb, it's like using the energy from the waves to keep you going" Becky explains. "It's about utilising the momentum from the upward turn to allow you to take advantage of wind currents. Watch me."

Becky demonstrates, flying up and down with the waves, using the wind currents from the waves to keep her going whilst barely flapping her wings. I watch her closely, trying to copy her movements. After a few tries, I find myself gliding across the waves in concave and convex curves.

"Okay, so we're currently flying over the Mediterranean. Not far from the island of Malta, off the Spanish coast. Migrants who make successful journeys will pass here on their way to the Italian coast in boats. To our west is Tunisia, and almost directly to our south is the Libyan coastal town of Tripoli, where the largest number of migrants leave from. We're going to head in that direction now. Follow me." Becky takes a slight turn to the left and I mimic her. She starts to show off a little bit, switching to swift mode from albatross mode and swooping, looping, diving and spinning through the air. She really is an impressive flyer. After a minute or two of this, she returns to albatross mode and rises further into the air. I follow her, tilting my hands backwards once again.

"It's fun being near the water," she says. "But for reconnaissance, height is everything. The higher you are, the more you can see. The Falcons are able to zoom in to an optical zoom of about times 200 relatively comfortably, so being high does not sacrifice visibility on a smaller scale, but it allows you to see what is happening over a much larger area of the sea."

She isn't lying, the higher I get, the more I am amazed at the expansiveness of the body of water below me. No matter how high I rise, it always seems endless. The only body of land I can see is Malta, which progressively shrinks as I rise.

"Use your Zoom," Becky tells me. "Use your Zoom and you'll see the Libyan coast in the distance."

"How do I zoom?" I ask. There is no zoom in The Evolution of Wildness, which is supposed to give you the authentic feeling of being an animal.

"Your gloves aren't the only thing which have sensors." Becky tells me. "Squint."

Really? Our headsets have sensors too? That's new. I squint, and as soon as I do, a small x, followed by the number one, appears in the upper right-hand corner of my field of vision. After a moment, the x is followed by a two, and the image before me zooms in towards the water. I continue to squint and it zooms more. I look ahead, and by the time I reach x30, I see a faint coastline start to appear, the outline of cliffs and beaches.

"Tell your Falcon to split screen and you'll be able to switch easily between watching a zoomed-in perspective and a regular perspective. You don't want to start crashing into things because you're lost in the details." Becky says.

"Falcon, split screen," I say, and immediately a vertical line appears down the centre of my field of vision. On the left side of this line is a zoomed in perspective from afar of what I assume must be the Libyan coast. On the right side of this line is my Falcon's normal field of vision. In the corner of it, I see Becky's Falcon, at this distance only just distinguishable from a real bird.

We fall into a rhythm of flight. And flying is therapeutic, there are no obstacles, there is no traffic to block the way or pedestrians to block my chair on the pavement, assuming right of way. This allows us to let our concentrations drift a little and discuss some more personal topics as we continue our journey to the Libyan coast.

"So how long have you been working here?" I ask Becky.

"A couple of years," she responds. "Two years. I joined when I was 15. But I have continued having tutoring and I'm still taking exams and stuff. How old are you?" she asks me.

If she started when she was 15 and she's been here for two years, then she's 17. Maybe even 18. I'm 15, but a sudden urge to lie about my age and say I'm older takes hold of me. I have to remind myself that I'm going to be working closely with all these people and my true age will not be a secret. I force myself to say 15.

"I would have said 16," she replies. "You seem so mature."

I jump at the opportunity. "I'm almost 16. My birthday's in two months."

"Ah, so you're 15 and five sixths. You should have been more specific. You aren't such a baby after all." She giggles and swoops upwards before turning vertically and looping behind my back to emerge again swiftly from underneath me. When she appears before me with her wings spread wide, there is only five or so metres between us as she passes. I see the detailed patterns of her metal feathers.

CHAPTER 14

I'm lying on my side, my right arm folded underneath my head as a makeshift pillow, my legs bent inwards to allow me to fit in the restricted space. There is no light except for the two solitary rays of thin yellow which filter in through the holes for ventilation. I can't see the road on which I'm travelling because I am in the boot, and each bump comes as a surprise. It is hotter in here than in the main body of the car, and there are no windows to open to allow for a cooling breeze. Moisture sticks my cheek to my bicep and my forehead to my forearm, and I lick my lips to be greeted with the taste of salt.

I concentrate on my breathing, trying to calm my nerves in the darkness and the heat. I must have imagined hearing the other man's laughter coming from the trunk earlier, as I cannot now make out the conversation of the others. Their voices are audible but muffled, and I am unable to distinguish individual words. The car dips sharply for a moment, probably going over a pothole, and my head rises for a second, then slams back against my arm, making my teeth rattle. I'm breathing though, that's what matters. The other guy survived his five hour stint and I can survive mine.

Without external stimulation, without the passing scenery of southern Niger visible through a window and the conversation of my fellow travellers readily available, my thoughts begin to drift. Everything has been so rushed, the whole arrangement, from my first conversation with Mustafa about his plans to leave, to setting off with the smuggler this morning. Even my goodbyes to my mother and sister were rushed. Alone in this car boot, with only my thoughts for company, I begin to think of them and their goodbyes.

Both Fatima and Karima cried. Karima tried to hide it and Fatima didn't. That's the difference between them. Fatima is younger and expressive and feels no need to pretend, whereas Karima has always wanted to exude an air of disinterestedness about everything. Karima, however, being closer to me in age, knows more about the dangers of the journey. This is what drove her to worry and to finally show how much she cares about me. I told them I would bring them with me, that they would follow me in a few years, and I so hope that that will be true.

Karima hugged me so tightly before I left, hugged me for a full two minutes. She hugged me in a way that she hadn't done since Dad died. She hugged me in a way that reminded me of how very close we always were, even when we pretended that we weren't, in a way that reminded me of when I was nine and she was five, how I would put her tiny hands in mine, grip them tightly, and spin myself around and around until her feet left the floor, and then we would both fall to the floor, dizzy and laughing.

Karima was always Dad's favourite. Well, when Fatima came along, of course she received all the attention. But that was because she was new. She was the baby. And at the age of six, she was still the baby when my father died. So with Fatima, it was never really a fair contest. But even before Fatima, and even once Fatima had been born, Karima was Daddy's little girl. He was protective over her, but he doted on her. Whereas I was to be moulded into a man, and not to be spoiled, and not to be doted over. Maybe he foresaw that he would not be around forever, and that one day it might be necessary for me to provide for my younger sisters. Isn't that what I'm trying to do now, in making this very journey?

The car comes to a halt, and I am brought back to the present.

I can hear the muffled voices again, and I realise I have been dozing. I can make out the sound of car doors opening and slamming shut, but I know not nearly enough time has passed for us to have arrived at our destination. The car remains stationary for a couple of minutes whilst the engine still runs. I wonder what has caused the delay. Then, without warning, we set off again. The sudden movement makes my body swing to the side, and I willingly continue the movement, shifting over onto my left, using my left arm rather than my right arm as a pillow, facing the other way. By this point, pins and needles have set in around my right shoulder and my arm feels numb and heavy. I close my eyes and try to drift off again, but the intermittent bumps and dips in the road mean that sleep comes in scattered and segmented snatches. Because of this, I am unable to have one uninterrupted dream, but instead have many, each short and vibrant and each abruptly put to an end by the capricious whims of the unmaintained road.

In one dream, I spin my sisters Fatima and Karima simultaneously, with Fatima holding onto my left hand and Karima holding onto my right. I spin them faster and faster and faster and then eventually I let go and they fly away from me out over the Sahara Desert. As I watch them drift further and further into the sky, I realise I am throwing them all the way to Europe. I then turn to my mother and grab her hand, planning to do the same, but a jolt in the road wakes me. For a few moments, I remember where I am, in the boot of a car, on my way to Zinder, before I drift back into a different dream. A dream where I sit with my father in our old home, and he teaches me Quranic verses. There is nothing supernatural about this dream. Nothing out of the ordinary. Nothing that would raise suspicion in my waking self, except for the fact that my father is alive within it.

Another of my dreams includes a large octopus, like the one described by the smuggler behind the counter at the electronics store. I have never seen an octopus, but somewhere I must have heard a description because I know that they have multiple arms and legs that are indistinguishable from each other and very long. I let my imagination do the rest. The octopus sits in the middle of the city of Sokoto and spreads its tentacles through the roads, pushing them into windows and doorways at night and stealing jewellery, money, goats and chickens, piling them sky high in the centre of the square beside the Sultan's palace.

Eventually, I am woken from a dream in which I am flying, not by the jolt of the car, but by an almost blinding light. I fly towards the light, but even as I fly towards it, my eyes flicker open and I see Olusola pointing a torch down at my face. The car boot is open and Mustafa stands next to him, looking at me with concern.

"See? He's just fine," says Olusola. "We are here in Zinder." He directs this second comment at me. "Let's get you out of the car, and we can make our way over to do the handover."

Mustafa offers me a hand and I take it gratefully, stepping out of the car and into the night. I stretch my arms and legs and take a few deep breaths of fresh air. The sky is darkening but is not yet dark. Olusola takes out a cigarette and lights it. The other three passengers are all standing beside the car: Abdulai, the giant who I nicknamed Dogo; the small man with tribal scars who was in the boot before me; and the spectacled man with the pencil moustache.

We are standing in a large car park, where a multitude of people are milling, arguing, bartering, and mounting and dismounting open-backed Ford pickup trucks. There is an air of urgency and confusion.

"Follow me," Olusola tells our group, slamming shut the boot of his car. He begins to snake his way through the throng, and we follow him, making our way through together. Six or seven trucks down, Olusola stops and greets a skeletal Tuareg man, whose face and hair are covered by a blue turban, whose eyes are covered by sunglasses, and whose cheekbones and hands are the only part of body visible. The man acknowledges Olusola with a nod and a wave, but continues shouting instructions in Tuareg at another turbaned man. The Tuareg language feels strange upon my ears, guttural and yet lyrical, throaty and yet melodic, a language full of secrets.

The second Tuareg man runs off in a hurry, to follow whatever instructions he has been given, and the Tuareg with the skeletal frame turns to Olusola. He waves in the general direction of those of us in the rest of the group without looking at or acknowledging us.

"For Agadez?" he asks Olusola.

"Yes," Olusola responds. "And then on to Libya."

"We have to take them two separate trucks, because of space," the Tuareg replies. "How we split them?"

"These two are travelling together," says Olusola, pointing at Mustafa and I. "The other small one can travel with them." He points at the man who was in the boot before me. "Take the other two in a separate vehicle."

"Okay," replies the Tuareg, briefly following Olusola's fingers with his eyes as our smuggler points out who exactly he means, but still not acknowledging us with any type of greeting.

"You pay?" he says to Olusola.

Olusola takes some notes out of his pocket, counts them, and hands them to the Tuareg, but in the dimming light and with the speed at which the transaction is completed, it is impossible to say exactly how much is paid.

"Separate into your groups," the Tuareg barks at us. Mustafa and I group together with the small man with tribal scars on one side of Olusola, the remaining two of our group move to his other side.

"You leave half an hour," he says, pointing at my group. "You leave one hour," he says, pointing at the other group. "Make sure you here. You want buy water for the journey? You go him." The Tuareg points out an old man whose face is also covered by a turban, but who does not wear sunglasses, allowing us to perceive the deep wrinkles around his eyes. He is sitting on a large rug next to a small mountain of plastic containers and bottles of water. "You want food before journey? You go her." The Tuareg points further to the left, at a plump woman in a headscarf who is stirring the contents of a large metal pot with a wooden spoon. The pot is perched over a small kerosene gas stove like the one we use at home. A queue of about 15 migrants hold onto plastic plates, waiting for her to finish the batch.

"Water and food not free," says the Tuareg. "You want water and food, you pay water and food. The journey is long. Eight hours to Agadez, then desert. So not good to be thirsting. Not good to have empty stomach." He points at my group again. "Half hour," he reiterates. He points at the other group. "Hour." He turns away from us and shouts across the car park in Tuareg at another man, without once asking our names. We are the product, I realise. This man's job is to move people en masse, constantly, day in, day out. Even if he did ask our names, he would forget them by the time our car leaves. He has no reason to remember them, none of us have the intention of returning.

The plump woman serving the food turns out to be friendlier than the skeletal Tuareg. The patterns painted on her face clearly mark her as of the Fulani tribe; painted whiskers at the corners of the mouth; vertical lines on the cheeks, forehead and nose; triangles around the collarbone and neck, all painted in a traditional Fulani mixture of shea butter, kohl, and other natural materials. Despite the fact that her English is non-existent apart from the few words and numbers needed to undertake her business, she speaks decent Hausa, and expresses interest in asking where we are from and where we are going.

When she turns to the man with the tribal scars and asks him, "Daga ina kake?" He looks at her blankly.

"Where are you from?" I translate to him.

"Oh, I am from Benin," he replies.

"Benin?" repeats the woman, her smile growing even wider, and she engages him in a conversation in rapid French, from which I am able to gather a few words and phrases, including "belle ville" (beautiful city) and "étudier en France" (study in France). At the end of the day, however, we are in a queue, and when people are waiting in a queue, such a conversation can only go on so long. The man behind us gives a loud false cough and raises his eyebrows defiantly when we look in his direction. He follows this not-so-subtle hint with an even less subtle, "Wetin you go do now? You go chop or you go just talk for here? I'm hungry oh." We say goodbye to the woman and move back towards the meeting point.

By this point, there is a group of at least 18 migrants gathered around this single truck, not including myself, Hasan and Mustafa, and I start worrying again about logistics. There doesn't seem to be a boot, which I'm thankful for, but there also seems to only be two actual seats that aren't the driver's seat, at the front section of the vehicle. It looks as though we are all going to have to squeeze ourselves into the large open space in the back. This suspicion is quickly confirmed when the skeletal Tuareg returns. He begins pointing at us in turn, saying "You move" and then pointing at the back of the pickup truck. In our group of what is now twenty-three, since two more migrants have appeared, there are four women and two small children, both accompanying the same woman. Another one of the women is pregnant.

The women and children get on first, and are closer to the centre of the pickup truck, presumably because it is assumed that they will be less apt at holding on to the wooden poles and ropes tied to the sides of the pickup truck to be clung to in order to prevent migrants from falling out. All four women have covered their hair, but only the pregnant woman wears a hijab. One wears a sort of blue woollen hat, one wears a turban not unlike that of the skeletal Tuareg, and the mother of the two children has draped a brightly coloured scarf with a chequered pattern over her curls. One of the children, appearing to be the younger of the two, starts to cry. The Tuareg tells him to shut up, but he only cries harder. His mother takes him in her arms, bounces him up and down on her knee and quietly shushes him, and he calms.

Before long, we are all squeezed onto the back of the jeep, some of us sitting on its sides with our legs hanging out, holding onto poles and ropes to secure ourselves, others jammed into the centre. We barely have enough room to move our shoulders. The two largest men are sitting in the actual passenger seats in the front of the jeep, whilst the Tuareg is in the driver's seat. I myself dangle at the edge, looking down at a drop of at least two and a half metres, very thankful that I managed to get some sleep in the boot. As we set off towards Agadez, I look towards Mustafa to my right and try to catch his eye, but his brow is furrowed in concentration, and he seems to be considering something, deep in thought. I close my eyes, take a deep breath, and prepare myself for the next stage of our journey.

CHAPTER 15

Rush Russell is a man of about 30. He's dressed in a black turtleneck jumper and a suede blazer. He has a well-groomed beard, a button nose, hazel eyes, thick eyebrows, and protruding ears. His hair is slicked back like a wave at the top of his head, and short at the sides. He heads the Combat and Control team, of which Tim Weibers is a member, and where I am doing my current rotation. I have started at a very busy time. Clashes between migrants at a large camp in Calais and the team have reached a high point. Rush, however, believes that this is a good thing - as it provides me with the opportunity for what he calls a 'baptism of fire', whereby I will be exposed to action, or at least be able to shadow the other team members, during a particularly volatile period.

Rush is not currently wearing his headset, but the rest of the team are. There are ten members, each of whom controls an Enforcer. Enforcers are crowd control robots that assist French police in controlling the floods of undocumented humans trying to make it from France to England, whether by jumping onto moving trains that travel through the tunnel, stowing themselves away in the back of, or even underneath, lorries and hoping to pass over the Channel undetected in the holds of ferries, and even those seeking to make the crossing by boat. From where my wheelchair is placed at the very end of the row of desks, next to Rush, I am unable to get a good view of what exactly is transpiring on the bowl like screens of the rest of the group. The other team members are all plugged into their headsets, wearing their gloves, moving their hands rapidly and their necks in every direction to take in their surroundings. Tim Weibers, who is three seats down, is giving a juvenile running commentary, exclaiming "POW! Take that! Not so quick, sucker! Weibers strikes again!" at regular intervals.

"So, you've just come from reconnaissance, right?" Rush asks me.

"Yes," I reply. "Last week I was doing a rotation there. Flying a Falcon on the Italian coast."

"Well," Rush replies, "forget everything you learnt last week then. Reconnaissance and crowd control are two very different things. Enforcers can hover and take off from the ground for short distances, but they don't have the battery to maintain sustained flight, as heavy as they are. You don't use Enforcers to find the target. You know where the target is, and you send in the Enforcers to disperse and control crowds, and enforce law and order. You have an arsenal of tools," he continues. "Pepper spray and gas are useful for dispersal. Say you have a large camp set up near the motorway, waiting to take their shot at stowing away. A good smoke or gas canister can send them on their way, at least temporarily. You have all the classical crowd control tools, tasers, sirens, extremely bright strobe lights, rubber bullets and, if necessary, real bullets too. There's also flame functionality, which can help to burn down tents and makeshift wooden structures once the inhabitants have been driven out, to stop them returning.

"The Enforcer itself is extremely sturdy. It's impervious to basic projectiles like rocks and even firearms, though the migrants rarely get their hands on firearms. Its exterior is constructed of a structured polymer composite made of alternating rubbery and glassy layers, with a flexible innermost layer designed to absorb shock and protect the Enforcer's delicate electronics. The Enforcer is equipped with a pneumatic gun mounted on its left arm, which can fire real bullets, rubber bullets or tear gas, as well as multiple cameras that allow it to monitor the crowd.

It also has a powerful loudspeaker and a bright searchlight mounted on its right arm, and is capable of moving quickly in any direction. The Enforcer is controlled via headset and gloves, with the controller able to see what the Enforcer is seeing, as well as manually directing its movement. The Enforcer can also be programmed to follow specific orders on autopilot, such as maintaining a perimeter around a crowd or patrolling a specific area. One of these cameras is a specialised infrared camera, which is particularly useful for identifying bodies inside lorries. It picks up on the heat, and makes the job of identifying well-hidden stowaways much easier. I know it's a lot of information. Are you following so far?" he asks me.

"I think so," I reply.

"Good," he continues. "So usually at this point, I would take you down the row and show you each teammate's individual screen from behind their desk, explaining exactly what they are doing and why. But I don't think squeezing your wheelchair down the aisle is the best idea whilst they are active in the field. What I can do is clone a live stream of their screens onto my own, so you can get an idea of what's happening in real time without us having to move."

Rush turns to his monitor and presses a small button in its bottom left-hand corner. A spiral, a yellow spiral, unfurls from the centre of the bowl-shaped screen towards its outer edge, accompanied by a generic four note jingle. The screen goes dark again for one moment before turning on, and a picture of Rush with his arm around a slightly chubby red-haired woman and what I assume must be their toddler aged son cradled in his other arm appears. In the centre of the screen is a small box, above which are the words "Enter password". Rush turns his head to me again, eyebrows raised, engaging in the age-old ritual of giving someone side-eye until they look away from the keyboard whilst you enter your password. I make a show and dance about looking around the room and humming. By the time I look back down at the screen, he has logged in. Evidently, his gloves are connected not only to his headset, but also to the screen itself, as he swipes through the different applications and programs available by flicking his wrist repeatedly before settling on a programme called Monitor team. He clenches his fist and the programme opens. He flicks through a few names, including Tim Weibers, before landing on the name Ricardo.

"Alright," he says. "Let's see what Ricardo's up to. He's five seats along, the one in the red jacket." I glance down the row and identify Ricardo, he seems very busy indeed, his gloved fingers tickling the air. Rush clenches his fist again, and the screen changes.

It's a first-person perspective. But glancing towards the bottom of the screen, whose curves allow me to see below, above, to the left and to right of the Enforcer as well as in front of it, I see that its arms are unlike human arms. The polymer composite that Rush described is a clear transparent material, and through it the metal beneath is visible, as are the small guns mounted on each forearm and the appendages resembling Swiss Army knives insofar as they contain an array of useful tools alongside strange metallic fingers. The setting is a motorway. Small piles of wooden pallets have been thrown onto the road in a number of places to slow down traffic. A French policeman is visible, gripping the pallets and throwing them from the road.

Dark-skinned people in unwashed clothes line the sides of the road and sprint between the lorries. Some have mounted them, and cling to windshields and roofs; others appear to be trying to break open the back doors and make their way inside. I glance at Ricardo and see his head turning from left to right, then glance back at the screen to see the image follow his gaze, drinking in the scene. Moments later, the image quality changes. It becomes the image of an infrared thermal camera, which I recognise from Final Facedown III. Though the outlines of the people and the lorries and the pavement all remain, the colours are much different. Greens, blues, reds and yellows replace the grey of concrete and the countless shades of yellow and brown skin. The redder the object, the higher the amount of heat it emits.

Ricardo continues to scan the scene, before locking his gaze onto a lorry, in which can be seen shifting red objects with human shapes. The perspective of the screen shifts slightly downwards but without tilting, not as if the Enforcer were bending its neck but rather as if the Enforcer were bending its knees. It then shifts forwards at great pace, as if driven by the leap of some ungodly beast, with legs of either muscle or steel. From the way that the movement continues for seconds, the Enforcer seems to be being propelled through the air. It lands at the back of the lorry after covering at least fifteen metres in one leap, and I assume there must be some sort of propulsion guiding it. When the Enforcer lands, this suspicion is confirmed.

To the left I see another Enforcer, also moving through the air - somewhat humanoid in shape - with two legs, two arms and a torso, but with the same glassy exoskeleton revealing a metallic machine beneath. Two streams of fire pour from its feet, not to guide it over oceans like the Falcon, but to allow it to leap from one side of a battle to the other. Designed not to rise into the skies, but to facilitate rapid passage over the Earth. The screen now shows the back of the lorry, which appears to be locked by padlock, Ricardo's Enforcer's arm stretches forward and I watch as a small pen from the Swiss Army knife type collection of tools sprouts from its end and emits a laser which cuts through the padlock like butter. The metal fingers loop around the handle and swing open the door of the lorry.

The Enforcer's other hand rises to join its brother, and from the small mounted gun that sits on top of the forearm, three small pellets emerge, surprisingly softly, and travel only about a metre before landing with a thud at the foot of the entrance to the lorry. I have only a few moments to take in the petrified faces of the migrants huddled within before the three balls explode, filling the lorry with smoke, but not with fire. Tiny smoke grenades.

Rush confirms my suspicion.

"Just smoke, hyper compressed to the level where it can fit in pellets small enough to fire from the arm mounted gun. The smoke is specially designed not to be harmful to any of the produce in the lorries, whether it's fruit or furniture, whatever's being imported will be fine, but for now the back of that lorry will taste and smell awful. The smoke will fill the nostrils and the throat and make it impossible to see. Driving out the stowaways, forcing them from the vehicle. Before you ask, the driver should be fine, there are no vents between the driving compartment and storage." Rush turns his head and shouts down the row. "Good work, Ricardo. Keep it up. Okay, let's have a look at what Jenny's up to."

Rush heads back to the team selection menu and swipes through until he gets to Jenny. He opens her field of vision up to the screen. A rudimentary camp is burning; makeshift tents and ramshackle wooden structures pitched along the edges of the road. No one appears to be there currently, either having been driven out by the fire, or the fire having been set in part due to the absence of the camp's residents. Again, the first person perspective allows for only the arm of the Enforcer to be visible, and from the same mounted gun which fired the pellets for Ricardo, a thin stream of fire is emerging, directed towards the burning encampment. Rush looks at the screen and gives a satisfied nod.

"They know not to camp there," he says shortly. "A lot of them will keep their most important belongings on their person anyway, in case something like that happens, or in case there are thieves in the camp. Shall we take a look at Tim? I believe you've met before. Both during your first visit to the control room and also in the VirtuWorld."

"Hmm", I think to myself. "So Tim has been telling the whole team about my defeat in Final Facedown III at his hands before I have even met them. Why am I not surprised?"

"All right," I say. "What's Tim up to?"

It turns out Tim is up to a lot. Weaving and dodging between the slow traffic of the motorway, he is aiming at any migrant who seems to get too close to a lorry and taking fire. The bullets seem to be rubber rather than metal, as they don't always draw blood or pierce through clothing, but Tim seems to be purposefully aiming for the body parts that would do the most damage. He takes out a young man with a shot to the head that leaves him unconscious in the street, quickly followed by another young Arab man with a shot to the groin which is accompanied by a jovial shout of "Right in the gonads! Go on baby! Tim Weibers strikes again!" Even a mother, with a small child clasped in her arms, is not off the cards for him, although he avoids hitting the child itself and is content to shoot the mother in her arm. He then approaches closer to her, with the gun still extended and pointed in her direction. She runs from the lorry, off the road, over the pavement and into the distance, her child still clutched in her one good arm.

At this point, I feel I've seen enough. I certainly prefer reconnaissance with Becky.

"I need the bathroom." I say to Rush.

"Go ahead," he replies.

But as I wheel my chair out of the aisle, he grips my wrist and looks at me directly.

"You can't be squeamish about these things," he says, eyebrows ever so slightly raised and head cocked perhaps five degrees to the side. "These people are not British citizens. They've made it as far as Europe, which they already had no right to do, and they were unsatisfied with Europe, unsatisfied with Italy, and unsatisfied with France. Britain is full, and Britain is great, and that is why those who have no right to be here wish to come. But Britain will not be great if we let in any old riff raff. Rubber bullets... a bit of smoke... a burnt-out tent... that is the price for your freedom."

Rush lets go of my arm and tilts his head ever so slightly to the left, returning it to a perfectly vertical position. He pushes his chin forward. "Go for your bathroom break," he says, "and then come back and continue with the rotation." He grins broadly and winks.

CHAPTER 16

Evening has truly descended, and moonlight provides the only illumination with which to discern our surroundings, apart from the truck's headlights, which carve out a yellow tunnel along the road. If we were static, this may well be the time to listen for the sound of crickets, but instead, the only sounds that greet us are our own breathing, the rumble of the engine, and the wind. One woman has spent a large period of the journey repeating a Christian prayer about giving people bread every day and forgiving sins. Eventually, the man beside her told her that God would hear her prayer just as well if she said it in her head, and thankfully, she got the hint.

For those of us who are Muslim, praying at the allotted time is quite impossible. The very idea of trying to stand and kneel in the direction of Mecca in a moving vehicle overloaded with human bodies is laughable. But one man did ask the group at large in which direction Mecca was. The car then took a sharp left turn, and the man seemed to realise the endeavour was hopeless. He chanted a few duas, with which myself, Mustafa and a few other migrants joined in, and that was it.

There is some scattered conversation, and at one point, the night was accompanied by the surprisingly soothing sound of a child's snores. The evening air provides some respite from the heat, and though the wind buffets our hands and faces, sitting as we are in the open back of the truck, its coolness is somewhat welcome. There is still the heat of our bodies, which mingles in the confined space. We are squashed together like sardines.

Before our car left, another five migrants arrived, bringing the total number up from 23 to 28.

My legs hang over the edge of the vehicle and I cling onto the wooden pole that emerges from between them, securing me to the vehicle. The wood is abrasive and rough, but thick and sturdy. Though it may give me splinters as the bumps of the road chafe my hands against it, I do not fear that it will snap, throwing my weight forward onto the road below. If I were to fall, would the smuggler stop and allow me to remount, for others to assist if I found myself injured, or would he continue and leave me, given that, in business, time is money? How would the other migrants even inform him of my absence? I don't plan on finding out.

The woman behind me has looped her arm through mine, either for comfort or balance, and I have not rejected her. She has the smell of a Nigerian marketplace, of tomatoes and kola nuts, of pungent spices and freshly cut leaves. I wonder how long into this journey until that smell is replaced by the odour of sweat, grime, and despair. Or will it take the ocean itself to wash away her fragrances? Mustafa is three places to my right and still brooding over something, pensive and troubled. I wonder whether he is simply contemplating the dangers ahead, or if he has caught on to some new troublesome development as yet unperceived by myself.

"Mustafa," I call across to him. "Everything okay?"

He turns to me, bites his lip, gives the smallest shake of his head imaginable and says, "Why did they separate us?"

"What do you mean?" I ask him.

"Think," he replies. "Me, you, and Hasan. What do we have in common that the others in the car didn't?"

Hasan is the small man with tribal scars who travelled in the boot before me. I put myself to the task of thinking. What do the three of us have in common that the others in the car did not? Myself and Hasan are small, but Mustafa is large in stature, so that can't be it. Myself and Mustafa are Hausa, but Hasan is from Benin, meaning he is most likely of the Yoruba tribal ethnicity. And he didn't understand a word of Hausa when the lady serving food spoke to him in it. I'm stumped, and for a few minutes I cycle through possibilities in my head, ruling them all out, unable to find a common thread that links myself, Mustafa and Hasan but not the other passengers in Olusola's car. And then suddenly it hits me.

I shift my weight and turn so that I'm speaking over my shoulder to the woman whose arm is linked in mine.

"Where are you going on your journey?" I ask her.

"Libya," she replies. "We are all going to Libya. Together. In this car. Are we not?"

"Yes," I reply. "But where do you hope to go afterwards? What will be the next step of your journey?"

"Europe," she says simply. "Once I have the funds, I will continue on to Europe. But I must work first. Hopefully as a housemaid. Or cleaner."

I make an involuntary groan of disappointment and the woman replies indignantly.

"What is wrong with housework? We all need to humble ourselves to survive. You're sitting here, boxed in, squashed together like fruit in a basket too."

"I don't mean to offend," I tell her. "We do what we need to to survive." I turn back to face forward and towards the scenery. I cannot make out details in the dark, but I can tell that the further north we get, the more the terrain resembles desert, the gravel replaced by sand, the buildings sparser, with larger open stretches between villages and towns. I think back to the conversation in the car. The man in the spectacles had said he wanted to go to Germany. That he had paid upfront to get to Libya and would have more money sent by his parents once he arrived to pay for the trip to Europe. Abdulai the giant had said he had a brother in Greece who would send money to him once he arrived in Libya, to make the next step of the journey.

Abdulai had said that Hasan, who was in the boot at the time, had spoken to him that morning and said that like myself and Mustafa, he was simply heading to Libya and hoping for the best. The smugglers have divided us between those who, once they arrive in Libya, will be able to follow up with further funds in order to continue their journey, and those who have paid everything they can already and have nothing left to give; those who are still an asset to the smugglers and those who are now expendable. Why?

My initial suspicion softens. It could just be a matter of logistics. Those who are going straight to Europe might end up at a different destination within Libya, they may go straight to the coast. That would make perfect sense. Dividing us by this criterion would make perfect sense if that was the case, but another memory still wriggles its way to the forefront of my brain, keeping the fire of doubt burning. When they split us, the skeletal Tuareg, now driving the vehicle, had told Olusola that there was not enough space. He had definitely said the reason they needed to divide us was because there was not enough space in this vehicle. He had then asked Olusola how best to do the divide. If space was really the issue, why would he have had to ask Olusola how to do the divide? And if space was not the issue, why would he lie?

The woman behind me has said that, like the three of us, she only has the funds to make it to Libya, and has already paid them, presumably. At the moment, I'm willing to bet the small amount that still remains from the money I reclaimed from the thieving first wife of my father that every migrant in this vehicle is in the same position, with nothing left to offer the smugglers but a few coins in their pockets. So what will they do? Take us as far as Agadez and then abandon us without taking us through the desert at all? Take us into the desert and abandon us to die of thirst? Or am I overthinking this? Is there some legitimate reason for the separation that I cannot currently see?

I turn to the man to my right. He is about 30 years of age, with large lips on a very slim face, sunken eyelids and an asymmetrical nose. He has pulled down the scarf he was using to cover his face and is squinting against the wind.

"How far are you going on your journey? All the way to Europe, or only to Libya for the time being?" I ask him.

"Don't understand," he replies in a thick French African accent. Hasan, who is sitting to my left, translates.

"Tu vas jusqu'où?"

"Seulement la Libye," the man replies. "La Belgique plus tard."

This I do understand. Just like us, he only has the funds to go to Libya. The man smiles at me, showing teeth that have been stained by Kola nuts and battered by the years.

"Toi?" he says. "And you?"

I try to smile back, and eliminate fear and confusion from my features.

"Libya," I respond. "We're all going to Libya."

But even as I say it, the words sound less and less true.

CHAPTER 17

Jim is overweight. The only exercise he gets is the daily walk from his desk to his pod and back. His pod is a small bedroom he has in the office out of which he lives most of the time. He tells me that he still has an apartment where he keeps his things and sometimes goes on weekends, but generally sees commuting as a waste of time.

"I have work and I have my games," he says. "I alternate between them. Both of them I can do from here. Why waste 40 minutes of every day?"

"You could always wear your headset and gloves and play your games on the bus," I suggest to him.

"And miss my stop?!" he says indignantly. "That happened to me once. Very unfortunate. Plus, all that movement affects my balance."

As I say, Jim gets no exercise. The only reason he is only 'overweight' and not 'morbidly obese', in my opinion, is that he doesn't seem too interested in sugary junk food, but he lives a sedentary life - like me. Sedentary. It's a strange word. The Oxford Learners Dictionary describes it as "spending a lot of time sitting down and not moving" or "inactive." I guess I live a sedentary lifestyle too, but not out of choice. Before the accident, I used to run, and play basketball from time to time. If I still had the gift of working legs, I would use them for more than walking between my pod and my desk. But I do like Jim. We bond over Arideth, which is one of my favourite games.

In Arideth, I am a warrior mage, meaning I utilise spells as well as weapons. This is the most common path. Players want to experience a bit of both styles and there are a number of quests available to those who have skills in both weaponry and magic that are not available to those who take a more one-sided path. Jim prefers the warrior route. He says he finds it more authentic.

"Magic didn't exist in mediaeval times, and it doesn't exist now," he tells me sternly. "But maces did, and arrows did, and swords. I want the real mediaeval experience, and the real experience doesn't involve freezing my enemies with a twist of my fingers. It involves bashing their heads in with spikes."

"Any sufficiently advanced technology is indistinguishable from magic," I respond, just something I once read on a poster. "How do you know magic doesn't exist? Can you tell me exactly how your VirtuWorld gloves work? How do you know they aren't magic?"

"They have motion sensors inside them. Everyone knows that." He responds "And I don't need to know exactly how a motion sensor works to know that a lot of smart people figured out how to make them without resorting to Delilah's tears and Hocus-Pocus spells. Yep, it's the Warrior Path for me. More realistic."

"But isn't the point of a game that it isn't totally realistic? Isn't the point to suspend your disbelief? Escape from reality to somewhere different?" I challenge him.

"Games are my reality," he says shortly. "Games and the Great Walls of Ceuta and Melilla."

Ceuta, one of two cities in the northernmost tip of Africa that technically belong to Spain, making it officially the southernmost tip of the European Union. The other city is Melilla. Between Ceuta and the southernmost tip of Spain is the Strait of Gibraltar, an expanse of water which many migrants see as their ticket to Europe. Much, much smaller than that between

Tunisia or Libya and Italy or Greece. Perfectly swimmable for a strong swimmer when currents are not too strong and water not too choppy in the area, though also a busy shipping lane, meaning any potential swimmer must avoid passing ships. Given the shorter distance, many migrants make the risky crossing in small boats and even makeshift rafts, haphazardly put together from bicycle inner tubes, plastic drums and bottles and wooden planks, with tarp and rope constituting a rudimentary sail.

Given that the Strait of Gibraltar provides a potential route for migrants to get to Europe through Spain, and also given that the standard of living in Ceuta is higher than those living below its border, the Spanish authorities, with the backing of the European Union, were always keen to find a way to keep the migrants out. In the 1990s, a low barrier was built along the border of Ceuta, and also Melilla. In the early 2000s it was reinforced with a second fence of razor wire and barbed wire with high walls. The third fence was built by 2013 with surveillance cameras and motion sensors to help detect those trying to cross the border illegally. In 2020, a fourth fence with thermal cameras and drones was announced. By 2030, it was decided that the fence was insufficient as, on some occasions, migrants had found ways to cut through, and huge groups continued to rush the fence en masse in the hopes that a few would make it. Construction of the Great Wall of Ceuta began, with a similar project in Melilla.

The wall was thick and constructed of bricks formed from a particularly durable and strong form of concrete. Initially, the work was done by humans, as was the maintenance of the wall. By 2040, maintenance of the wall, which was under continual threat of damage, was undertaken by remote building assistance or RBAs, which were controlled remotely by headset and gloves. Now, as we approach 2060, pro-migration groups and migrants themselves are constantly attacking the wall. A deterioration of relations between the European Union and Morocco (who have always believed that both Ceuta and Melilla should belong to them, and are vestiges of an outdated Spanish colonial empire) mean that Morocco does very little to stop attacks on the wall. The RBAs now have a dual purpose. They continue to play their role as builders, constructing and maintaining the wall when it is damaged, but also now are equipped with certain defensive capabilities - and can be dispatched to defend the wall in case of an attack.

This second purpose, however, is not their principal purpose, and there are a group of Enforcers that have been dispatched to Ceuta and Melilla to deal with the crowds of migrants and their attempts to breach the walls in the same way that Rush's team deals with the crowds in Calais. These Enforcers, however, are controlled by workers for the Spanish Home Office rather than the British Home Office.

Jim has explained to me why we, working for the British Home Office, work on projects all across Europe, and in conjunction with the governments of countries on the periphery of the continent, such as Italy, Greece and Spain. Apparently, a long time ago, when the migrant crisis really started to take off, there was some kind of European rule in place which said that if a migrant arrives in Europe and claims asylum, meaning that they claim they're getting persecuted or something in their original country, they had to do that in the country they first arrive in. It was called the Dublin rule or Dublin regulation or something. This meant that countries like Italy and Greece, which were coastal and the first port of call for migrants coming in boats, had many more migrants staying in their countries than countries deep into Europe like the UK did. When Britain first left the European Union, years ago, this was the beginning of a fragmentation of European unity which eventually led to these countries on the edges of Europe saying 'screw you' to the countries deeper into Europe and pushing, actively pushing, migrants through their territories and towards these countries in northern Europe.

These countries in northern Europe were often the preferred destinations as their economies were stronger, and as many more migrants from Africa and the Middle East speak French or English than speak Greek or Italian. It took the UK Government and the French Government dedicating a significant amount of money and investment into assisting these peripheral European countries in their quest to keep migrants out before they stopped actively pushing the floods of humans arriving at their shores towards countries like Britain and France and Germany. That's why Becky from Brixton is involved in reconnaissance on the coast of Italy and Jim from Bolton is maintaining a wall at a Spanish border at the northernmost tip of the African continent.

We are on our lunch break, one of the few times, apart from when he sleeps, that Jim is not wearing either of his pairs of gloves, neither his work gloves nor his VirtuWorld alternatives. He has not yet found a way to feed himself pizza without the use of his hands. Jim is a messy eater, and a dribble of tomato sauce runs down his chin which he wipes away with the corner of his wrist. So far today he has been showing me the basics of wall maintenance, and explaining to me the specifics of how the two Great Walls of Ceuta and Melilla work. The walls are constructed of concrete, but within that concrete is reinforced rebar steel.

This rebar steel, also known as reinforcement steel, actually consists of a carbon steel alloy. It is constructed in the shape of long cylindrical bars with regular horizontal grooves, which sit within the concrete and provide it with additional strength, protecting it against cracking, shrinkage and other forms of damage to which it is vulnerable in the coastal regions of Melilla and Ceuta, with their shifting temperatures and salty sea air. The bars are bent to the required shape and tied together to create a reinforcing cage within the concrete. The concrete in turn provides a barrier against moisture and oxygen for the steel, slowing the rusting process. However, given that sometimes the concrete can crack or become damaged, allowing moisture in, an extra epoxy coating provides a further barrier against moisture and oxygen for the metal.

The initial excavation and foundation work that was undertaken on the Great Walls of Ceuta and Melilla involved deep trenches that went below the frost line, the depth to which the groundwater in soil is expected to freeze. This means that the foundations of the walls are not vulnerable to the soil beneath them freezing and expanding, and do not crack or shift. It also means that tunnelling under the wall is not a feasible undertaking for migrants, especially given that generally the tools available to them are not likely to be more sophisticated than handheld shovels and picks. Machines such as backhoes, excavators or tunnel boring machines, which would make the undertaking feasible, if still challenging, are generally not at the disposal of those fleeing Somalia or Eritrea on a rubber dinghy.

Some pro-migrant groups have occasionally managed to get their hands on basic explosives and blast a hole in the wall above ground level. This allows migrants to rush through until the Enforcers swoop in to secure the area and block off the hole, allowing Jim and the RBAs to repair it. But this does not happen at the same frequency as before 2030, when the wall was simply a number of fences, and it was much easier to use power tools such as angle grinders and heavy-duty bolt cutters to cut through the metal mesh. There are still two fences beyond the wall itself, providing an extra layer of protection against those who permeate the largest barrier.

The most common approach by those trying to get past it remains the most simplistic: climbing. Ladders, ropes, hooks, all of these tools are used to climb the 25-foot concrete barrier and descend safely on the other side. Infrared cameras, motion sensors and various other forms of surveillance mean that an individual trying to climb on his own would easily be identified and detained, but the migrants rely on the power of numbers. They identify weak spots in the wall, areas where the thick slippery anti-climb paint has begun to thin and dry up, or the sharp coils of barbed wire which sit atop the wall have snapped or rusted to a degree that makes them easier to cut through. Then one day, without warning, they emerge in their hundreds from their encampments in the forests of northern Morocco, often in numerous locations simultaneously, knowing that by storming the wall in numbers - perhaps two, three, or even five percent of them may manage to breach it.

A large part of Jim's job is ensuring that these potential 'weak' spots do not actually become weak. Maintaining the wall, re-concreting where the concrete has cracked, and looking out for areas where the anti-climb paint has begun to dry up under the baking Moroccan sun, or the barbed wire has been snipped and then put back in place discreetly, to allow it to be taken down quickly at a later date. The RBAs themselves are optimised for climbing vertical surfaces. They utilise the most modern climbing technology. For example, though they have 'hands', 'arms' and 'legs' of sorts, alongside a large range of relevant tools (and can reconfigure themselves to take the general appearance of a monkey); they are also equipped with a powerful motor, suction cups, and a sophisticated control system that allows them to climb with great accuracy, and suggest efficient and manageable routes.

The robot's onboard processor uses algorithms to detect the best route, suggest which direction to move in and detect obstacles, making Jim's job easier. When moving across the wall, an RBA takes the shape of a climbing rover resembling an insect more than a monkey, holding itself in place with micro spine grippers on the end of six extendable legs, each tipped with hundreds of tiny hooks which can grip onto almost any surface, and function even when taking the anti-climb paint into account.

RBAs are also equipped with an array of sensors that allow them to detect and monitor changes in the environment. These sensors provide information on temperature, humidity, air pressure, and other parameters, which the robot can use to identify potential hazards or areas of interest where the wall may have been subject to extra environmental stress. Although I'm reporting directly to Jim and shadowing him for this rotation, other members of the RBA team include Dylan, Victoria and a smattering of other individuals. Dylan has never been into video games, but grew up as a drone enthusiast and somehow ended up in the control room. He's about 25, with close cropped hair, a thick monobrow, and a mildly squeaky voice. Victoria is a Chinese-British girl of about 20 who is very quiet, keeps to herself, and spends her lunch breaks on the phone, always with either her boyfriend, her sister or her mother.

They seem like a nice bunch, but I'm not feeling a spark, and in all honesty, repairing barbed wire and painting walls does not get my blood running in the same way as sweeping through the skies between Malta and the Mediterranean Sea.

Jim chomps through his last slice of pizza and smacks his lips with a satisfied sigh. "Right," he says to me. "I've still got..." He looks at his watch. "Thirty three and a half minutes of my lunch break. As have you. And I plan to use it. Have you ever done the quest of the folded scroll in Arideth? I'm about a third of the way through and could use a fresh perspective..."

CHAPTER 18

We've been on the road for about eight hours by the time we eventually arrive in Agadez. According to one man's watch, it is 04:22am when our truck pulls up outside a large metal shipping container, flanked by two turbaned men in faded blue robes and sandals holding AK47s. The skeletal Tuareg steps out of the truck with his pistol in hand and starts ordering us to alight in his brusque and impersonal way. Those of us at the edges jump down and land on the ground below, softly, kicking up grains of sand. I stretch out my hand and help the woman in the blue hat, who looped her arm around mine for most of the journey, to descend. The mother of the two children passes them to a fairly broad-shouldered man below, he grunts as he lifts the first child over the side of the jeep and pretends to grimace, acting as though the child weighs much more than its wispy frame suggests. The little boy giggles indulgently and the child's mother smiles before passing over his sister too.

Soon enough, the jeep is empty, and we all stand around its perimeter, awaiting instruction from our guide. I turn to look at the shipping container and notice one single porta-toilet at its side, presumably to be shared between us. The two men flanking the shipping container take their hands off their AK-47s, which are attached to their bodies by leather straps slung over their shoulders lazily like children's backpacks, they unlatch the thick metal bolts of the container. The skeletal Tuareg turns to us and begins to speak, and the rest of the group falls into silence.

"You enter container," he says. "You wait in container 14 hours.

Desert too hot in day, better to travel at night. After 14 hours we leave for Libya. One toilet you share. Man only use toilet for poo. If man needs piss, man piss in plastic bottle or sand. Woman use toilet for both. Long drive to Libya through desert, 20 or 30 hours. Sleep now. On drive, difficult sleep." He repeats the same instructions in French, then turns to the two guards and motions for them to open the container.

The group enters hesitantly. Inside, it's dark and the air is thick with the smell of sweat and urine. The internal walls are corrugated iron, and a single dim light bulb flickers into existence when one of the two guards pulls a cord that dangles from the ceiling. The floor is lined with thin stained mattresses and blankets without covers, some of which are caked with the dull reddish brown of dried blood. A collection of empty plastic bottles is piled in the corner, from which comes the worst of the smell. This, I assume, is to be the principal toilet for men.

The skeletal Tuareg points around the room with his gun, "Women and the two children on right, Men, left. Only leave for toilet. Later, you have some food drink. I come back 14 hours."

He turns on his heels and walks back out through the doors, and the two guards follow him, enclosing us in metal arms. The clicks of the bolts sliding back into place behind the doors are clearly audible.

I gravitate towards Mustafa and Hasan, towards the comfort of familiarity, and we move towards the back of the room, sitting together on one of the mattresses. Hasan is still unaware of our concerns, but given that he travelled with us, and was witness to the split with the rest of the group just as we were, it seems natural that it is to him we raise our concerns. His own English is not perfect, and his Hausa is non-existent, but he is able to understand us. As the significance of our questions hit him, creases of worry spread out across his face like highways on a map. We make sure to keep our voices down, muttering softly between ourselves. Even given the language barrier, informing the rest of the migrants about this could be our downfall. We are at the total mercy of our smugglers. If we are seen as the ringleaders of some kind of rebellion, or to be stirring up some kind of foment, our troubles could become much more immediate than the troubles that are currently just the subject of speculation.

Our murmuring does not bring suspicion. With 28 people crammed into a shipping container, it seems that the general consensus is that murmuring in our individual groups is good etiquette. Space is so restricted that, if we were all to speak in our regular voices, each group's conversation would drown out the conversation of the next. The Christian woman who was praying in the jeep has recommenced with a subdued voice, and the Muslim man seems to have decided to guess the direction of Mecca. He kneels, prostrating on the ground towards the front of the container, murmuring softly. At one point we are interrupted by the young boy, the child of the woman in the scarf. He waddles over to us and holds out his palm, in which is a small Lego action figure, missing an arm and half a leg.

The boy can't be more than six or seven, with thickly coiled curls of coal black hair and a cheeky smile which reveals a number of missing teeth. The thin vest he wears is a little too small for him, and doesn't quite cover his nipples or lower belly. His trousers, on the other hand, are a little too large, and have been secured by a makeshift belt fashioned from some blue synthetic rope. His mother quickly snakes through the mass of bodies to grab him and take him back to their own corner. She smiles at us as she does so, in a way that is half apologetic, and Mustafa waves his hand dismissively as if to say, 'There is nothing to apologise for.' She leads the boy off and sits him back down with his sister, and our conversation turns back to the topic at hand.

"There are two possibilities." Mustafa murmurs, "Either we are stuck in this container for the foreseeable future, or we do set off for the desert, but something might happen to us while we're out there. Maybe they abandon us. Or maybe there is something else in store. If it's the first option, and we're stuck in this container, I don't see any real solution. But if it's the second option, we set out for the desert. I think we have a chance to ensure we get to Libya."

"So, what do you suggest?" I ask him.

Hasan is following the conversation intently. He doesn't seem to be picking up everything, but he is certainly trying. His brow is furrowed in concentration. Growing up in Benin, he never had the need to learn English particularly well. But he told me in the jeep that he has a love for American hip-hop music and British neogrime, and listening to these rappers in his teenage years has allowed him a decent level of comprehension. When he does speak English, he does so with a strange accent somewhere between French and Afro-American, and says "dawg" and "dun kno" at regular intervals.

"The two big guys, the ones even taller than me, that sat in the passenger seats rather than on the back of the jeep, we need to get them involved. We need to inform them of what we suspect. When the Tuareg is driving, he'll be using his hands for the wheel. If one of the big guys can get his hands on the pistol, then we're in the position of power. He can't leave us in the desert. He can't drive us somewhere we don't want to go," Mustafa continues.

"But we only tell those two," I interject excitedly. "The smugglers can't know we suspect anything. Until we are back in the vehicle and back on the road with no guards with AK-47s in sight. Once we have the gun, once we have the pistol and we have the vehicle in our control, then we can inform the rest of the group why we took the decision we did."

"Big guys. *Des gros gars*. Take pistol. *Prenez le pistolet*. Take control. *Prendre le contrôle*. I like this plan dawg, gangsta plan. I need to get to Libya dawg," Hasan says softly.

"Okay," says Mustafa. "Then the first thing we need to do is talk to them."

He gestures with his head towards the centre of the room, where the two men, who seemed to have bonded somewhat during their time in the front of the car together, sit side by side on one of the mattresses in conversation, their backs towards us. One is as large as was Abdulai. The other is both tall and wide, with broad shoulders over which matted dreadlocks hang like curtains.

"Do we call them here or go to them?" I ask.

"Let's bring them here," Mustafa says. "There's a little more space."

He stands and carefully makes his way around a few people and mattresses, stepping over one sleeping man and tapping the man with dreadlocks on his shoulder. Another murmured conversation ensues, and I see Mustafa point towards myself and Hasan. I wave and nod my head when the two large men look round at me with expressions of curiosity. After a moment or two of further conversation, they stand and begin to make their way over towards us. Mustafa himself is quite tall, and these men are taller. There is something impressive about the sight of them, the three largest men in the group, moving in unison, and a few of the other migrants glance up in curiosity. However, it does not take long for them to reach myself and Hasan and, once they are seated, the attention of those who had looked up dissipates again.

The man with the dreadlocks has a thick beard and ears that are slightly outturned. There is something boyish about his face, despite his immense size. The other man is tall and lanky, without a huge amount of muscle on his frame. There is something in his demeanour which reminds me of a spider.

They both sit down opposite us and the man with the dreadlocks speaks up. 'Hello,' he says. "Your friend tells me you want to speak to us." He gestures with his hand towards Mustafa, who has sat in such a way that he faces everyone, somewhere between myself and Hasan and these two new accomplices to our plotting.

The man with the dreadlocks continues. "The problem is that my friend here does not speak much English." He gestures to the other large man, whose close-cropped hair could not be more different to the matted threads of rope emerging from his own head. "He is from Cameroon, but not the English-speaking part, the French part. I don't know any French either, but we were together in that car and the smuggler himself, the Tuareg, was not very talkative. I have been trying to teach him a little bit of English and he has been trying to teach me a little bit of French. It may come handy in Europe after all."

"That's not a problem," I tell him. "Hasan here is from Benin, the country, not the state." There are two Benins. One is a state in Nigeria, the other is a separate country which used to be a French colony. "He can explain the situation to your friend and we will explain it to you."

"That makes sense," replies the man with dreadlocks.

"You got it, dawg," interjects Hasan.

"What are your names, by the way?" I continue.

"My name is Eloka," replies the man with the dreadlocks. "And this is Paul."

He gestures at the man from Cameroon, who nods with a start as though for the first time understanding a part of the conversation. The man points at himself and confirms, "Moi, Paul."

"Great," I continue. Hasan, please explain the situation to Paul.

The two conversations begin concurrently in the two separate tongues. The same conversation happening in parallel. Our murmur is even quieter because now we are careful not to speak over each other as well as not to give away the game to the larger group. Two conversations in parallel. Two parallel responses confirming that both men have only paid so far to travel to Libya and do not yet have the funds to continue into Europe. Two darkening faces. Two sets of eyebrows curving inwards in doubt. Four eyes shifting to the side as though considering the various possible eventualities.

Once it's clear that both of the men now understand the situation, the man with the dreadlocks whose name, Eloka, tells me he is probably Nigerian, of the Igbo tribe, goes very quiet. The man with the close-cropped hair continues conversing urgently with Hasan next to us. After 30 seconds or so, I open my mouth to speak, but the man with the dreadlocks lifts up his finger and taps his head, indicating that he is thinking. He holds out his palm and his eyes ask for more time to consider. I go quiet, and from the murmured conversation in front to my left, manage to salvage a few words; *voiture*, meaning car; *abandonné*, meaning abandoned; *l'argent*, meaning money. But I am unable to follow the underlying meaning of the sentences as a whole, especially given the urgency and speed with which the interlocutors are speaking. Eventually, Eloka speaks up.

"I am from the Niger Delta," he says. "From the south of Nigeria. I can tell you both are also Nigerians, though you seem more like northerners to me."

Myself and Mustafa both nod our heads in confirmation. Eloka continues.

"As you know, in the Niger Delta, we have oil, and we have many types of oil extraction. There have always been vigilantes that have, shall we say, recaptured some of the oil from these pipes and the big multinational companies that supposedly own it.

Drill a hole in the pipe and syphon it off. Use pumps to syphon the oil from storage tanks. After all, the oil should belong to the people of Nigeria. I am one of those vigilantes, so to speak. Or I was before I made the decision to travel to Europe."

I look across at Mustafa, and he seems equally engaged by the story, though I can tell from his features he also doesn't quite know the relevance to our current predicament.

Eloka continues.

"The authorities knew what we were doing a lot of the time, but they accepted bribes. We would pay them bribes and they would let us do what we needed to do. But we always knew that they had their superiors to report to, and that every now and then, even those who had paid bribes would have to be arrested and prosecuted for stealing the oil, in order for them to save face, and claim they were doing their jobs."

The pieces of the Jigsaw start to come together. Eloka's tongue flicks at the corner of his mouth and a piece of spittle disappears. He talks on.

"Imagine that we are the oil, the illicit product, and the smugglers are the oil thieves. They probably pay bribes to the Libyan authorities to let them make the journey without interference. What if they have an understanding with the Libyan police? What if both of them know that they have to have a certain amount of migrants intercepted at the border, and so they choose those of us who are no longer an asset to them, who no longer have any funds to pay, to be the fall guys to be intercepted at the border and sent back to where they came from?"

CHAPTER 19

I am both blind and deaf to the scenery of the road. The only indications that I am travelling through the streets of London, driven by Jeffrey, are the occasional jolt of my chair over a speed bump, and the forward thrust against my seat belt when stopping at a light. My eyes and ears are dedicated to very different surroundings.

The Melancholy Fountain, sculpted in the oval shape of an eye from stained stone and marble, hexagonal steps leading to its waters. The basin of the fountain emerges from the iris of the eye. Its base tapers off but then widens again to produce the bowl over which the water of the fountain flows, back into the pool below. Delilah sits within. It is said that the water of the fountain consists solely of her tears, fed to it in a constant stream over the centuries, both in moments of joy and melancholy, salty to the taste.

Cursed with immortality, Delilah has long lived within the fountain, and her tears have the power of healing. But she will only sell them at a price, not because she has some great love of money, and not because she has some great need for it. She will not give out her tears too freely because, having been denied the ability to die herself for many centuries, she understands death to be a part of life, and does not see an unlimited supply of healing tears as the solution to mankind's problems.

She will grant you her tears only if you impress her, only if she looks into your soul and sees something she believes deserves to live. There is a secondary market for her tears, of course, but it is small, as so few of those to whom she decides to grant her tears are those that would seek to profit from them. Her back is turned to me, and her shoulders emerge from the water, her red hair floating in ringlets on its surface. She stands and turns towards me, her red hair now covering her breasts. Arideth, after all, is a game that's often played by children. Her lower half remains submerged within the water, bathing in the salty tears of centuries.

"Traveller," she says neutrally, and a droplet of water rolls down her face and drips into the pool below. "How may I help you? Have you come with a petition?"

I dismount from my horse and move towards her, running my fingers along the earth's thin floor before me and rubbing a small amount of soil into my character's eyes. It is seen as a mark of respect to approach Delilah with eyes that are at least watering. And if you can openly weep, this is even better, but weeping without provocation is a skill only available to those who have attained a level seven skill rating in deception.

Delilah only chuckles. "False tears are no tears at all," she tells me. "Only a mask to hide behind. True tears do not come from earth, or anything external. They do not come from some irritation of the eye. They come from understanding. Pain and joy. Do you have understanding?"

"We all have understanding," I reply. "We all have understanding of something. But I'm not sure I have understanding of your question. To what do you refer?" I venture.

"Do you have understanding of yourself?" she specifies. "Do you have understanding of your relationship to others? Your positionality within this game we call reality?"

She spreads her arms wide and I chuckle. The makers of Arideth certainly tapped at the fourth wall with a hammer without quite breaking it there.

"Are you an agent of the light or of the darkness?" she concludes.

"I am an agent of the light," I assert firmly. "I seek to aid others in their quests, to share my fortunes. I travel through the lands of Strognir as a mage, healing, and assisting the peasantry in their fight against the barons of this land. I seek your tears so as to better fulfil my need to spread the magic of recovery."

"You say you are a mage, and yet a knife sits at your belt," she responds questioningly.

"This knife I took from a bandit," I tell her, "so as to prevent him from attempting to steal from others. I admit that I know how to use it. But I would not use it for ends that are unsavoury. And I will drop it at your feet if you will grant me my desire."

"I have no need for knives," she responds firmly.

"You say you are a friend of the peasantry. Do you distinguish? From which region do you hail? Do you assist all peasants, or only those that are your kin? Those linked to you through blood, through language, through geography?

"The light is visible to all," I tell her. "And its brightness, when spreading through the world, cannot distinguish and choose on whom to fall."

"That is true," she responds. "But you have not yet proven to me that you are an agent of the light."

Suddenly, though my eyes, hands and ears are still in the world of Arideth with Delilah and my body is still moving through the streets of London, strapped into Jeffrey's car within my wheelchair, my mind is in Calais. I am watching a smoke bomb explode in the back of a truck, watching a woman fleeing with her child as Tim Weibers giggles and exclaims "Pow, pow, pow."

I shake the image from my mind, I am speaking on behalf of my character, not myself. But Delilah's words nestle themselves within me, somewhere where they will not easily be forgotten.

"And what proof can I give you?" I ask her.

A smile plays on her blood-red lips. "None," she replies. "Despite my many years in Strognir and beyond, across the ocean of snakes, no one has ever proved to me, nor ever will, what lies within them. You can never know the depths of another's soul. You can give me no proof, but I am rather good at making educated guesses. Tell me more about why you deserve my tears, traveller."

The red outline of a rectangle with another small, vertical rectangle within it to the left side flashes in the top right-hand corner of my field of vision, and a disembodied voice tells me, "Low battery. Saving game." Both Delilah and the droplets of her tears, flowing over the edge of the bowl of the fountain into the pool below, freeze in mid-air, before quivering out of existence, my surroundings suddenly nothingness. And as the headset turns itself off, its noise cancelling capabilities do the same, allowing the sound of the car's engine to filter through. I remove my headset and gloves and place them on my lap, kicking myself (metaphorically, of course, kicking anything is physically impossible for me) for not having charged them last night.

I call out to the front of the car through the intercom that connects both sections. 'How far to the office, Jeffrey?' I ask him.

"10 minutes or so, we're close," he replies from the front.

I've been lucky. Most employees don't get this privilege. A free chauffeur service taking them directly to and from the office. The exception was made for me due to the fact that, in my case, commuting can be so difficult. On the days that I go to school, my mum still drops me off and picks me up. But, Marsham Street is a little bit further than my school and she doesn't really have time to do that drive before her workday begins. And also the fact that I'm only in the office two days each week at the moment probably helped too. The ride to and from Marsham Street is one of the times I can catch up in the VirtuWorld. Jim's complaint, that there's a little bit of movement when playing on the road which can distract you from the game, is true. But I requested for Jeffrey to try not to drive too haphazardly and he has accommodated my request extremely well. The wheelchair tie-down system which holds me in place is also fairly solid, meaning that, once I'm wearing my headset and gloves, I can focus on the game.

Jeffrey only really speaks when spoken to, and I doubt he would have many opinions on how I can convince Delilah to grant me her tears, so I open up a conversation with him on a different topic.

"How long have you been doing this, Jeffrey?" I ask him. "How long have you been working as a chauffeur?"

"Oh, I've been driving for about 14 years now," he says proudly. "Before that, I worked in a kitchen. But I always wanted to be behind the wheel, so I knew this was the job for me." He pauses, then adds, "I'm glad I made the switch. It's been a great experience."

"Almost as long as I've been alive." I muse thoughtfully. "Have you always worked with the Home Office or did you start off somewhere else?"

"I started out with a private chauffeur company, back in the day," he says. "But I eventually moved on to the Home Office, as a full-time driver. I've been here for about five years now. It's been a great ride. I'm glad I made the switch."

Something tells me that, even if Jeffery did not enjoy his work, he would be contractually obliged to tell me that he did. I go for a slightly more direct question. "Have you had any difficult clients?"

He chuckles softly and opens up a little. "Of course. You get all sorts of people when you're driving. Some of them are polite, some of them are rude, some of them are demanding. But I do my best to stay professional and make sure everyone gets where they need to be on time." He pauses, then adds, "The toughest client I've ever had was a woman who wanted me to drive her to five different locations in one day, each on the opposite side of the city to the last. Back and forth, back and forth. I was exhausted by the end of it, but somehow I managed to do it." A slight pause, then his voice comes out from the intercom again. "How are you enjoying the new job?"

"If I told you I'd have to kill you," I joke, and chuckle in turn. "No, seriously, I am quite enjoying it. They have me doing different rotations at the moment. This week I get to be an octopus."

"Intriguing," he says. "But I like being alive, so I won't push you for more details."

"Wise decision," I respond, a hint of humour in my tone. We leave the conversation there and my thoughts drift to the upcoming rotation.

What exactly will this rotation entail? Will it be more like Becky's rotation? But instead of flying through the skies, I travel through the oceans, exploring the Aegean Sea as an octopus and discovering its beauty, or will it be like Rush's rotation, controlling large groups of migrants in coercive ways so as to direct them away from their destination. This time pushing them back to Turkey in their boats, rather than blocking them from the tunnels of Calais. Probably somewhere in between.

Jill, the 50-year-old woman who heads up the team, is somewhat of an unknown quantity. Unlike my three previous rotations, I did not visit her desk during my first visit to the control room. I have not met her yet and have no idea of her own temperament or who constitute the members of her team. I must admit I am a little nervous. This is also my last rotation, after which I will have to give Thomas Rutchers and Joe Gradle feedback on which desk I prefer, and each desk will also give their opinion on me. Even though it was Becky that showed me the ropes on the reconnaissance team, the head of the team is a 33-year-old man called Gregory. I can only hope that, since he didn't see my flying much personally, Becky is able to talk me up to him as, unless my experience with the octopus is particularly mind-blowing, I think reconnaissance is still my number one choice.

"We're here." Jeffrey's voice comes from the front of the vehicle through the intercom as we pull up into the car park once again. He hops out of the vehicle, comes round so as to assist me in detaching myself from the wheelchair tie-down system, and rolls me to the small lifting platform at the back of the vehicle, which descends to ground level; soon enough I am outside of the car.

"Have a lovely day Mr. Octopus," he says mysteriously, before getting back in the vehicle. I roll myself towards the elevator, my VirtuWorld headset and gloves in my lap. As I roll towards the control room, Delilah's words bounce around in my head. "Are you an agent of the light or of the darkness?"

CHAPTER 20

Eloka and Paul have returned to their own section of the container and reclaimed the mattress on which they had been sitting before we called them over. This is not because we have fallen out in any way or because they were not on board with our plan. The plan has been discussed, developed and is ready to be implemented. The space in our corner of the container, however, which had already been restricted before we had called them over, became more restricted still in their presence. Eventually, the need came for us to take the advice of the skeletal Tuareg and catch some sleep. Even with Eloka and Paul returning to their own mattress and myself, Hasan and Mustafa staying in our corner, we have had to alternate when we would lie down. There isn't enough space for all three of us to do so simultaneously, even with one of us lying on the hard floor rather than the mattress.

Given that myself and Hasan are particularly small compared to the others – we were, after all, those that were chosen to travel in Olusola's boot – we shared the mattress first, sleeping simultaneously whilst Mustafa sat awake. After a while we swapped places, Mustafa got some rest and myself and Hasan sat. We are at the back of the container and are lucky in so far as we have been able to lean against its walls. Though the walls have been hot to the touch, they are not so hot as to burn skin, and the thin barrier of our clothing protects us. Those sitting at the centre of the container are not so lucky, and a few duos have taken to sitting back to back, leaning against each other and counter-balancing one another's weight, to give the semblance of having a backrest. Sitting cross-legged and supporting your weight with your spine, or leaning on a hand or an elbow is perfectly fine for a short period, but after some hours becomes very uncomfortable.

We are going to try to swap Mustafa for Paul in the front seat. The language barrier is a problem. It's all very well and good, Paul and Eloka teaching each other a little bit of French and English, but if they are to take the Tuareg's gun and force him to follow through on his commitment of carrying us to Libya, they really need to be able to communicate with each other. This is something which is not possible currently. Paul speaks no English, and Eloka speaks no French, apart from the few words they have managed to teach one another by pointing at their faces and saying "nose," "eyes" and "lips." Further, from what I have managed to gather by talking to Hasan about his conversations with the Cameroonian, Paul is deeply Catholic and very reluctant to engage in any type of violence, very reluctant to follow through on what may need to be done.

I have known Mustafa for years. He is a religious man, a Muslim, like myself, a man of peace. He would never have joined the Boko Haram jihadists or raised his hand to one of his siblings, but he is not one to allow his religion to get in the way of doing what must be done. He has a family to support, brothers, sisters, parents back in Nigeria, like me, like my own, counting on him. I know him and trust him. I do not know Paul. I am not able to speak to Paul directly, despite my small understanding of French, and what I have heard from Hasan does not fill me with confidence that he is the one who should be in the front of the vehicle with the Tuareg.

The fact that he himself seems more than happy to swap with Mustafa only bolsters my conviction. Mustafa is the third largest person out of the whole 28-strong group of migrants and not much smaller than Paul. Given Paul's lanky, spider-like frame, it is perfectly possible that Mustafa is the heavier of the two. If he and Paul were to talk to the smuggler and find some excuse for why they wished to swap- maybe Eloka wants someone he can actually speak to for the next stretch of the journey, or perhaps Paul and Eloka have fallen out during their time in the container- surely this would be permissible.

Once we are on the road with Mustafa and Eloka in front, they have to take control, then the Tuareg must be made to admit the situation and other migrants in the back of the vehicle will have to be informed. I will explain what's going on to those who speak English and Hausa, Paul and Hasan will tell those who speak French and Yoruba. There will be other languages spoken amongst the group, but we do not know them. Paul speaks Ewonde, his own native tongue, but believes that he is the only Cameroonian in our cohort. We will make sure that everyone understands that as a group we have all become disposable, and that this is an action which is necessary for us to reach our destination.

We must get them on board with the plan, have them in agreement. Once we are in agreement, it is 28 against one. And with those odds, out in the lawless desert, I see much more likelihood of the Tuareg taking us where we need to go. Once we are in the desert, the skeletal Tuareg should not be killed. He should believe that the threat of death is there, but he should not be killed. If he is killed, who else will guide us through the dunes, the empty, endless field of golden sand, with no paved roads or signposts or directions?

If he must be hurt, then he must be hurt. A bullet in the leg, the arm, the foot. But he must live, as knowledge of the desert is essential, and he is the only one we have any reason to believe possesses it. But we will be firm with him. No checkpoints, no passports, no bribes, no officers, no border security. Direct to Libya, evading all officials. The only other humans we should see are other jeeps of migrants making their own journey through the dunes.

The Christian woman who annoyed some during the initial drive from Zinder with her incessant praying has begun to sing hymns. She is the fourth woman, not the lady in the blue hat who looped her arm through mine on the journey from Zinder, nor the woman in the chequered scarf with her two children and her apologetic smile, obviously not the woman in the hijab - as she is singing Christian hymns. She is the woman who wore a turban not unlike that of the Tuareg's own to protect her face in the back of the moving vehicle. Now she has removed the turban, and her face is visible. She is older than the other women, perhaps around 40. Her nose is not protruding, but protuberant, rounded and thick. The beginnings of crow's feet adorn the corners of her eyes. Her eyebrows themselves are short and lack the ridge that traditionally characterise these features, stopping abruptly directly above her pupils. Her lips move in time with the hymn, opening softly, but not excessively, just enough for her to enunciate the consonants and vowels of her devotion.

"In Christ there is no east or west,
In Him no south or north,
But one great fellowship of love,
Throughout the whole wide Earth."

At the beginning, she sang very quietly, not wanting to disturb the sleep of those with whom she was incarcerated, and likely remembering the sharp words of the man that had sat beside her on the journey: "God will hear you just as well if you pray in your head." Earlier, her spoken prayers seemed urgent, and almost abrasive to those that do not share her faith, or do not feel it with the same fervour. Now, in contrast, the sweetness of her singing voice, its silky timbre and innocent clarity, have filtered through the room and encouraged a sentiment of permissiveness, to which she has responded eagerly.

"In Him shall true hearts everywhere,

Their high communion find,
His service is the golden cord,
Close-binding humankind."

She has augmented the volume of her vocalisations, not to the point at which she is belting out her words and echoing them off the metal walls of our temporary prison, nor even to the point at which they overpower the conversations which still take place in murmurs around her, but at least to the point at which the words she speaks are clear, despite her location on the other side of the container. At least to the point at which the fullness of her voice provides some relief from the heat, and the stench, and the worry about where exactly we have landed ourselves and what exactly are the intentions of the skeletal Tuareg.

"Join hands, united in the faith,
Whate'er your race may be!
Who serves m..."

You speak of the Devil and the Devil appears. The sound of the bolts on the door of the container sliding brings the woman's singing to a halt. The soft murmur of conversation filters out as the doors swing open and the skeletal Tuareg, his turban still covering his features, strides into the room. The wrinkles in the cloth which covers his mouth and nostrils are mirrored by the wrinkles that appear just above it on the bridge of his nose when he takes in the smell of the container. "And whose decision was it exactly, to put us in this sweatbox with bottles to piss in and minimal water?" I think bitterly.

"Time to go," the Tuareg says brusquely. "If you want buy water, buy water and clean container outside. Desert very hot. Journey long. Buy water good idea. After journey finish, Libya. New country. New ..." he pauses for a second whilst trying to remember the word "...prospect. New prospect." The creases of his turban shift around where his mouth must be and I imagine he is smiling at his own use of a fancy English word.

Could this be another motive? Keep us in a sweltering metal box so that, by the time we're ready to go, we're all in need of hydration, and then sell us the water we crave, squeezing out those last pennies?

"Stand!" he barks. "Come!"

Paul stands almost immediately, and I see him push through the room and begin a conversation with the skeletal Tuareg in French, pointing over at Eloka and then at Mustafa in turn, evidently putting the first stage of our plan into practice. As this conversation takes place, the other migrants around the container begin to rise, stretching their limbs, twisting their torsos, waking their sleeping companions. Given the mass of standing bodies, the Tuareg and Paul are momentarily obscured from my view. Once I myself have stood up, I am able to make out the sight of Paul giving Mustafa the thumbs up sign, something I am fairly certain is standard across both French and English. I allow a small ripple of relief to pass through me. A ripple, not quite a wave, as this first stage in the plan is really the most straightforward, the least risky and the most likely to succeed.

We shuffle out of the container, into the open-air group by group. The smell of fresh air and the feel of the breeze on my cheeks are deeply welcome. As the hour shifts from afternoon to evening, the aggressiveness of the sun is diminished. For a moment, I close my eyes, gulp in the untainted air and iron out the wrinkles of my body, standing on my tiptoes and stretching my limbs, squeezing my buttocks together and swivelling my hips, profiting from the privilege of space before I am again compressed like a packaged good.

A few of the men have filtered off to relieve themselves in the sand, and two of the women have made a direct beeline to the porta potty along with a number of other men who evidently need to do more than just urinate. During our stay, the guards would come in every few hours or so to check if anyone needed to use the porta toilet, but it has been at least two and a half hours since their last visit. As promised, a man stands next to a selection of water bottles and containers, from small 500 millilitre bottles which could fit in a decently sized coat pocket to 10 or 15-litre jerry cans full of life-giving water. Most people decide to pair up with three or four others and buy a larger container together, as it works out cheaper. Myself, Hasan and Paul are trying to decide whether to buy 10 litres or 15 between us when the woman in the blue hat who had looped her arm through mine, and who seemingly is travelling alone, appears beside us.

She asks if we would be willing to share our water with her if she chips in for 15 litres. It seems she plans on travelling next to me again, perhaps holding on to me for stability once more. There is no reason for me to turn her away. After all, before long, I will need to get her on side. And so, we buy 15 litres between us, a large and heavy container, which I happily allow Paul to carry. Hasan looks pensive for a moment, and then asks the merchant whether he has any empty bottles, in case we wish to divide the water up between us at a later time. He asks this in French but I manage to follow the gist. The vendor shakes his head and presumably says something along the lines of, "If you want small individual bottles, you pay for small individual bottles." He obviously is not in the business of helping his customers secure a cheaper deal. Unsurprising, as he's probably in the business of trying to turn a profit.

Hasan bites his lip, and his eyes shift from the merchant to myself, to the woman in the blue hat, as though steeling himself for a decision. He then turns on his heel and disappears back into the shipping container. I look at Paul in confusion and he raises an eyebrow at me. A few moments later, Hasan re-emerges from the shipping container carrying a number of smaller water bottles containing small amounts of yellow liquid. He pours out the liquid, shaking the bottles to evacuate them of every last drop. The urine soaks into the sand at his feet. Hasan looks up at our horrified expressions and shrugs.

"The desert is desert. In the desert, water is life, *l'eau est la vie.* Cash money is money. *Argent liquide...* no point wasting cash, dawg, none of us have much... *nous sommes très pauvres...* maybe we have to separate. Just in case.. *au cas où..*" He squashes the empty water bottles, evacuating them of air, and replaces the lid on each, before folding them and placing them in his backpack.

CHAPTER 21

Jill smiles, and when she smiles dimples appear on her cheeks and in the space between her chin and her bottom lip. Her teeth are rather large and her face is wide and angular. Her hair is beginning to grey, it seems that she dyes it a coffee brown, but the snow is still visible, pushing through at the roots. She's dressed rather plainly and cradles a metal flask of an unidentified hot drink between both hands, fingers overlapping.

"Hello Elijah," she says as I roll down the row towards her. "It's lovely to properly meet you. I hope you're looking forward to working with our team."

"Hello," I respond. "It's lovely to meet you too. I've been anticipating this rotation eagerly for the past few weeks."

"Well," she says jovially, "let's hope it lives up to expectations. What do you know about what we do here at the OctoBot team?"

Jill's screen is currently off, and we are tucked away in the corner of the control room. There are two members of the team sitting further down the row. Both have their headsets on, but do not seem to be wearing any gloves. They are sitting rather still, as though watching a film or engaging in some other passive activity. I notice that their headsets are slightly different in shape than those used by the reconnaissance, combat and control, and RBA teams, and slightly larger in size. Just as had been the case during my rotation with Rush, I am unable to see exactly what is happening on their screens from my vantage point at the end of the row.

"I have heard a little about what you do," I respond sheepishly. "You work in the Aegean Sea and the Mediterranean, helping to control the flow of boats and ensure that they remain near the waters of the countries from which they departed, guarding the European shore. I'm not much sure about the specifics beyond that, but octopus mode is one of my favourite modes in The Evolution of Wildness. I'm sure I could get my head around it quickly."

Jill's eyebrows raise. She does not smirk in a way that is supercilious, but the way she squints almost imperceptibly, and the slight shift in her smile, indicate a type of knowing scepticism.

"An octopus has an entirely different biological structure to our own, they are not mammals, they are not even vertebrates. They are molluscs belonging to the order Cephalopoda, meaning head-foot in Greek. Their brain to body ratio is similar to that of a whale, an intelligent mammal. However, whereas our neurons are mostly centralised in the brain, the central brain of an octopus only contains about 10% of its neurons. Its two optic globes contain 30%, and the remaining 60% are in its tentacles. You might think your hands are sensitive. You might think your hands are the most sensitive part of your body. Have you ever heard of a cortical homunculus?"

"Yes," I reply. "I know what they are."

"Well," she continues, "When compared to an octopus tentacle, your hands, so large on the cortical homunculus, are nothing. Imagine each of your limbs having its own little brain. That is the experience of an octopus. Yes, in The Evolution of Wildness, you may use your fingers as rudimentary tentacles, propelling you through the seas, but this is not The Evolution of Wildness. This is no video game, Elijah. This is real. The research that has gone into this is ground-breaking. It is not possible to mimic an octopus using the body of a vertebrate, an animal with bones, with joints, our fingers are rigid and inflexible compared to their tentacles. The only way to control the OctoBot is to bypass our insufficient bodies altogether, to pick up the signals of the brain directly and transpose them, translate them into something different."

"But surely," I respond. "Surely that requires somehow rewiring the brain, learning how to move in an entirely different way, changing our very understanding of what movement is and building up from the basic blocks. Like a baby learning to crawl, to toddle, to walk from scratch."

"Yes Elijah." Jill says softly. "Yes, it's almost like learning to walk again." She glances at me and raises her eyebrows, complicit in the irony. "I heard about how you strode... sorry... rolled into the control room and wowed everyone with your first flight of a Falcon. Apparently even the insufferable Tim Weibers allowed himself to compliment you. Congratulations. It won't be like that, however, if you choose to join the OctoBot team. The learning curve is much, much steeper. And your experience with The Evolution of Wildness is not easily translatable. You will have no need for gloves."

There are a few moments of silence as I ingest her words, but I respond with a confidence worthy of Tim himself.

"I do like a challenge." I say. "I love to stretch my boundaries."

"Well," she responds, "It seems you should follow me."

Perhaps it's because of the fact that fewer of her team are currently in the office taking up space along the row; perhaps it's due to the fact that, unlike Rush during the 'baptism of fire' in Calais, her team is not currently in a high stakes situation in the field; perhaps it's simply because they are different individuals. Unlike Rush, Jill does not simply share her screen and clone the screens of her team members, but rather leads me down the row, pushing in chairs as she walks, to give my wheelchair room to roll, until we arrive behind one of her colleagues. Given that they are wearing a headset, only the lower half of their face is visible. Puffy cheeks and puffy lips. Pale skin with freckles. Shoulder length auburn hair.

"This is Sophie," Jill says, "I'll introduce you shortly. But first allow me to describe what you see on her screen."

"This is the Aegean Sea, underwater," she says, gesturing towards the screen. I don't quite know what I expect to see intuitively, whether I expect to see reefs and crabs, schools of fish, sea turtles, and coral reefs or perhaps just emptiness (I'm thinking again of Mum's C-food stew), but instead, I'm greeted with the sight of a shipwreck, illuminated by artificial light, presumably produced by the OctoBot itself, which must be at a depth where the sun's rays do not penetrate sufficiently. Rotting timbers and beams are strewn about the sea floor. Ancient coins, pots, and tools lay scattered about, while the remains of ceramics and glassware, covered in green weed and algae, add to the mystery of the site. Huge tentacles are visible, streaming out from the bottom of the screen and moving through the wreckage, wrapping onto anchors and masts.

"Now, exploring shipwrecks isn't technically part of our job here, of course," Jill says frankly. "But I always find that, with new recruits, it's better to start with something cool. We do want you on our team after all. This particular wreckage is a Classical Greek shipwreck, found around 60 years ago in 1999 at Tetkas Burnu. The Greek vessel was transporting wine, pine tar and butchered beef, but sank to a depth of 45 metres around 400 BC. You're looking at a piece of history. Incidentally, the wreckage is very close to the city of Bodrum, which is where many of the migrants leaving from Turkey, hoping to get to Greece, set off on the waves. As a lot of our job involves waiting to hear from reconnaissance and jumping into action once we have news of a boat on the move, little gems like this, which are close enough for us to dispatch ourselves to the necessary site quickly, are sometimes where we spend our downtime."

"And ... and those tentacles," I ask slowly, "those are Sophie's tentacles... They belong to the OctoBot."

"That is correct." Jill confirms.

"And they're moving."

"That is correct." Jill confirms again.

"But she's not moving at all. She's perfectly still. So how is she controlling them?"

"And that is the question." Jill smiles. "Neuroscience," she continues "Is a complicated and magnificent thing. But how to explain it to a school child?"

I feel myself bristle at this comment, but remind myself that I am, in fact, a school child. There's nothing factually wrong about her statement. And science isn't really my best subject.

"Simplify it to a level I can understand," I tell her.

"Neuroscience is my life's work," Jill explains "I am a scientist, I designed the system. Sophie is not a scientist, but I have explained the theory to her at a level that she understands. Now it's time to see how well she can explain the theory to others. Let's allow her to tell you exactly how it works."

Jill places her hand on Sophie's shoulder, and I see one of the octopus's tentacles twitch in response before all of the tentacles become still, attaching themselves to the ocean floor with their suckers. Sophie removes her headset, but does so in a way that is slow, deliberate, and much more complicated than expected. After first detaching the outer casing of the unit, including the virtual reality goggles and headphones, underneath is an unfamiliar sort of fabric cap, strapped beneath her chin, with a number of green and yellow tabs attached to wires leading to a small box behind her ear. She unstraps the bottom of the chin strap, which seems to be attached by a type of Velcro, and pulls off the cap itself. Glancing between myself and Jill, and pouting her puffy lips, she clicks her tongue and asks,

"Is it time for me to put on my teaching cap then?"

"The student becomes the teacher," Jill replies.

"Nice to meet you, Sophie," I say. "It would be good to get an explanation. How do you control the octopus without moving any part of your body, without using gloves?"

"Well Elijah," Sophie responds, "this here," she holds out the cap and places it on my lap. "It's called an EEG cap" she says as she points to it. "It monitors my brain activity, specifically my alpha, beta and gamma waves, those associated with wakefulness. As I focus on a specific action, like moving my left arm, my brain produces a specific pattern of alpha, beta and gamma waves. The EEG cap detects this pattern and sends the signal to the Octobot, which then moves its tentacles accordingly. It's a form of mind control, but rooted in technology and data rather than any psychic powers. Not everyone uses a cap, Jill has actually had a chip implanted permanently, but the cap doesn't require any surgical procedure and can be used by anyone with some basic training. It's all about understanding how your brain is producing these waves and being able to control them to control the Octobot. Does that make sense?"

"I guess so," I reply.

"Great," responds Sophie. "The issue is that controlling an octopus's body is a completely different kettle of fish to controlling a human body. No pun intended. The idea of joints, knees and elbows for example, is non-existent. There are eight limbs instead of four. And things such as suckers are controlled independently. Did you notice before I took my headset off that my tentacles tend to move in pairs? That's because I haven't quite yet got the hang of independently moving eight separate limbs. My brain isn't used to it yet. Even after working on this desk for more than a year. The only way I've been able to really... I'm still... working within the frameworks of a mind which is used to human motion. And they're very difficult to break, habits.

Once you learn to do something one way, it's very difficult to get your head around doing it in a way that's totally different. That's why learning a language like Chinese, which depends on the pitch of the voice rather than just the sounds themselves for meaning, is so difficult for people from England or France. That's why it's so difficult for me to control the tentacles separately. It's a different kind of motor skill entirely, like a guitar player trying to play the violin, they have to start from scratch."

I think of my mother and my promise to her that I would pick up an instrument. The violin could complement her guitar quite well, but I haven't yet quite decided.

"A wonderful description, if I may say so," says Jill. "You must have had a wonderful teacher." A wry smile visits her lips. "This science has been around for decades now, but we're only just getting to the point where it's really accurate, and where the readings we are able to receive and the speed with which we are able to relay the data to a remote location allow for a project such as the OctoBot to be viable. This is the cutting edge, Elijah. This is the future."

"And Jill is helping to build it." says Sophie admiringly.

The wry smile playing across Jill's lips gives way to a pensive look, and the three of us fall into silence for a few moments before Jill blinks and begins to speak again. "I wouldn't want to get your hopes up prematurely, Elijah. As I have just told you, even after decades and decades of work, EEGs and brain control implants are still experimental. But there is another use case for them. It's actually the reason I got into neuroscience in the first place. But research needs funding. And the people willing to fund my research, who had the money to do so, turned out to be the Home Office. So I'm here, paying back my pound of flesh." She glances around surreptitiously as if expecting Joe Gradle to jump out from behind a computer monitor. When he does not, she continues. "As I say, the reason I got into this branch of neuroscience originally was interest in another particular use case of EEGs? Could you guess what that might be?"

I don't know. I have no idea what the other use case might be. I'm not a neuroscientist. Is this some sort of test or rhetorical question? The only answer I can give is one of ignorance. "I don't know," I respond.

"Well, try to remember. When I first told you about the OctoBot being very different to octopus mode in The Evolution of Wildness, what did you say it would be like?"

I push myself to remember. This is no rhetorical question, nor is it a test. But I still feel the need to demonstrate that I have been paying attention, and can remember our conversation thus far. The memory comes to me.

"I said it would be like learning to crawl again. To walk." I say blankly.

Out of nowhere, Jill spills a little of her still hot drink on my leg, and I let out an exclamation of indignation. She smiles in response.

"A partial spinal lesion. Your motor fibres have been severed, but some sensory fibres remain. You can still feel, but you cannot move. The signals from your brain don't quite make it all the way to your legs. But if those signals could somehow be read, and redirected, sent through the sensory fibres, or skip over the spinal cord entirely to a wireless receiver just below the waist, well then Elijah, anything might just be possible..."

CHAPTER 22

The stars are spheres of gold. There is no artificial light except the headlights of the jeep, and each constellation is beaded through the sky like the jewellery of a traditional Hausa bride. The desert is open emptiness. All life, all activity in the area is compressed into this jeep, which rumbles through the sand at speed, somehow carving a path through the labyrinth of sameness.

The seating arrangements are much as they had been on the first leg of our journey, with a few minor adjustments. Paul has taken the place of Mustafa, a few seats to my right, of course. Like myself, he clings to his wooden pole, Catholic prayer beads slipping between his fingers. Hasan has placed himself in the centre of the open backed jeep, alongside the women and children. The idea is that, given he is the member of our group of conspirators with the best overall grasp of both English and French, he may well be the best placed to address all of the migrants at once from that location, standing in the middle with the ability to turn and speak to the crowd as one.

For those of us like Hasan, Paul and myself, who dangle off the edge precariously, addressing those on the other side whilst the vehicle moves would be difficult. Though our voices would probably reach them over the noise of the engine if projected over our shoulders, it may well be muffled or drowned out by the objections of others. The way we are sitting, with our legs dangling from the side of the vehicle on either side of the poles, we would not be able to look at those to whom we speak, to express the sense of urgency with our eyes, to gauge their immediate reactions and react accordingly.

The woman in the blue hat is gripping me tighter than ever, her nails digging into my forearm, clinging to me as though she were Karima clinging to my hand as I spun her, knowing that to release my hand mid-swing could well result in injury or harm. Karima. Fatima. How is Fatima? Has the medicine worked? Has she begun to come back from the fevers of malaria once again? Has she begun to shift once more from the shivering lethargic child who coughs between her giggles to the bundle of energy and joy that chases lizards along the walls and clambers up the trees like a monkey?

Will I ever see her again? My sweet, sweet sister. When I next see her, will she still be the child that giggles at the voices I put on when I recount my father's stories? Will she still recollect our bond, or will she be a woman, separated from me by the years? My phone has little signal in the desert and I was unable to call my mother and sisters from the shipping container. And what would I have said? That I have not yet reached Libya? That I suspect I have been scammed? I cannot call them until I have advanced in my journey. Until I have something positive to say. Until I can show them that the decision I made was wise and judicious, for it was my decision. What was it my mother said? She 'consents' but she does not give her blessing. But I know they are thinking of me. My sisters' older brother, my mother's son, gone from them, but not gone in the same way as our father. Gone to a place where they may well one day follow.

Our faces are all covered by cloth. The dust of the Sahara is ever present, kicked up by the wheels of the jeep, flicked by soft jets of wind to settle over our clothes and in the space between the straps of our sandals. Hasan had a spare set of sunglasses which he has lent me, for which I am extremely grateful. Not only do the glasses provide some protection from the dust, and stop me from having to squint constantly against it, but once the sun has risen again, they will provide a different sort of comfort.

My body is uncomfortable. The thin metal side of the jeep over which my legs hang has started to dig into the underside of my thighs. My bottom hurts, and my buttocks have begun to chafe. The way we are squeezed into the jeep means my shoulders are hunched ever so slightly forward and my upper arms are not quite at my side but rather rest against my ribcage, skin squashed against cloth squashed against cloth squashed against skin. My armpits, moist repositories of sweat that they are, have little room to breathe unless I extend my arms directly out in front of me, but doing so is not really an option. My left arm is trapped in the grip of the woman in the blue hat, and my right arm clings to the wooden pole before me, providing me with the very stability with which she herself hopes to cling to.

But I am used to feeling uncomfortable. How many nights have I slept with a belly that gnaws at me, demanding food we do not have? How many days have I spent in the sweltering sun, seeking relief from the small fan our family shares between us, powered by the same rays of sun it seeks to provide relief from? The uncomfortability of my body is secondary. I spend much more time contemplating the situation at hand, the need to ensure I reach my destination.

My mind flits regularly to the front section of the jeep. Where does the skeletal Tuareg keep his pistol? In the glove box? On his person? When will Mustafa and Eloka have the opportunity to get their hands on it? Each time the vehicle shudders, or unexpectedly swerves with slightly more vigour than usual, scenarios play out in my head. The jerk of the steering wheel as both the Tuareg and Mustafa simultaneously lunge for the weapon. The jeep turning suddenly into a sand dune as they wrestle for the piece of metal which converts its possessor into a menace, a threat. A shot ringing out in the desert, taking another brother and son from the world.

The longer Paul sits a few places to my right and whimpers,

clutching his beads and shivering, not from cold but from fear, the happier I am with the decision to replace him with Mustafa in the front. For Paul, this section of the journey is a downgrade, I guess. On the journey from Zinder to the shipping container in Agadez, he had had a seat belt, leg room, somewhere to rest his feet, possibly even air conditioning, as I assume the skeletal Tuareg would not have denied himself that luxury. I look at the way that Paul seems to be chewing at the fabric that covers his face compulsively, and wonder if he is scared of heights, and the possibility of falling over the edge of the vehicle or if, like myself, he is simply worried about where the journey will take us in reality.

It's been agreed that, once Mustafa and Eloka have been able to get the gun from the Tuareg, they will allow him to drive a short distance further, explain why they have taken the action they have, and then order him to stop the vehicle. He will then exit the jeep and admit to the larger group of migrants that our suspicions are well founded. At this point, myself, Hasan and Paul will address the rest of the migrants, and Eloka and Mustafa will ensure the Tuareg behaves by the simple expedient of pointing the pistol at his face. Hasan, who along with loving rap music and neogrime in his youth, had a particular love for urban gangster films set in the inner cities of London and New York, was quick to point out that it is essential to make sure the safety on the gun is off, and that the Tuareg is not concealing a second weapon.

The reason we have decided to wait until the Tuareg himself has admitted guilt before informing the rest of the group about our plan is simple. I myself remember the deceptive conversation between the Tuareg and Olusola, and have connected the dots to know for sure that on some level I was being deceived. I am not, however, aware of what conversations between smugglers the others in the back of the jeep have been privy to, if any, or if they will remember them correctly, if they were there when the words were spoken, or if they spoke the language in which the words were said.

When I first realised that everyone in the jeep only had the funds to take them to Libya, did I not try to rationalise it and allow a desire to believe in and trust those who were transporting me to muddy my judgement? Did I not wonder whether it was all just a question of logistics, and if the reason for the split was due to the migrants who had money to go all the way to Europe being transported directly to the coast? Unity between the migrants is essential. If any of the migrants don't believe us, and take the side of the smuggler, it could spell trouble. If the Tuareg refuses to admit his part of any plot, that is a road to cross when we come to it. But with the facts laid out and the added incentive of the threat of a bullet, the hope is he will cave and clarify our predicament, perhaps confirming Eloka's theory about an agreement with the Libyan border guards to give us up.

The Christian woman has begun to sing her hymns again, but given that she does so quietly, some of her words are lost under the rumble of the engine. I hear enough to know that she is singing about a star in the east, guiding some travellers through sorrow and grief in the night, helping pilgrims follow the route to the place where they aim to travel. Travellers. Grief. Stars. It seems fitting.

But not quite as fitting as before. Yes, the stars have definitely dimmed. They are no longer the beads of jewellery adorning the robes of a Hausa bride, but seem to peek through a thicker haze of dust than before. The wind also feels a little stronger, and the temperature has dropped slightly, not to the point where Paul's shivers might be excused as being rooted in the cold rather than cowardice, but still to the point where the shift is noticeable.

It happens in a matter of minutes. As the jeep continues to roar through the desert, a building sandstorm begins to gather on the horizon. At first, it is only a faint haze, but it soon begins to grow, becoming a wall of sand that stretches from the ground to the sky. The wind picks up, kicking up more dust and sand and making it difficult to see more than a few feet in front of us. The air becomes thick with particles, and it is difficult to breathe. The sunglasses transform from a convenience to a necessity, and the woman in the blue hat tightens her grip on my arm. Her fingernails may well be drawing blood. She seems to think that if she releases me the wind will blow her into oblivion. Paul begins to pray, his words are inaudible over the roaring of the wind, but the movement of his lips, the threading of the beads between his fingers, the rocking of his shoulders tell me he is asking for salvation. The two children in the middle of the jeep begin to cry; the woman has stopped her singing.

The vehicle swerves erratically, and with the reduced visibility, and the effect of the wind buffeting against it, the thought passes my mind that the driver must be struggling to stay in control, and that this may be the ideal moment for Mustafa and Eloka to make their move. But the thought is fleeting, and is quickly replaced again by fear and by the taste of sand. The t-shirt I have used to cover my face has slipped, allowing sand to crawl into my nostrils and my mouth. I spit. I close my mouth and push air out through my nostrils, trying to clear them. I release my grip on the pole, place it within the nook between my bicep and my forearm, and close my elbow around it, freeing up my hand and attempting to secure the t-shirt more firmly around my face. It's difficult with one hand, but when I try to free my other from the woman's grip, her voice behind me is full of panic, and her second hand closes around my wrist.

"Don't let go of me!" she exclaims in a way which is both an order and a request.

I manage to re-secure the t-shirt more firmly with one hand by twisting some of the fabric and looping it under itself at the back of my head to create a very rudimentary and questionable knot. Just as I extend my arm, releasing the grip of my elbow on the pole with the intention of returning it to my hand, the jeep swerves erratically. Without the stability of the pole to secure me, I lunge forward, smacking my shoulder painfully against it, and almost tumbling over the side of the jeep, the glasses fly off my face and are lost in the Sahara. Perhaps it is only the woman's grip on my arm which saves me. She clings to me and pulls me backwards, giving me time to regain my grip. I immediately squeeze my eyes shut, surrendering myself to the darkness as the sand beats against their sensitive lids. As my heart beats frantically, I am sure I hear a gunshot.

CHAPTER 23

The EEG cap is tight against my scalp. The Velcro strap digs in underneath my chin. The headset is heavier than I am used to, and currently audio is disabled, allowing me to hear the voice of Jill as she guides me through the training exercise. I see four rudimentary tentacles in my field of vision, marked with the numbers 3 to 6. I know that four more lie behind me in the virtual space, labelled 1, 2, 7 and 8. Geometrical lines form cubes that extend endlessly in every direction, filling the space that surrounds me. The lines themselves are translucent, but extend outwards in regular parallel intervals, like the graphs we have been studying recently at school in GCSE mathematics, but in three dimensions rather than two. This is to help me keep track of the distance of movement. If Jill asks me to lift the tentacle labelled 2, three boxes upwards, or to pull it back by four, I am able to see in a clear and measurable way if I am doing so correctly. Her voice comes to me somewhere from my left.

"Okay Elijah," she says, "I hope you're ready for the next stage of the process. We are going to start to realign the parts of the brain you use for movement, so that they control these tentacles, rather than your own body. You only have one brain, however, and your whole life, the parts of your brain controlling movement have been used to moving your arms and legs, torso and toes. We have to rewire them in such a way that a particular command, say the command to twist your wrist at an angle of 30 degrees, results in a different output, say bending tentacle number three a third of the way down its length at a 30 degree angle to the left. Since this command still aligns with you twisting your wrist, in order for you to truly will it, it would still have to be accompanied by the corresponding action in the real world as well as resulting in the virtual counterpart. We don't really want this, we don't need you accidentally knocking over your monitor or punching a colleague in the face."

"Where's Tim when you need him?" I say jokingly. She pretends not to hear me.

"So what we're going to do is induce a temporary blockage of signals from your spine downwards, by way of a small electric pulse just above the back of your neck. The effects will be similar to the effect of the real spinal lesion which demobilised your legs. From the neck down, you'll be unable to move. But this, of course, won't be permanent. There will be a signal. In this case, the combination of pursing your lips together and wrinkling your nose acts as a switch of sorts. When you do these two actions together you will find yourself unable to move from the neck down, and therefore able to focus entirely on learning how to use your body to control the OctoBot. Do these actions in combination again and you will free up your body. Do you want to try it?"

Not particularly, I think. The idea of willingly paralysing the rest of my body sends a small shiver down my spine. But hey-ho, I think, apparently this device will block any further shivers from heading down it. I purse my lips and screw up my nose. I feel nothing, no small electric buzz at the back of my neck and accompanying click. Nothing. I wonder if I pursed my lips hard enough.

"Okay," Jill continues, "now I want you to try and beat your chest like a gorilla."

"What?" I ask her.

"Like a gorilla. Beat your chest. Go for it. As hard as you can," she pushes.

"Okay." I respond, and will my arms upwards, but they do not come. I do not feel the corresponding thump of my fist on my chest, I remain as still as silence.

When I was a child, I would sometimes suffer from sleep paralysis. I would have a nightmare about a dragon, or a clown, or a talking shark and would wake up from the nightmare cold and try to move, but I wouldn't be able to. My heart would be racing and I would feel terrified. I would try to call out to my brother, since as kids we shared a room, but I was unable to make him hear me. Eventually the paralysis would pass and I would regain the ability of motion. When my accident happened, I kept waiting for the moment when the paralysis would lift, when I would wake up from my dream and move my legs again. But, of course, it never came.

For a long time, I abandoned hope. I came to terms with the fact that I would not walk again. I allowed myself to become lost in the VirtuWorld. Ever since Jill informed me that this EEG technology is also being tested as a way to help those without the ability to walk regain their ability, I've become a little obsessed. When I got back from the office yesterday, I didn't play games, but I spent the whole evening on the Internet. I was looking at videos about brain implants and neuroscience, and reading academic papers that I didn't understand about medical trials, allowing hope to start bubbling up in me again. I want to spend every minute of this rotation asking Jill about it, finding out if it would be feasible in my own case, what I would need to do to become involved in one of these trials. But at the end of the day, in the control room, the purpose of the technology isn't to help me walk. It's to allow me to control a different type of body, under the sea.

"Okay," Jill continues. This time, somewhere slightly off to my right, as though she's walked to my other side whilst I was lost in my contemplations. "Now, we're going to connect you to your virtual octopus. I want you to raise your eyebrows and flare your nostrils if you can."

I carry out these actions simultaneously, feeling like an idiot, and again there is no visible, audible, or sensory indication that anything has changed.

"Have you done it?" Jill asks me.

"Yes," I respond.

"Okay, now I want you to kick the desk in front of you. You can't see it at the moment, but you know where it is. Kick it for me, Elijah."

My eyebrows, which moments ago were raised almost as if in surprise, descend into a frown. Is this a joke? If so, it's in bad taste. She knows I cannot kick. But even though my frozen body and my covered eyes can give no signal of my indignation, Jill somehow seems to sense it.

"Trust me, Elijah. You used to be able to kick, did you not know how before your accident? Well, your brain still knows how. You can still have the intention and your brain will send the signal. It just isn't able to get to its destination. But this time we are recording the signal at its source. Kick."

Well, what's the worst that can happen? I screw my face up in concentration and will myself to kick, pushing with all my might in the same way that I did in those first few weeks after the accident when I somehow believed that, through sheer willpower, I could force my legs to move. They didn't move then, just as they don't move now. But I see tentacles number four and five flick upwards abruptly at the very moment I try, and when they land back down, I feel two soft points of pressure in a spot at the top right hand side of my scalp.

"Good," says Jill, evidently watching my progress on the monitor. Good. You made that happen. You intended to kick, and to do so in a particular way. The intention was picked up by the cap and relayed in the form of information to the virtual octopus. If you were to try and kick more softly, the tentacles would move more softly. If you were to try and move your leg in a different way, the tentacles would move in a different way. If you were to move your arm or chest, or if you intend to thrust your hips forward, all of this will have an effect somehow on the virtual octopus. And of course, despite the fact you are not wearing gloves, your fingers and hands remain the most sensitive part of your body. Just like in the VirtuWorld, a huge amount of the octopus's functions are controlled through hand movements, the only difference is this way your real hands do not move. It's literally the thought that counts."

"And what was that pressure on my scalp?" I ask, interested.

"Well, a lot of our understanding of movement, balance for example, and the ability to hold things, throw things, touch things... it's to do with pressure. We respond to the pressure of the world around us. When the pressure or impact is high enough, we feel pain. It helps us navigate the world around us. That's something you don't get with your VirtuWorld games, and they find their ways to compensate. If you're shot or hit with a sword, you lose points or your character automatically flees when a certain threshold of damage has been reached. With this technology, however, the cap itself is able, through the use of needles, to provide a degree of sensory stimulus.

"The scalp is rather sensitive and actually covers a decent surface area. Thus, the area of your scalp which the needle hits represents a certain part of the octopus's external body. Its skin, so to speak. And the amount of pressure the needle applies corresponds to the amount of pressure applied on the octopus. To a certain threshold, of course. Were your OctoBot to be attacked by a great white shark, the pressure in your scalp would certainly not be proportionate. But to a reasonable extent, and even to a certain level of uncomfortability and pain, it will. For those of us with implants, of course, The process is much more immersive. We feel the pressure and pain as though throughout our whole body. But getting a chip in your brain is a large step. Sophie hasn't even had an implant yet and she's been here for a year. We don't even know yet if you're going to join our team."

I hesitate, then decide to ask the question that is bothering me.

"The research you mentioned into using this technology to help paraplegics, to help people walk again. Does that use EEG caps or implants or both?"

"A combination," she responds. "But many participants hoping to use this technology to help them walk again don't want to walk around all day wearing a great big EEG cap. And also, as I mentioned, accuracy, responsiveness and the real experience of pressure are all enhanced with an implanted chip. Most of the trials looking to use this technology to help people walk have been done utilising a surgically implanted chip. But that's by the by. Let's focus on the octopus for now. Do you dance, Elijah?"

I'm thrown by the question. Do I dance? I used to dance. I still do sometimes. Shake my arms, roll my shoulders, listen to my favourite songs alone in my room. I decide to stop being so defensive and give an answer she can work with.

"Sometimes, if the music's right," I say,

"Cool," Jill responds. "And how did you learn how to dance?"

"Just by doing it, I guess."

"Okay. I want you to dance, to just move bits of your body. Forget yourself and start to move your fingers, your toes, your elbows, your neck, your knees, your ankles, and observe. Observe how the virtual octopus moves in sync with your own dancing. Take note of what movements do what, and where the pressure is on your scalp when your tentacles touch the ground or each other. If you want to see behind you at the other tentacles, you can do so. Simply look as far to the right or left as possible with your eyes and the image will track around for a full 360 perspective in total. Get to know your new body. Meanwhile, I'm going for a coffee."

So coffee is her beverage of choice, then. It was coffee that I was cleaning out of my jeans last night.

"Jill," I blurt out, "before you go for your coffee, could I ask you something?"

"Ask away," she responds.

"If I don't end up at this desk. If I was to choose one of my other rotations, could we still talk sometimes, about the medical side of this technology, about the possibilities of it helping me get my legs back?"

"Elijah," Jill responds, her voice much softer now, the scientist in her giving way to something more gentle and less academic, "I told you that the very reason I got into this field of science was in the hopes of helping people in your situation. You are not obliged to work with this team, and even if you don't you'll still be my colleague. I'd be happy to talk to you about the medical applications of the technology. I'd even be happy to show you some of the applications. And if we can find the time, perhaps after work sometime, we can try out a few basic experiments and tests. But for now, we need to make sure you understand the technology as it applies to your new potential job."

Jill has one last question for me. "Before I go, what type of music do you like?"

"I'm a fan of a band called Midnight Monkey," I respond.

I feel Jill's fingers push underneath my headset on each side of my head, popping some earbuds into my ears underneath the cap.

"Enjoy," she says, "I'll be back in 20 minutes or so."

The album starts to play. Baboon Business, their third album. Not their best work, but not their worst either. Jazzy undertones with a little bit of neo soul and hip-hop intertwined. I start to dance.

CHAPTER 24

The storm has raged for hours. I cannot say how many, but I know the line between minutes and hours has long been crossed. The jeep stopped moving through the sand shortly after I heard what I believed to be a gunshot. We have been static ever since, huddled against the wind and sand. The t-shirt with which I cover my face is now draped over even my eyes. No part of my face is left uncovered. The sound of the wind rebukes all thoughts of murmured conversation, though - occasionally - indistinct shouting can be heard from those behind me. The pincer-like grip on my arm remains. But I am sure that the sandstorm is softening.

And once it has softened, what course of action shall we take? What course of action should I take? In our briefings, Mustafa, Eloka, Hasan, Paul and I did not discuss this precise eventuality. If I heard the gunshot, then it's almost certain I was not the only one to hear it. Will the others have deduced its significance, or brushed it aside as the sound of the engine backfiring, or some other unlikely but comfortable explanation. In the panic of the moment and with the howling of the wind, it's safe to assume that it will have passed unnoticed by some of the group. But all 28 of us? No.

People will be asking questions and the answers to those questions will depend partially on the particulars of the situation. Who fired the gun? Did the Tuareg use it on Eloka or Mustafa when they tried to take it from him, or were they successful in acquiring it and firing a warning shot? None of these things were open to investigation whilst the thin sand of the Sahara permeated our every fissure, but as the storm softens they are to be contemplated with increasing urgency.

Five minutes pass... 10. The wind grows calmer still. I pull down the neck-hole of the t-shirt covering my face and peek trepidatiously, I find that squinting through the haze is bearable. Visibility has improved, but it is still night time, and, of course, all that is visible is an endless stretch of sand. The murmur of conversation begins to bubble up again. People uncover their faces. Suddenly, the night is pierced by a pitiful, choking scream.

"*Mon frère*"

I know that word. I know what those words mean. My brother.

"*Mon frère!*" shouts the voice, choking up. "*Où est-il?* Where is he? *Mon frère?*"

It sounds like I wasn't the only one to have trouble keeping my body in the vehicle. It sounds like someone's brother fell during the chaos, but for some reason or the other, they weren't sitting together. Only now, without the distractions of the wind and without the storm-induced blindness, have they realised their brother's absence.

"*Mon frère!*"

I make a snap decision. This is the moment to investigate. All the attention currently will be on this man and his missing brother. I place my hand on top of the pincer that grips me, turning to the woman and murmuring, "The vehicle is not moving now. I need you to let go." I am ready to pry her fingers off me if the occasion requires, but such measures are unnecessary. Her fingers loosen and she releases her grip wordlessly, also un-looping her other arm from mine. I stretch my arm and splay my fingers before placing both hands on the wooden pole in front of me and using them to pull myself to my feet. I turn, placing my feet on the edge of the jeep, whilst facing inwards towards the larger group.

Every person is covered in a thin film of dust and sand, the hues of their skins and of their clothing filtered red. Some of them are huddled together, the woman with the two children seems to have been trying to use her own body as a shield, of sorts. The Christian woman who sang hymns has her arms wrapped desperately around her face, clinging with each hand to her shoulders. I lower myself down the side of the jeep as though abseiling, maintaining a hold of the pole until I am at the height where it is fairly easy to allow myself to fall to the ground. I walk towards the window of the driver's seat and open the door. No skeletal Tuareg. Eloka and Mustafa, their own clothes and faces untouched by the dust and sand, look towards me gravely. The gun lies in Eloka's lap. I step into the vehicle and for a moment we all sit in silence, waiting for the others to speak, then Mustafa begins.

"The gun was at his belt. He was driving, wasn't really speaking to us, seemed lost in his own world. It looked like he was studying the dunes and the trees, looking for markers which let him know exactly where he was at any time, to help make sure he was going in the right direction."

Mustafa is sitting closest to me. He would have been the best placed to have attempted to take the Tuareg's weapon. Eloka sits in the other window seat, his locks flowing over the back of his seat, his eyes filled with a fearful and contemplative stillness.

"I was just waiting for the right moment," Mustafa continues. "It was all very theoretical when we discussed it in the shipping container, but when I was actually there, waiting for the right time to try and grab the gun from his belt, it was much scarier. When the storm came, you could tell he was totally focused on the road. From the windscreen you could actually see the shapes of the dunes in front of us shifting, remoulding themselves as the sand disappeared into the sky. I told myself it was now or never and I lunged for the gun. But his reactions were quicker than I'd ever expected. He saw me going for it, or maybe my nervousness had given us away. He went for it himself with his left hand, keeping his right hand on the wheel.

We struggled for a moment, but since I had two hands and he only had one, I was more in control. Somehow as we fought for the gun, someone pulled the trigger. And it hit him in the leg. Only in the leg. He slammed down the brakes at that point, bringing us to a standstill. Opened the door on your side of the jeep and got out into the building storm. Maybe he thought our plan was to kill him. I don't know. But I didn't follow him. I couldn't in that storm."

"So, where is he?" I ask.

"He has to be somewhere. He can't have gone far in that storm. And he should be alive. We only shot him in the leg. Only in the leg. We ended up following our own rules by accident."

"You shot him in the leg three hours ago." Eloka chimes in, pointing at the clock on the dashboard of the vehicle. "You don't know that he's not dead. You can lose a lot of blood in three hours."

"We need him," I say despondently, feeling a stab of panic push into my stomach like an icicle, the only icicle for hundreds of miles, somehow un-melted. "We need to find him now."

Out of nowhere, Eloka slams his hand down on the counter in front of him. "Why on earth did you look so suspicious?" he growls. "Why did you look so nervous? You gave the game away. And there were opportunities earlier, when he opened his window, when his seat belt got stuck. You chose the wrong time."

"The storm was as good a time as any," Mustafa responds. "And you were the one who chose the window seat, the position of safety, so don't lecture me about nervousness."

"This is the seat I sat in on the first stage of the journey from Zinder!" Eloka replies defensively. "If I had swapped now, it would have just seemed suspicious."

"Nonsense," replies Mustafa. "The Tuareg had no problem with Paul leaving the front entirely. Why would he care about you swapping seats?"

I slam my hands down on the dashboard in turn. "Shut up!" I yell. "We have a very serious situation here." Silence falls again for a few moments before I speak once more. "We need to find the Tuareg ASAP. A man outside has lost his brother. I think he fell off the vehicle while the storm was brewing. I almost fell myself. The storm will have covered any vehicle tracks and the jeep was swerving so much during it that there'll be no way for him to know which direction we came from. If we get out and offer to help him - we'll say that we'll take three directions and he can take the fourth - that's the perfect cover for us to look for the Tuareg. The man speaks French, so we'll ask Hasan to translate."

"And what do we say about the missing driver to the others?" Mustafa interjects.

"Nothing," says Eloka.

"Nothing yet," I concur. "They're not yet aware of what we know, and telling them we've shot our driver is not likely to warm them to us. They'll probably assume he's still in the front of the vehicle, and find out he's not whilst we're off searching for him. When we bring him back, we will make him explain why we did what we did."

"Why Mustafa did what he did." Eloka mutters.

"Why we did what we did," I respond emphatically. "We agreed on this together."

"And what do we do if the Tuareg has died?" responds Eloka.

"I only shot him in the leg," reiterates Mustafa. "He'll be fine."

"And if he has died," repeats Eloka.

"Then Allah help us,' I say shortly, before stepping back out into the Sahara.

The man who has lost his brother has descended from the back of the jeep and is pacing nervously around its perimeter. Another man seems to be attempting to console him, but each time he places his hand on the man's shoulder or approaches him, his hand is shrugged off and his consolation brushed aside. Mustafa and Eloka circle around the front of the vehicle to join me, and together we approach him. The sand, so successful in covering the tracks of the vehicle's tires, has had no likewise success in covering the tracks of tears across his cheeks.

"Do you speak any English?" Mustafa begins, but the man pushes past us, avoiding our gaze. His pursuer follows, a look of helplessness plastered on his features. As he shrugs towards us despondently, I turn first towards the jeep and then towards Mustafa.

"Give me a leg up," I say.

Mustafa kneels, threading his fingers together to produce a step in which I place my left foot.

I count down "three, two, one" and spring myself up whilst he lifts with his hands. I'm not quite able to reach the upper edge of the outer section of the vehicle.

"Again," I say, after descending back to the ground. We get back in position. "Three, two, one." This time, I am just about able to grip the upper edge of the jeep, and pull myself up so that my head pokes over the side. I'm not very strong, but I'm also not very heavy, and I'm able to support my own body weight. Given the way that we were packed into the back of the vehicle side by side, my hands are squashed together, my thumbs touching, and I shout towards my companion through a gap between the thighs of two men.

"Hasan!" I exclaim.

"Yes?" His voice comes to me through the thighs.

"We need your help. Can you come down here? We need you to translate."

"Okay," comes the response.

I slacken my arms, take a look down, and allow myself to fall, landing clumsily but not losing my balance. Hasan follows shortly after, swinging himself over the side of the jeep, and landing a little more gracefully than myself.

He glances behind him towards the floor, then looks towards me and says, "What's the problem dawg?"

I lower my voice.

"We've lost the driver. Mustafa shot him in the leg during a struggle for the gun."

I make a gun with my fingers and point it towards my leg, lifting my fingers quickly and making a soft 'pfft' sound with my front teeth and lower lip for emphasis. "We need to find him. We're going to offer to search for this man's brother, and use that opportunity to find the Tuareg."

"No need," Hasan responds frankly. "Ain't no need, dog."

"Why not?" I ask, frowning. Hasan steps to the side and points down towards the spot behind him, which he had glanced at moments before. Poking out from underneath the jeep is a male human hand, a softer paler brown than the sub-Saharan cocoa of my skin, Hasan's or Eloka's; fingernails caked in sand, framed in the sleeve of a blue turban.

I hear a sharp intake of breath to my left and know that Mustafa has also seen. Eloka's voice arises from its slumber, "Let's get it over with."

He approaches the hand and grabs it, tugging at it with unnecessary force. A whimpering sound comes from underneath the vehicle, and Eloka looks up towards us in surprise. I kneel down beside him. "Careful." I mutter. "He's still alive. Careful. Let's get him out slowly."

The man with the missing brother can wait. His brother will not guide us through the desert. Were the Tuareg to die, but his brother to be found, their reunion would be short and joyless. Slowly, carefully, we extricate the whimpering man from beneath the vehicle, starting with his hand and arm, followed by his head and torso. Eventually his hips begin to appear, and it is clear that Eloka was correct when he stated that a lot of blood loss can happen in three hours. The thin blue fabric of the man's robes is stained a deep and vibrant red, a sticky pool of moisture that puddles in the folds between the fabric. He appears to be only semi conscious, wincing in a way that is involuntary. Eyes closed. Breathing coming in shallow, jagged, jittery gulps.

Once we have extricated him completely, before we can fully assess the damage, a scream comes from the sky. Well, no, it doesn't. Of course it doesn't. The night sky does not scream. Least of all in the desert. Nor do its vultures. I should say that the scream comes from above, but for a moment it feels as though from the sky. I glance upwards and see three faces looking downwards. The Christian woman with her hymns, who must have squeezed her way over from the centre of the jeep. A man with angular cheekbones and a heavy jaw. Another with thick eyebrows and pencil thin lips. All looking down at the Tuareg beneath them and the pool of blood. All three faces knotted and twisted and tugged into expressions of consternation, shock and fear.

The scream draws more attention, and more faces appear,

emerging over the side of the vehicle like desert moles from the sand, glancing to their neighbours in confusion, muttering to those behind them. Chaos is seconds away. I stand, look towards Hasan and nod. He nods back. No further communication is necessary.

"Listen!" I shout. "*Écoute!*" he echoes. The rumbling of those in the vehicle does not die down.

"Listen if you value your lives." I shout again.

"*Écoute maintenant!*" Hasan echoes. Not a perfect translation, I don't think. I should speak slowly and clearly. Allow him time to take in my words.

"The intention was never to bring you to Libya," I say, and Hasan echoes me.

"Ask your neighbours. If you are going to ask your neighbours anything, ask them this. How far along the journey have they paid? And do they have more money with which to pay? You will find that everyone in this vehicle has only paid as far as Libya and has no more money waiting for the smugglers to take. You are of no use to them."

"That's not true," a voice comes back from somewhere above, before Hasan has the opportunity to translate. "I have paid as far as France!" The rumbling starts to bubble up again and I look at Mustafa in confusion.

Mustafa returns my look with eyebrows raised then speaks, "And have you paid all of it up front, or have you made some agreement with the smugglers that, when you arrive in Libya, your family will send them the balance?"

A few seconds of silence and the man replies. "I have paid all of it up front. I have no one in Ghana I trust enough to send money for me."

"Then," continues Mustafa, not quite triumphantly, but with a firmness to his tone, "you are of no more use to them. You have paid them all you have."

The man above falls silent.

"Take a moment. Ask your neighbours. That is why they separated us. In my group, those who had more money went in a different vehicle. Ask yourself, did they separate your own groups, wherever you came from? This is why." I start to speak again, pausing periodically whilst Hasan resumes his translation. "In the shipping container, we formulated a plan. We didn't tell you all because we didn't know who we could trust, but the idea was to get our hands on the Tuareg's weapon and force him to take us to Libya. There was a struggle for the gun during the sandstorm, and the Tuareg has been injured. Though he is a liar and a cheat, we still need his knowledge to get us through the desert. If anyone here is a doctor or knows anything of medicine, of treating wounds, please, help us. Come down and help us keep the man alive."

Silence follows, and I start to feel the real beginnings of despair, to imagine Fatima and Karima awaiting my call eagerly. Awaiting the news of my arrival, to be greeted by only silence as my bones gather dust amongst the millions of granules of valueless gold. A doctor, what am I thinking? A doctor may well wish to make this journey, but a doctor would be educated, from a well off family, would have some money, some funds with which to follow up, some savings for their family to send at a later date. A doctor would be of use to the smugglers. Even if, for some reason, the doctor found no way to emigrate legally, and felt the need to flee, they would not be in this jeep. They would be with Abdulai and the pencil moustached man with his endless sniffling. There is no doctor here.

After what could well be seconds or years, the hymn singer calls down. "I am not a doctor, but my mother was a traditional healer. I used to help her with her remedies. Often wounded men would come to her. She dealt with many a bullet wound during the second Biafran war, and I observed. The hands of God were with her. Healing hands. Let me examine him."

I'm reluctant. I know about faith healers. They exist both in Islam and Christianity. Charlatans who believe they can pray away an illness or cure a bullet wound through the power of Christ or Muhammad. I myself am Muslim and the woman is Christian, so we already have different gods, but even if she were Muslim, this talk of healing through the hands of God would make me think twice. We are in the middle of the desert and the man who knows how to get us out of it is bleeding to death. We need more than the hands of God, we need someone who knows medicine. The hands of God did not cure Fatima of malaria, medicine was needed. But no one else has spoken and this woman seems to be all we have, so I don't protest as she descends, aided by Mustafa and Eloka and a few men from above.

The man who has lost his brother appears to have taken the sight of the Tuareg as a sign that we will not be going anywhere anytime soon, and has chosen a direction in which to wander off in search of his own lost companion. I hope he will find his way back but, again, he is not the priority here. Once the woman has descended, she leans down over the Tuareg, before looking up and asking those of us down on the ground if anyone has anything sharp. When nothing is forthcoming, I head back to the driver's seat and retrieve the keys from the ignition, bringing them back to her. She uses them to cut at the fabric around the Tuareg's leg, opening it up so as to examine the bullet wound.

She inspects the wound, then reaches into her bag and produces a bottle of white liquid. She pours some of it on the wound and then grasps the Tuareg's leg firmly. The Tuareg whimpers and I immediately jump forward, thinking she is doing more harm than good. But as if from nowhere, she produces a pair of tweezers, and begins to extract the bullet from the wound. The Tuareg whimpers harder, eyes screwed up in indignation, but I can see that the woman is skilled and experienced in her craft. Once the bullet has been removed, she bandages the wound with some of the fabric she has cut from the Tuareg's turban.

"Water," she says. "He needs water. All this blood he has lost contains water, and it needs to be replaced." A few moments, and a bottle of water falls from the sky. I catch it and hand it to the woman, she trickles it into the corner of the Tuareg's mouth and he swallows greedily. Once he has drunk his fill, the woman hands me back the bottle. I haven't drunk in hours and I'm feeling thirsty myself. I lift the bottle towards my lips, but before it can reach them, angry shouting in French comes from above.

Hasan translates, "They say you should drink your own water. They threw down the bottle because the man was in need and we all need him. But you have not been shot. They say they bought the water with their own money."

A fair point, I think to myself. Even fairer given that we do not know how long we will be stuck here. I put the lid back on the bottle and throw it upwards, and it is plucked out of the air by the same hand that dropped it.

The woman looks up at me, concern visible in her gaze. "The spirit of the Lord is going from this one," she says gravely. "He has lost a lot of blood. I think the bullet hit a vein. There are important veins that run through the legs and arms. There is some chance he may recover, but the chance is slim. And he will need time we do not have. The Bible tells us Jesus spent 40 nights and 40 days in the desert, tempted by the Devil. We are all children of God, but we are not all divine and without sin. I do not wish to spend 40 nights in this hell. We must choose someone else who can drive us."

CHAPTER 25

The sounds of the Amazon surround me as I stand amongst the leaves, perched between the branches of its trees. My fifth limb, my tail, is wrapped delicately around one of these branches, my young offspring is clinging to it, her own tail wrapped around mine, securing her to me. My task is to protect her. My hands and feet are thumbless, and my curved fingers make hooks with which I swing. I am a spider monkey of the Amazon. I am queen of the trees.

I am in desperate need of particular minerals that are essential to my survival, and the only place I can get to them is a mineral lick on the jungle floor. A mineral lick, or "salados," is a specific site in a tropical or temperate ecosystem where a large diversity of mammals and birds come regularly to feed on soil or salt, minerals such as sodium, calcium or potassium. Essential for their... our ...survival.

A single place in the jungle where a variety of animals are compelled to gather compulsorily for their own survival naturally pulls in the predators. Descending to the mineral lick is the only time I leave the safety of the trees and broach the danger of the jungle floor. This journey is a dangerous one and it requires lookouts. I travel with not only my offspring, but also with a friend. We set off through the trees in unison, leaping distances of up to 30 feet. A small red bar in the upper left hand corner of my field of vision indicates my level of fatigue and stamina, how much energy I have left at any time. I slow down and take sporadic breaks at times, allowing it to recharge, nibbling on the fruit that adorns my environment, my offspring clinging to me, my lookout never far.

I think of Jill and her implanted chip. Would she require a bar to indicate that her virtual spider monkey is tired, or would the chip allow her to actually feel its exhaustion, to become as immersed in the world of the Amazon as she becomes in the world of the Aegean Sea. I keep moving, using my thumb (my real thumb, as I have mentioned, spider monkeys are thumbless) at just the right moment to trigger a flick of my tail, which twists around an overhanging branch and propels me forward, with momentum, into another tree. Birdcall trills above, but quickly fades into the distance as I move forward urgently. We have chosen to make this journey at the height of day because we know that, with the daylight streaming through the coverage of the trees, we will be better able to see the predators that roam the area, better able to scope out the jungle floor and emerge from our venture intact and living.

My tail twists around another branch and my feet curl around its sister, gripping it tightly. The mineral lick is ahead, and I can see the animals on the jungle floor, gathering around it and feeding; harmless birds and mammals of all shapes and sizes, just like me. In a way, their presence is reassuring. Not only does the fact that they are feeding unmolested indicate the absence of predators in the area, but were a predator to approach, it would have lots of choice of potential victims and snacks. But I remain cautious. My companion lowers himself further still through the trees and perches in a particular spot with excellent visibility, eyes darting left to right, on high alert despite the positive signs below.

As I approach the mineral lick, I notice that my lookout is staring intently at something on the jungle floor. He is shaking a nearby branch and making a low, guttural vocalisation, which is a sign of alarm. I know from experience that this could only mean one thing: a predator is nearby. I follow his gaze and see a large, spotted jaguar approaching the mineral lick from the other side.

The animals below are oblivious, and I have no way of warning them. Even if I could, it's not my job to warn animals of another species of the presence of a predator. If the jaguar manages to take one of them as his prize, he will no longer be hungry, and I will be in less danger. I stay in my position, high enough that I remain out of reach, watching as the action unfolds below me. Through the leaves, my eyes follow the dappled black markings on the golden coat as it weaves its way through the undergrowth, silently, towards a capybara.

The largest living rodent in the world. At first glance, a capybara might look like a cross between a beaver and a guinea pig. It has a stocky, barrel-shaped body with short legs and a blunt, rounded head. Its fur is short and dense, and ranges in colour from brown to reddish-brown. The capybara's ears are small and rounded, and its eyes are set high on its head, giving it a slightly comical expression. One of the most distinctive features of the capybara are its teeth. Like all rodents, capybaras have sharp incisors that never stop growing. However, the capybara's front teeth are particularly prominent. Despite the capybara's strange appearance, the jaguar is not squeamish, and has its eyes set on the creature as a potential meal.

I've hunted as a big cat before and know the procedure well. There are slight differences depending on which cat you are playing as. For example, lions are social animals that live in prides, and they often hunt in groups. They use their strength and teamwork to take down large prey, such as zebras, buffalo, and giraffes. They typically use an ambush strategy, where they work together to encircle and attack their prey from multiple angles. You can actually play as lions in multiplayer mode, hunting with your friends in the VirtuWorld.

Tigers are solitary hunters, and they prefer to hunt at night. They are opportunistic predators, and their diet can vary depending on what is available in their habitat. They are known for their powerful pounce, where they leap onto their prey from a distance and deliver a fatal bite to the neck. They were one of the first big cats to go extinct, dying out by 2040. The game will often tell you these tidbits as it's loading.

Before they went extinct, cheetahs were the fastest land animals, known for their incredible acceleration and manoeuvrability, their ability to change direction quickly to catch their prey. They typically hunted smaller prey, such as gazelles and impalas. Leopards are also solitary hunters, and they are known for their stealth and agility. They stalk their prey and wait for the perfect moment to pounce. They are able to take down prey much larger than themselves, such as antelopes. Jaguars are similar to leopards in their hunting strategy, but lived in South America rather than Africa and Asia, they are known for their powerful jaws and ability to crush skulls with them. They are also excellent swimmers, one of the reasons I love playing in jaguar mode.

The jaguar is metres away from the capybara. It bends its hind legs, ready to pounce, and then leaps, plunging its jaws into the neck of the helpless creature. The surrounding animals scatter in all directions. Parrots and macaws, that have nestled on the ground too, flutter away in a flurry of wings and a few spider monkeys from a rival family clamber away into the trees. A tapir scampers away into the bushes, its short trunk flopping around pathetically. The jaguar drags its prey off to a more secluded location, and once it is clear that its hunger might well be sated, a few of the more confident animals start to recongregate around the lick. But there is now a sense of wariness that pervades the air, and I remain on high alert as I descend, my lookout scanning the area once more with twitchy, calculated glances.

Trees in the Amazon are distinctive, with thin trunks and broad leaves. Typical tropical rainforest trees: mahogany, rubber, and kapok. I descend to ground level, shimmying down a knotted rope of thick vine. I intuit that the air is humid and thick with the smell of decay from the leaf litter beneath my feet, but these things my headset cannot tell me, only my imagination. Above are the crowns of the trees, intertwined with one another to form a canopy overhead through which scattered beams of sunlight dapple the jungle floor below. My lookout remains above, ready to warn me at the first sign of danger.

Before me is the mineral lick, pooling around the mouth of a narrow cave. A shallow, muddy pool filled with mineral-rich water and soil. In this game, it's not Tim Weibers I have to worry about, but a very different type of predator. Despite the sentinel watching from above, my eyes are peeled, darting from left to right and even behind me as I lumber forward using my hind legs and tail to move, whilst also curling my fingers and balancing my weight forward onto my knuckles, clumsily moving forward in a typical diagonal primate gait.

Spider monkeys are arboreal beasts. They spend their lives in the trees and are not comfortable on the ground, not in their element. Were a spider monkey to suffer the same partial spinal lesion I suffered in the accident, there would be no wheelchair that would replicate the ability to swing, no way of rolling between the branches of mahogany and rubber, and rolling through the jungle floors would leave it open to predators. Looking down, I note that the jungle floor is totally unsuitable for wheels, with roots and fallen branches, a soft and treacherous terrain of obstacles and sticky mud that sucks your chair in like quicksand. I am safe in my chair, when rolling through the streets of London, and the spider monkeys are safe in the canopy.

I catch myself and shake off the distraction. Examining the jungle floor is not the best use of my attention and time currently, not in the presence of danger. But I don't chastise myself. When you've been in a chair long enough, it becomes second nature to assess the terrain before you; from bumpy gravel, which jitters and jolts your joints as you roll over loose pebbles and shallow potholes; to Astroturf, which can offer an even and smooth experience; to the big no-no's of sand and snow. I arrive at the pool of muddy water and begin to drink. I sense my offspring lower herself, dangling by our connected tails, drinking too.

The small yellow bar which measures mineral intake directly below the red bar measuring energy and stamina begins to fill, and before me I see the ripples in the water that result from the steady lapping of my virtual tongue. Looking left to right now is pointless. Each direction reveals only water, and the pool is far too shallow for alligators. I allow myself the luxury of closing my eyes whilst I drink, but keep my ears peeled, both for the sound of an approaching predator and for any warning from my lookout.

Loud, high-pitched screeching sounds. A series of loud, rapid barks and shrieks, "Eeek-eeeek-eeeek!," the sound of fear, not a warning, but a petition for help. The sound is moving in the air above me. My eyes fly open and I stand erect on my virtual legs, pulling back my virtual neck to look upwards. A giant harpy eagle flies above, winding through the foliage, my lookout monkey is trapped within its claws, having been so intent on scrutinising the jungle floor that it forgot to also scrutinise the skies. Even from this distance, it is clear that the harpy is huge- judging by its relative size to the spider monkey gripped within its claws, its wingspan is at least two metres wide. Its feathers are grey and tattered, it drops my companion from a considerable height and he crashes through the foliage, landing with a heavy snap, bleeding and unresponsive.

The eagle swoops again, and I know in that very moment that I'm its next target. I lunge forward towards the narrow opening of the cave, hoping to squeeze my way inside. But the eagle is swift, and though I do not feel its talons in my back, I see myself lifting from the ground, see the leaves and the muddy pool shrinking below me as I rise, the thin tree trunks snaking their way into my peripheral vision, then rapidly snaking their way back out as I plunge towards the jungle floor.

"Game over," comes the voice. A light flashes red before me and my surroundings disappear. "Character deceased. Offspring deceased. Mission failure. Hunted by harpy eagle."

CHAPTER 26

The Tuareg's soul has all but left us. The cloth bandage wrapped around the bullet wound in his thigh was insufficient to staunch the glistening stream of red that bubbled from it. His breathing has shifted from laboured to shallow, as though his lungs have now resigned themselves to their fate. Were he to have died at home amongst his family, Islamic law would require him to be buried within 24 hours, at a depth of at least three hand-spans. I still remember my father's Islamic burial at home, the washing and shrouding of the body, performance of Salat al-Janazah, the funeral prayer, the prayers and supplications of the mourners, and the Imam's recitation of Surah Yaseen. The performative weeping of the first wife, her crocodile tears as she publicly grieved with us and consoled us at the very time she plotted to deprive us of all that he had left us. The quiet composure of my mother and Karima, and Fatima's innocent, youthful incomprehension of the magnitude and nature of our loss.

Not until the body is buried can the two angels of mercy, Munkar and Nakir, be invited to question the deceased in preparation for the afterlife, asking the three essential questions: Who is your Lord? What is your religion? Who is your Prophet? Without a proper burial, the angels will be unable to question the Tuareg's soul, which may have a more difficult path to Jannah in the afterlife, or even worse, be at risk of being cursed to Jahannam.

But having seen this Tuareg alive, however briefly, having been witness to the cold and calculating nature of his character, perhaps even with a proper burial, he would have been condemned to the depths of Jahannam. As his chest rises and falls slowly one last time, I find myself worrying not of him, but of the rest of us travelling in this jeep. If we too are to find our only burial under a thin layer of sand blown up by the North African winds, what will become of our souls? Who will answer the three questions for us? Would we even have a chance to make it to Jannah?

The man who had so hopelessly searched for the direction of Mecca on the first leg of our journey has descended from the jeep and approached the body. A thick beard adorns his chin, his kufi and his thobe sand-stained, he gently closes the body's eyes with his fingers, murmuring the Shahada, "La ilaha illa Allah, Muhammadun rasulullah."

Eloka spits on the sand in repressed fury. "He does not deserve such respect," he mutters. "He saw us as expendable. Whatever plans he had for us were not the plans we paid for."

The bearded man looks up towards Eloka. He looks to be in his early thirties but holds himself as would someone older. The prominent ridges of his brow form dimples with his forehead. "Be that as it may, we no be the ones to to judge him. God alone can do that."

The woman who removed the bullet from his thigh, who I have since learned is called Princess, responds "Jesus said 'Blessed are the merciful, for they shall receive mercy.' It is better show mercy than seek revenge."

The bearded man's face remains impassive, but Eloka spits again.

One of the voices shouts down from above, "Look at this man spitting at the dead, he is volatile! Whoever the driver be, he was taking us some place. Even to return home would have been better than this. Why are we allowing the man who shot him to still hold the gun?" I turn and notice the Tuareg's gun tucked into Eloka's belt.

Eloka looks up in the direction of the voice and shouts back angrily, "It was not me that shot this man! Mustafa was the one that shot him." He points towards Mustafa.

"It was an accident," replies Mustafa urgently. "We were struggling for the gun and the trigger went off. He may have even pulled it himself."

The man from above shouts again, "But you plotted it together, didn't you?" He looks towards Eloka. "None of you told us of this plan. You plotted it together. And look where you've gotten us. I don't trust you with a gun."

Another voice comes somewhere from the top of the jeep. The speaker is not visible from my vantage point. "Why do any of us need a gun? Remove the bullets. Throw them to the sand or distribute them amongst us. Then make there be nothing to fear."

A third voice, that of a woman. Something in French, too fast to be understood. Another deep male voice responds and the word, '*L'arme,*' French for gun, is distinguishable. The same male voice then switches to English.

"Bandits," it says with a slight accent. "There might be bandits in this area. Looking for people come rob. We should keep the gun. But someone else should hold it."

"Give the gun to Princess," I interject.

"Who is Princess?" comes back the voice of the first man above that spoke.

"Princess is here. Princess is down here with me," I say. "Princess is the woman who tried to save the Tuareg. The woman whose songs gave us some relief in that container. The woman who has tried to help, and who wasn't part of our plan. Princess can hold the gun and will not hurt anyone."

A brief pause, then a general murmur of assent from above. The man with the deep voice says something in French, relaying the conversation. Eloka frowns slightly, his eyes darting between us. After a moment's hesitation, he removes the Tuareg's gun from his belt and hands it to the singing healer. She looks at it disparagingly, as though it is some sort of diseased but venomous serpent. For a moment I wonder if she is simply going to toss it away into the sand, but she opens the small bag from which she took her tweezers and nestles it amongst the rest of her meagre possessions quietly.

"Now we have dealt with that," she says diplomatically, "we need to decide who is going to drive us, and in which direction."

The bearded Muslim man coughs intentionally and speaks, "That's actually why I came down, not only to help his passage," he gestures towards the dead body at our feet, "but also because I think I may be able to help. For about 12 years I was a taxi man in Ghana. I have plenty of experience driving. I've never driven in the desert. But during my years in Accra, there was an older retired taxi man, a friend of mine, who spent many years in Mali and Burkina Faso. He told me of his experiences in the desert, of how when you're approaching a dune, you can't slow down at its tip or the middle of the car will get stuck in the sand, both the front and back tires freewheeling in the air. It's called high-centering. He told me that when the sand is too soft, deflating the tires can help by increasing their surface area and spreading their weight. I can't make any promises but, Bismillah, I can try to drive us."

Those of us on the ground look at each other sombrely, confirming our agreement, and no objections come from above.

The man continues, "Now I happen to know that Saudi Arabia is directly to the east of northern Niger. To get to Libya, we would have to go in a similar direction, but slightly more north. So if anyone can answer the same question I've had all journey, which way is Mecca? That will also tell us which way to Libya."

My own phone is too cheap to have an inbuilt compass, as is Mustafa's, but Eloka draws a smartphone out of his pocket, looking at its screen hopefully. This hopeful expression turns to another scowl. "My phone is dead," he says simply. There was no opportunity for us to charge our devices in the shipping container.

Hasan takes in the conversation attentively and then shouts up towards those still in the back of the jeep. "Anyone got a charged phone? *Quelqu'un a-t-il un téléphone chargé?*" he says loudly.

"A phone with GPS," I add, making sure to also project.

"*Oui, pourquoi?*" comes a female voice. The deep voiced bilingual man in the jeep above explains and, after a minute or so of murmured French, the woman agrees to pass down her phone for the new designated driver's use. He opens up the GPS and determines that we are very close to the Aïr Mountains, slightly southeast of the city of Arlit. The jeep is currently facing in the wrong direction, towards the southwest and Niamey. It will have to turn.

Eloka speaks. "Should we get going then? What are we waiting for?"

Mustafa replies, "The man that went searching for his brother. Shouldn't we wait for him to come back, even if his search is a failure?"

Our new driver speaks. "We should, but we shouldn't wait long. My friend also told me that the nighttime is the best time for driving in the Sahara, as long as the headlights are strong, because the desert is much cooler then. At night, the sand cools down and becomes more compact, providing more traction for the vehicle's tyres. We have already lost much of the night to the sandstorm, we shouldn't waste any more. Let me pray. Pray with me, brother. If the man returns by the time we have finished, let him come with us. If he returns with his brother, better. But we cannot afford to wait for him for hours."

I quietly agree. The man was inconsolable. He will not return until he finds his brother, and finding his brother could take him hours or longer. If he does find his brother, in what state would he find him, having fallen from a moving vehicle in the middle of a sandstorm? We are all facing possible death. We can't afford sentimentality. I nod my agreement, and join the man in prayer.

In Islam, Wudu is a ritual ablution performed before certain acts of worship, such as Salah (prayer), and it requires the use of water. However, if water is unavailable or if using it would be harmful to a person's health or well-being, then a person may perform Tayammum instead. Water is available, but we have no knowledge of how long it will have to last us, and so we agree to instead perform Tayammum, striking both hands on the sand and then wiping a portion of the face and the hands. "It is permissible," says the new driver. "The Prophet said, 'The earth has been made a place of worship and a source of purification.' It was recorded in the Hadiths set out by Ibn Majah."

I nod as though I have read the book of Hadiths set out by Ibn Majah, but I haven't. As a young child, I never really got the hang of Arabic during my brief time in Quranic school. My knowledge of the words of Muhammad is largely limited to Quranic quotes my father told me in Hausa rather than Arabic, often slipping them in at the end of his stories as a way of highlighting whatever moral or lesson they had been intended to convey. Princess eyes us wearily as we prepare for prayer, but does not comment, remembering our permissiveness when she had sung her Christian hymns.

Some grumbling does come from above, from those who seem dissatisfied by the fact that we are not leaving immediately. Perhaps if the delay was only to allow time for prayer, objections would be raised, but the fact that the man who lost his brother could technically return at any moment gives another reason for a limited degree of communal patience. Once our prayers are concluded, Eloka and Mustafa retake their places in the front of the vehicle along with the bearded Muslim, our new designated driver, and the rest of us who have descended from the jeep make our way back up and seat ourselves among the murmured and distracted conversation of our very worried fellow travellers. A few seats to my right, Paul looks as though he himself has been shot, his face contorted in a mask of fear, regret and pain, his eyes squeezed shut. His knuckles protrude like tiny black hills topped in sand, the scattered valleys of which form irregular patterns.

After a few false starts, the vehicle's engine springs back into life, and the jeep manages a full 180 turn, meaning it now roughly faces the correct direction. We set off again in the desert, but it quickly becomes evident that, despite his years driving taxis in the streets of Accra, our new driver does not have the same feel for this terrain as the man whose body has been left behind us. Our progress is jolty and unsteady, and I find myself gripping harder to my own pole too, questioning whether we will lose more of our fellow travellers over the side of the jeep as the journey progresses. The woman in the blue hat no longer grips my arm, perhaps remembering how it had been she that had pulled me back, and considering the possibility that, were I to fall again, I may pull her closer to falling rather than help save her from it.

A few minutes of slow and fractured progress and the vehicle stops in front of its first major challenge. A moderately sized sand dune stretches before it, clear under the illumination of the headlights. It must be perhaps 10 or 15 feet high, but it's impossible to tell the exact height. The vehicle revs its engine and begins its ascent. It navigates carefully up the dune, taking its time to ensure it goes up safely, but maintaining enough momentum to take it over the ridge. Once the jeep reaches the top of the dune, I feel the vehicle shift slightly as it begins to descend. As gravity swings me from my left to my right, my fingers reflexively tighten their grip on the pole in front of me and I tense my upper body and my core in an attempt to hold myself in place. The steep slope causes the tires to slip and slide a bit, but it seems the driver is keeping a steady hand on the wheel, using gentle corrections to keep the jeep on track. I hear a few audible expressions of relief behind me and imagine them to be accompanied by a number of nervous smiles.

The vehicle continues but seems to move with more confidence, now approaching the second, slightly shorter, dune, which lies a short distance from the first, steadily and without the shaky and halting movements of before. As we ascend it steadily, a movement in front of me demands my attention, and I see a human figure sprinting through the sand, its arms waving. Behind it, another man seems to be limping quickly towards us. It seems that this was indeed the same direction the man chose to look for his brother, and he did in fact find his brother, and he has now seen us leaving without him and is chasing us desperately down. I wonder if either the driver, Paul or Eloka have also seen them. Once they descend over the other side of the dune, the two men will be obscured from vision by the mound of sand itself, and I have no way currently to communicate with those in the front of the jeep. A few of the other migrants have also noticed, in the corner of my eye I see one man, a few places to my left, point his finger and say, "*Regarde, ils arrivent!*"

My question is quickly answered. Just as we approach the crest of the dune, the vehicle seems to slow and turn slightly to the left in the direction of these two men. The driver seems to realise almost immediately the mistake his reactions have drawn him into, and overcompensates for the reduction in speed by accelerating a little too vigorously to avoid getting high-centred, pushing it over the edge with force, making those of us in the back jerk erratically to the side and propelling the jeep downwards into an unseen sand hollow. The front tires hit the bottom of the hollow and sink deep into the sand, kicking up clouds of dust as the rear wheels continue to spin uselessly. The engine roars as the driver tries to reverse out of the hole, but it's no use. The jeep is stuck. I hear a chorus of groans and curses and supplications from every side.

CHAPTER 27

I emerge from the elevator onto the polished floors of the 19th floor. The highest in the skyscraper, where the offices of the Heads of Departments are located- the big fish- reportedly even the Home Secretary herself. Just like the corridor that leads into the control room, the corridor in which my wheelchair now sits ends abruptly in a translucent glass pane that stretches from floor to ceiling, from wall to wall. But I have been briefed on how to approach it. I roll my chair towards it and place my hand on the glass. The disembodied voice greets me.

"Hello Elijah. What business do you have on the 19th floor?"

It has recognized my palm. After all, I use it to gain access to the control room every time I enter. But it knows that I do not have access here.

"I have an appointment with Thomas Rutchers," I respond. "And Joe Gradle. About my choice of team."

"How wonderful. I'll just call Thomas now and confirm." Perhaps a minute passes before the voice pipes up again. "Mr. Walker, welcome to the 19th floor. If you take the second left and make your way down to the end of the corridor, you will find Mr. Rutchers' office."

"Thank you." I reply, now used to the spectacle by which a seemingly invisible seam suddenly appears in the glass and a door separates itself and slides backwards and to the side, opening up my path for forward movement.

I start making my way down the initial corridor, ready to

take the second left, as per the woman's instructions. Glancing around me, I notice that I am passing more glass-paned rooms, some of which have transparent panes, allowing their contents to be seen, whilst others have opaque panes, blocking out their contents to the eyes of visitors. From those with transparent panes, I can gauge that these are cavernous offices, with large desks on which sit stress balls, folders, and pictures of children, husbands and wives. Also present are large ornate rugs, sculptures and even, in one office, an exercise bike. The ample space apportioned to the residents of these offices could not be more different to the claustrophobic desks of the control room, where the team sits almost shoulder to shoulder in a row, with enough space for some personal effects and to control their drones with their gloves, but no real privacy and certainly no grandeur.

As I pass one room I look in to see a bald, plump man of about 60 sitting at his desk. He looks up and his eyes meet mine. He is wearing a yellow bow tie dotted in purple, and his round stomach spills onto the edge of his desk. He frowns, raises his fingers, snaps them, and the glass turns opaque immediately. I turn at the second left and continue to the end of the corridor where, sure enough, I find a glass pane on which the words are engraved.

'Thomas Rutchers, Head of Recruitment.'

The glass is currently opaque, so I rap three times on its surface and wait to be invited in. After a few moments, a portion of the pane of glass slips inwards and to the side, and the voice of Tom Rutchers beckons me in.

"Come in Elijah, come in. My assistant, Jemima," Thomas says, gesturing towards the woman. "Jemima, if you wouldn't mind moving these two chairs, I don't think Elijah will have need of them. And then, could you prepare him a drink? What do you drink, Elijah? I have coffee, tea, soft drinks. I think you're a little too young for me to offer you anything stronger."

"I'll take an orange juice, if you have it," I reply. Thomas nods and twirls his hand towards Jemima, adding another request. "And prepare Joe his favourite as well. He'll be here shortly."

Jemima nods, takes both of the small chairs and moves them to the side of the room, before moving to the corner and busying herself around a mini-fridge and a small table, on which a number of colourful bottles sit. Thomas beckons me forward and I roll towards the opposite side of the desk.

"I did tell Joe you were almost here as soon as I got the message you had arrived on our floor. He should be here in a matter of moments," Thomas says. "Speak of the Devil..."

I turn my head to see Joe Gradle entering the room.

"Hello Elijah," he says, moving over to pick up one of the two chairs which has just been moved and placing it next to me, before seating himself. "It's great to see you, I hear you've been getting quite stuck in."

Jemima comes over and places a large glass of fresh orange juice in front of me, and what seems to be some sort of whiskey in front of Joe. We both thank her, before Thomas nods slightly, smiles and follows up with, "You can take a break now, Jemima. I'll buzz you when I need you next. Time for some boys' talk."

Jemima's nostrils only slightly flare as she returns the smile, nods and makes her way out of the room.

Thomas picks up a sheaf of papers from the desk in front of him and moves it towards me with a twirl of his wrist, not unlike that of an orchestral conductor. "We have here the feedback from your rotations over the past few weeks, and it's generally very positive," he says. "Rush did express some concern as to whether you quite had the stomach for the combat and control team, but as I like to say, the stomach is like any muscle. You work it out and it gets stronger."

Joe Gradle coughs lightly. "The stomach technically isn't a muscle, Thomas. It's an organ. A muscular organ, yes. The stomach walls are made of smooth muscle, which contracts and relaxes to mix your food and move it. But the stomach itself is an organ."

"A muscular organ, as you say, Joe. What does it matter whether the word 'muscle' is used as an adverb or a noun? The point is that Elijah will easily toughen up. No need to ruin a perfectly good analogy with semantics."

"An adjective, I think you mean," I say, and Thomas turns his gaze from Joe to me inquisitively. "'Organ' is a noun, so 'muscular' would be an adjective, describing a noun, not an adverb," I continue timidly, regretting having opened my mouth to speak. Thomas looks disgruntled for a fraction of a second, a flicker of annoyance passing over his shamrock-green eyes, but he quickly composes himself.

"It seems that everyone's correcting me today," he says with a smile. "Well, you obviously have some stomach. As I was saying, we have your feedback in front of us, and all four of the teams with which you did rotations were suitably impressed, and would be happy to have you on their team. The choice really is yours, Elijah."

The choice may well be mine, but I haven't yet been able to make it. I'm still torn between reconnaissance and the OctoBot team. But I haven't come into this meeting without a plan.

"That's great news," I say. "I was wondering if I could ask you both a few questions before I make my choice."

"Of course you may," responds Joe Gradle, tilting his head forward to deepen his smile. "We're all ears."

"Well," I continue, "the thing is, as you said earlier, I haven't really had the opportunity for a full internship because of school, and also because of the fact that you placed a lot of faith in my VirtuWorld scores. So far, I've only got to spend two days with each team, and I have narrowed down my choices, but I'd still really like to explore both reconnaissance and the OctoBot team further. Also, Jill did tell me that eventually you guys might be looking to roll out the EEG technology to other teams, once it's been polished in the OctoBot department. I thought it might be useful for me to get a bit of experience with both, and that I might at some point be able to help the reconnaissance team transition from using gloves to using the EEG helmet or implants. It's just an idea, but if possible I'd really like a bit more time on both teams."

Both Joe and Thomas glance at me appraisingly before looking at each other with thoughtful expressions.

"I don't see any problem," Joe says. "After all, the initial internship would have seen each rotation around two weeks in length, rather than two days. You can alternate working between the teams. What do you think, Thomas?"

"Well, I don't see any harm in him taking a bit more time to choose. I have no issue with it, as long as the teams themselves don't."

"How's your little bet with Becky going, then?" Joe asks, smirking at me. Despite his inability to smile properly, he seems perfectly capable of smirking. I look back at him blankly. "Your bet?" he continues, "Well, not quite a bet, but more of a challenge. About you guessing four of her outfits in a row."

I feel myself start to blush. "Oh, that little thing," I say. "I'd almost forgotten about it, to be honest. It's going well. Apart from the Mario outfit, I haven't got anything wrong yet, and she let me off that one."

"I quite remember," Joe continues, still smirking, "Gregory tells me that Becky had nothing but glowing feedback to report about you. It's good to see you're already integrating yourself into the team. And of course, we all saw how excellent a flyer you were the first time you stepped into the control room! And Jill, what do you make of her? She's a clever old dame, isn't she?"

"Definitely," I say. "Too clever for me to understand half the things she talks about or works on, but also clever enough to find a way to explain them to me simply. I really enjoy working with Jill."

Thomas chuckles, "As long as you are happy, we're happy. Now, we were wondering whether you would be interested in increasing your hours, perhaps moving from two days a week to three? We'd be happy to provide tutoring in the evenings to make up for the lost time. Of course, your salary is pro-rata, meaning it's proportional to the time you spend working. So you earn a little more too."

I shake my head softly, an apologetic intake of breath accompanied with a raise of the eyebrows that says my hands are tied.

"My mother won't allow it," I say. "Not yet, not at this stage. I would love to, but I don't want to push things with her at the moment. She wants me to ease my way into the job and still attend school for at least four days out of five. Sunday might be an option in a few months' time, but I think for now it will be a difficult sell."

"Not to worry," says Joe. "Two days is better than one, and one is better than zero." He sips at his small glass of whisky and looks away, out towards the French doors and balcony. "After all," he continues, "we do hope to have you with us here for a long and illustrious career, Elijah."

"Now, moving on to the matter of your salary," Thomas continues, leaning over the table as if about to spear me on his beak-like nose. "We do have a few options available to us. As you're still underage, we aren't able to pay you directly. However, we can give you a choice between the two following options. The money can go into a trust, which nobody will have access to, and which will accrue interest until you reach the age of 18. Alternatively, the money can go to your parents, as your custodians, who will look after it for you, and give you whatever allowance they deem appropriate from it until you come of age. We have had a few situations in the past where overzealous parents have spent a little too much of their children's money, and so we do give you the option of going with the trust for your own protection. Please let me know what you would prefer, and I will make sure that the necessary arrangements are put in place."

"I trust my mum," I say simply. "The money can go to her for the time being."

"Great!" Thomas responds. "We'll arrange your internship pay and have a full time contract drawn up and sent to your home address. I'm sure you'll find the terms to be more than suitable. The arrangement with the chauffeur... Jeremy."

"Jeffrey," I correct him.

"Yes, Joffrey," he continues. "I have spoken to transport, and they've said they can make that permanent."

"Great!" I smile. "That's one less thing for me to worry about then. I get along rather well with him."

"Always good to have a working relationship with the help," nods Thomas.

"Well, Elijah," interjects Joe. "I think that's all we had to cover here today. Unless you have any other questions for us."

I shake my head.

"Well then, it's nearing 5pm and I have an appointment with my lawyer. Why don't we wrap up here and you start off home?" Joe suggests.

"Of course," I reply.

We all shake hands before Joe and I leave the office. As we make our way down the corridor, he gives me a parting remark. "We all see lots of potential for you here, Elijah. And I know I questioned his semantics, but just remember what Thomas said, the job can sometimes take some stomach. But what we're doing here is important. We are the guardians of Britain. We are the warriors at the gate. Be proud of that." He turns left at the end of the corridor and I turn right, passing back through the glass panel and taking the elevator back down to the control room. Though it's home time, once I get to the control room, I don't collect my things from my desk, but rather I make my way over to Jill.

I pass close by the reconnaissance desk on the way over to Jill and glance hopefully towards Becky's chair, but it's empty. It seems she's already on her way home. The head of the team, Gregory, a muscular man with buzz-cropped hair, a pointed chin and high-set cheekbones, notices me looking and looks back questioningly, moving his thumb from a thumbs-up position to a thumbs-down position, back to thumbs-up, back to thumbs-down, oscillating between possibilities. I smile at him and give him a thumbs-up, having informed him before my trip to the 19th floor of my intentions.

I arrive at Jill’s desk. On her monitor is a complex spreadsheet of data with rows and rows and columns and columns of numbers. On my approach she looks at me expectantly.

"So, they've agreed to allow me to work both with the reconnaissance team and you guys for the moment, as long as you're fine with that," I tell her sheepishly.

Her face, already wide and angular, broadens further into a genuine smile. "Why, of course I'm fine with that, Elijah. Why wouldn't I be? We're all looking forward to working with you more." I smile back.

"And," I continue, "do you still have a bit of time this evening, perhaps? To talk me through some of the science on the medical side? I've asked my ride to come at six-thirty rather than quarter past five. So I've got a bit of time to play with."

Jill looks at her watch, looks at her monitor, and looks at her watch again. "I'm a little busy today, but you know what? I'll make time. I'm a scientist after all. I'm used to late nights at the lab. Pull up your chair. Let's talk."

CHAPTER 28

Digging has been fruitless. At first, we had only our hands with which to dig. Eventually Mustafa located a small shovel, presumably intended for this purpose, underneath the driver's seat, but even with the shovel progress is slow. It is no longer night time. The Saharan sun has settled in the sky and beats down on us relentlessly, and the sand seems to shift and collapse in on itself as fast as we can move it. Pushing the jeep from behind is not an option, given that its nose is embedded in the sand hollow, and therefore pushing it would only propel it further into the groove of the hollow itself. Pulling the jeep, even with 28 of us, is far too difficult a proposition. It would mean fighting gravity, uphill, feet slipping in the sand. Given that the two back wheels are exposed and freewheeling in the air, reversing has no effect. Every salty bead of sweat that results from the labours of our bodies and the heat under which we ruminate on our woes is now precious, but we have no way to bottle them. Running out of water will mean running out of hope.

Given that the jeep is stuck at an awkward downward angle, sitting inside its open back has been rendered even more uncomfortable, with those nearest to the front of the jeep weighed down by those further back, as gravity pushes their weight to the side. For this reason, and also in an unsuccessful attempt to lighten the vehicle and make it easier to shift, most of the migrants have now descended to the desert floor. Some are inconsolable.

Paul has succumbed to shivering as though he were in the

Arctic rather than the desert, sitting with his knees pulled up to his chest, arms wrapped around them, eyes fixed somewhere in the distance. The woman in the blue hat is lamenting in her native tongue, her voice thick with anguish. The woman with two children has taken them aside and appears to be playing games with them, using her finger to draw animals in the sand, perhaps in the hope of distracting them from the weariness and resignation on every side. They giggle at the drawings, oblivious to the graveness of their fate.

The man who had saved his brother seems to be in shock. The brother's leg was badly injured in the fall, and trying to run on it in order to catch up to the jeep does not seem to have done his injury any good. He sits tenderly on the sand, leaning over on one buttock and extending his damaged limb before him. At moments, his brother tries to soothe him, putting an arm around his shoulder and gripping his arm tightly in brotherly affection. But at other moments, the uninjured brother stands and begins to pace again, some primordial confusion flickering in his eyes. Princess and the bearded man pray incessantly, separately, differently, to different gods and different prophets, but both with the same petition.

A man attacks Mustafa with his fists, bellowing that he has killed us all. Eloka restrains him heavily, and the deep-voiced bilingual shouts that it is stupid to waste our precious energy fighting; that we must preserve our sanity and our reserves and formulate a plan. But what plan can we formulate? We with our plastic jerry cans and plastic bottles? We who are surrounded by miles of emptiness? We who have no vehicle, and no driver, and few provisions, and no shelter from the heat of the day.

As the following days wear on, we will begin to succumb to exhaustion and dehydration. Slowly we will lie motionless on the sand, unable to summon the energy to move. Slowly we will crawl on our hands and knees, searching for a scrap of shade or drop of water. Princess and the bearded man will continue to pray, but their voices will grow weaker with each passing hour. And then we will be taken by the desert. Its sands will swallow us. Its dunes will devour us. Our fellow travellers' bones will be our tombstones and our bones theirs. Europe? What a joke. Europe? We did not even make it through Niger. My family will await my call and be greeted by an endless stretch of silence. How long will they cling to the mirage? The illusion that I somehow still continue on my voyage. Will I meet my father in the afterlife? Will he greet me? Hold me as he once did? Tell me more stories? Stories gathered in his years beyond the grave. Or will he chastise me? Berate me? Condemn me for having been unable to provide for my sisters, to survive and to thrive and to fill the void his absence left?

Mustafa's voice rises through the thickness.

"We have to separate," he says quietly. And then, again, louder, "We have to separate!"

A few heads turn towards him, others ignore his words, preferring to sit in their despondency and grief.

He continues. "Our only hope is for another vehicle to see us and to help. There's a rope in the same place as the shovel. Even if another jeep is not willing to take us with them, they'll probably be full of passengers themselves, we still have a working vehicle. If we can get a tow, that could pull it out of the pit in which it's stuck. But in order to maximise our chances of another vehicle seeing us..."

As he speaks, I snap myself back to reality. Karima, Fatima, my mother, they need me just as much as Mustafa's family needs him. Mustafa has not given up. He is not spending his precious minutes plotting out the specifics of his demise, imagining meetings in the afterlife. He is looking for a solution.

"We need to separate." I finish the sentence for him. "The more ground we cover, the more chance of intercepting another vehicle."

His nose has bled as a result of the blow, and speckles of glistening red sit on his collar like rubies. The man who punched Mustafa chuckles derisively. Eloka has now released him, but stands close by watching him distrustfully. Despite his outburst about the shooting, it seems he still has some protectiveness or concern for Mustafa.

"And how we dey trust each other if we separate?" the man chuckles. "This man," he points at the uninjured brother, "go find im lost broda and we quick quick forget about him when another driver was chosen. You wan make we all separate, go find our way back and trust say we go wait for each other?"

"You get better idea, big man, or you just sabi violence and criticism?" Eloka says, kissing his teeth.

"The horn." The bilingual man has both eyes shut as though in deep thought as he speaks. His head is tilted downwards and to the right. He looks about 26 or 27. Like Hasan, he has tribal scars, though whereas Hasan's scars form whiskers from the corners of his mouth along his cheeks, this man has two parallel vertical lines on each cheek. A large birthmark covers half his forehead.

The chuckling man chuckles again. "What horn you dey speak? I no see cow here."

"The car horn, you idiot," replies Eloka, venomously. "If we manage to free the vehicle or find another jeep to help us, we press the car horn. The noise should be loud enough to let anyone in the area know to return, and also give them an idea of direction if they find themselves confused."

We all digest the plan. It seems dangerous, risky, unlikely to work. But it's the only straw we have at which to cling.

"Who's willing and able to go for a wander?" asks Mustafa. The bilingual man translates, making sure to add the context of the plan and reasoning for it. 10, 12, 15 out of 28 raise their hands, Princess amongst them. But not the woman in blue. Nor the pregnant woman. Nor the woman with two children.

Eloka makes a reasonable point. "If a jeep is to stop for us, it might be more likely to do so for a woman or child."

We all stare at him.

He continues: "It's just a thought. A suggestion. If they see someone they perceive as weak or vulnerable, a jeep might be more likely to stop."

The suggestion is met by silence.

"He's right," says the woman in the blue hat, after a few moments. "Of course he's right. I'll go. We should tell her it's the best way to save her children. She speaks French, no?" She gestures at the woman with her children, still drawing figures in the sand, rubbing them out and starting again.

"We should tell her." The woman in the blue hat addresses the comment to Hasan rather than the bilingual man with tribal scars. But the bilingual man takes up the task nonetheless. The woman with children looks up confusedly and appears to think over the matter. But after a moment's hesitation, she stands and gestures at her children to do the same. If they walk for five minutes in another direction, the sand will still be there to play with after all. As she stands and her face turns away for a moment from the faces of her children, she allows a modicum of fear to ripple through her features. Her lips purse slightly. Her eyebrows curve inwards, creating a furrow of worry on her brow. She takes a steadying breath and turns back to them, her fear hidden beneath a mask of serenity.

"*Allons nous promener*." She says to her daughter and son, and they both giggle indulgently, the son hitching up his oversized trousers, which have started to slip down his bottom despite the makeshift synthetic rope belt. The pregnant woman decides to stay, and no one feels like forcing her.

And so we split. Before we do, Hasan retrieves the small bottles taken at the shipping container from his backpack and, using a page from a magazine wrapped tightly at the bottom but loosely at the top as a funnel, decants water from our large container into the individual bottles, handing them out between our group.

We arrange ourselves in a circular formation around the outer edge of the jeep in groups of two, equally distant from one another and facing outwards. We agree to walk in a straight line, as best we can, for around 10 minutes each, in the hopes that this will cover the largest amount of surface area. It is agreed that if no car has come by the fall of night, we will turn and follow our footsteps, if they have not yet been erased by wind, back to the vehicle. If there are no footsteps to follow, we just walk straight again, but in the opposite direction. The horn will be blown at dusk, in case anyone finds themselves lost. The reason for returning at night is simple. Visibility will be poor, and it will be less likely that, unless we were standing directly in the headlights of a passing jeep, they would be able to see us anyway. Were some of us to fall asleep, we might miss the horn anyway, and end up stranded whilst the others continue on their voyage.

We travel in groups of two rather than on our own because, though walking alone could cover a larger overall area, we are thinking of safety, and company. Bandits roam the Sahara, and if these are to be our last hours on earth, most of us would rather not spend them alone. The woman in blue has asked to partner with me and, given our history, I agree. Mustafa and Hasan will walk together. Eloka is partnered with Princess. All in all, by the time the power of peer pressure has kicked in, there are 20 or so volunteers, and those remaining at base include the brother with the damaged leg, the pregnant mother, and Paul. I have not eaten in more than a day, and my stomach is insistent, but food is a secondary consideration. The little we have should last us. We only take our water. As if by some unspoken agreement, I grasp hands with the woman in the blue hat and, when Mustafa gives the call, we march off in our own direction, trotting away into the dunes.

CHAPTER 29

Jill's pod is much smaller than the opulent offices of the 19th floor. Like Jim, she has her own personal room within the control room, into which she retreats on the nights in which the pressure of her work and the research she undertakes beyond her work for the Home Office take up a little too much of her time for the trip home to be worthwhile. We have gone to her pod in order to have our discussion about my legs and the potential for the rebirth of their functionality- partially because Jill thinks it better to talk about issues not related to work away from the control room floor, and also for a modicum of privacy. A small bed sits in the corner of the room; single, not double, economising space. A wooden desk embedded with a set of drawers is peppered with papers- well-thumbed, stapled together and bound- books, electronic gadgetry, motherboards and metal chips.

Above the desk, open-fronted shelves contain an array of interesting objects. A half-constructed EEG cap, wires emerging from it like twigs, unconnected to sensors. A silver life-size model of a human foot. An oversized, life-like model of a tarantula beside an undersized, life-like model of a squid. Beside the desk, an interesting contraption stands erected. I say stands because it seems literally to stand. At its base is an old, black shoe from which thin parallel metal bars run up vertically. On either side of the shoe, two parallel metal bars run up for around 30 centimetres, before meeting a pivot and connecting to another metal bar, which runs off at a slight angle for another 25 centimetres or so. A few leather straps circle around the bars at intervals. Tattered leather. Old leather. Leather that has stood the test of time.

Jill moves forward and sits on the chair that accompanies the desk. I roll my chair so as to position myself next to her, facing her. On the desk there are four framed photographs, three photographs of women and one photograph of a young boy, perhaps 14. He has dark hair, a gap-toothed smile, and cheeks still full of the chubbiness of youth. But his eyes are Jill's eyes.

Jill catches me looking at the photos.

"My ladies," she says. "Women who have blazed a trail in science. A few of my inspirations."

Jill gestures at the first photograph. An older white woman sits against a black background. Her eyes are deep set and wrinkles criss-cross the concave space underneath them. Her lips are thin. She has a small nose, and an angular, almost square face, not unlike that of Jill herself. Even though the photograph is black and white, you can tell that her hair is greying by the contrast between the white and black strands.

"Marie Curie." Jill introduces her. "The first woman to win a Nobel Prize and the first person to win two. She was a pioneer of radioactivity. Worked with her husband, Pierre, on radioactive elements; the same elements that eventually killed her. She has been an inspiration to me since I was a child."

Jill moves to the second photograph. A young black woman is smiling at the camera, her upper teeth visible. She has short afro hair and an infectious smile. She is wearing a large orange spacesuit, with a circular black ring orbiting her neck at the top of the jacket.

"Mae Jemison. The first African American woman in space. I just love her story, it's so inspiring. She was an astronaut, a doctor, an engineer and a teacher. Her mum was a primary school teacher and her dad was in charity. So it's not like she came from wealth, but she excelled against the odds."

Jill moves to the third photograph. An Asian woman wearing a beaded necklace and a lab coat, perhaps about 40, her hair combed back into a barely visible bun. "Chien-Shiung Wu. A Chinese physicist. She was a pioneer of radioactivity and particle physics. She was the first to disprove the Law of Conservation of Parity, which was a major breakthrough in the field of physics. Unfortunately, her research was used to create the atomic bomb, but it also set the groundwork for a lot of the progress we're making in nuclear energy today.

Sometimes we scientists have to be involved in things that aren't as savoury as we may wish in order to be given the opportunity to uncover important knowledge." Jill pauses for a moment, her eyes locked on the photograph. "It's the way of the world," she adds thoughtfully.

"And the boy?" I ask her. "Is he your son?"

"No," replies Jill, a sigh hidden somewhere in the single syllable. "He was my brother." Her use of the past tense discourages further prying.

"So, Elijah," Jill says, regaining her normal, upbeat tone. "I'm sure, very sure, that you have not simply been sitting around waiting for me to tell you about the possibilities of this technology as they apply to your predicament. You must have done some research these past few days, since our initial broaching of the topic. Tell me what you found out. It lets me know where I need to start, rather than covering ground you've already covered yourself."

"Um," I say, shifting in my chair, not out of uncomfortableness, but necessity. When you're in a wheelchair, it's good to shift your weight every 20 minutes or so to prevent pressure sores, which are the result of prolonged pressure on one area of the body and can be excruciatingly painful.

"Well, I have actually been looking into it. I've seen two types of ways it can be done. One is with what I think they call an exoskeleton; some kind of exterior metal device that goes around your legs like ... like metal trousers, and follows the signal sent to it by the chip. The other, like you told me, is to implant a receiver chip just below where the spinal cord was cut, which receives the signals and relays them to the nerves below the lesion."

Jill smiles broadly. "Well done, Elijah! It looks like someone has been doing their homework. That's correct. There's also a third method. Instead of jumping over the lesion, they try to use neurostimulation and training in order to try and reroute some of the neural instructions through the sensory nerves, but this only works with some lesions and is less holistically effective than the secondary chip. The exoskeleton is a useful training tool in the beginning stages, and sometimes the only way to go long term if a patient's legs have atrophied to the point at which recovery is no longer viable. To atrophy means for the muscle mass to waste away, by the way."

I nod. I'm fully aware of this. How many times has the physiotherapist used that term to me?

Jill continues, "But I don't think you will have reached that stage yet. How long has it been since your accident?"

"Just over a year," I respond.

"Then I assume you will have undergone severe atrophy, but not irreparable atrophy. We will, of course, in the meantime, have to find a way to prevent further deterioration. I would suggest some FES, Functional Electrical Stimulation, as a way of preventing this. It's a type of stimulation that sends electrical signals through electrodes to the muscles to make them move. It's used to help people with spinal cord injury or other neurological conditions regain some of their muscle movement.

It's not a cure, but it can help to maintain muscle strength and prevent further deterioration."

I nod. I had heard of FES, but I hadn't really considered it as an option for me. Such treatments are expensive and healthcare in Britain is not free. Apparently, there used to be some sort of government-funded healthcare service, but Dad says it was sold off long before I was born. Just the regular costs of life in a wheelchair, including the chair itself and accessibility modifications at home, have been expensive for my parents, and until very recently I haven't had a swanky job with the Home Office bringing in any extra money to the household. I also didn't really see the point in stopping my legs from atrophying. It would just be delaying the inevitable. I thought I would never use them again. But now things are different.

"The very first exoskeletons used to look like this, don't you know?" she says, gesturing towards the shoe with its parallel, thin metal bars protruding upwards. "Callipers. Metal and leather orthoses. In World War I, they were used to help soldiers with injuries to the legs. By World War II, they had become even more advanced and were used to help soldiers with spinal cord injuries, amputations, and other physical impairments. The 1940s and 50s also represented the global peak of polio, a disease which crippled many by weakening and deforming their limbs. These devices helped. Years ago, before either of us were born, I believe they made a film where the main character wore them, called Forest Lump or something like that. Today, they are obviously much, much more advanced and less clunky, shall we say. However, it's still much preferable to be able to use legs of flesh and bone, don't you think? Would you mind if I touched your leg, just to gauge how much muscle is left? On which side is your leg bag? I'll go for the other one."

Jill's last question surprises me. Most people who aren't wheelchair users themselves don't know what a leg bag is, and those who do are usually uncomfortable talking about it.

When they think about it, it makes perfect sense. Of course, someone paralyzed from somewhere between their shoulders and their waist downwards might have problems controlling their bladder. But the key thing is, they don't think about it. But Jill is a scientist, and Jill has thought about it, and factors it into her question, considering my own comfortability and embarrassment whilst displaying no embarrassment of her own. She follows up further.

“Suprasacral, I assume,” she asks.

“Yes,” I confirm. The sacral portion of the spinal cord is the very lowest, closest to the waist, and above it are three others. My accident led to a lesion in the lumbar section, directly above it. Most spinal cord injuries are suprasacral, i.e. above the sacral portion, and this has major implications for how the injury affects our ability to pee. The reflex pathways that control bladder and sphincter function are located in the sacral spinal cord, so an injury to that section means you can't release your bladder at all and it backs up into the kidneys. Any injury above it, like mine, cuts off the signal from the brain that blocks the release reflex and holds in pee, meaning that- quite the opposite- you can't prevent yourself from weeing as soon as your bladder starts to fill.

“Good," she replies, "then it would be much easier for the chip to help you regain normal bladder function. Now which leg is bag free?"

"The right one," I respond gesturing towards it with my hand. "Go ahead, touch it."

She reaches out and grips my leg, I feel the warmth of her fingers, and her eyebrows knit together in an expression that is not easily decipherable. It could represent concern, curiosity or even confusion.

"Not terrible," she says. "Not terrible, but a little more atrophy than may be expected after just a year... Now Elijah," she looks up at me with seriousness plastered on her gaze. "Elijah, I told you when I first mentioned this technology to you that you should not get your hopes up prematurely. It's still experimental, and most effective when utilising a chip, which involves neurosurgery, something which is not in any way cheap. One of my goals has always been to find ways to make it more accessible to those who need it. I am a neuroscientist, not a neurosurgeon. Though I work for the Home Office and still engage in research highly relevant to these innovations, I no longer work directly in the field, and cannot guarantee you access to the lengthy training process, surgeries and machinery which would be necessary for you to utilise the technology effectively.

“I will make no promises, but in the longer term I will try my very best, especially given that there may be grounds for getting the Home Office to cover the cost of the surgical implantation of the chip itself, if also used in your job in order to control the robotic octopus. Of course, this wouldn't include the costs of the second implant below the lesion, but I'm sure that Mr. Gradle has offered you a generous package."

Jill raises her eyebrows at me in question, but it is a rhetorical question physically posed, and she requires no answer before continuing.

"What I can do for you at the moment, Elijah, is work with you perhaps once or twice a week outside of office hours, with an EEG cap and some electrodes, to start a program of FES and ensure that your legs are engaging in some contraction and movement. If we halt the deterioration and atrophy in its tracks now, then, if and when the option arises in the future for you to take advantage of the more advanced technology, you will be in a position to take the leap- so to speak... but remember," she wags her finger doggedly at me, "I make no promises."

I don't need a promise. A promise is a 100% guarantee, a verbal commitment to ensuring that the outcome of the promise is reached. I don't expect Jill to give me a promise. What Jill has given me is hope, and that- in spite of its nebulous and unreliable nature- is sometimes enough.

CHAPTER 30

We walk in silence, side by side, the sound of our fellow travellers' footsteps pattering into the distance as we branch away from them. We try to walk in as straight a line as possible, in order to make our return journey more easily navigable. The desert sand is soft beneath our feet. After a few minutes of walking, we come across another sand dune, and silence gives way to debate.

"We've gone far enough, don't you think?" she asks me.

"Not quite," I respond. "If you look behind us, you can still see the jeep in the distance. Anyone driving past on the other side of this dune might miss us. If we climb this dune and descend on the other side, we open ourselves up to a whole new field of visibility. The whole point is that we get ourselves seen. We should climb over it."

I hear her sigh, beside me. She knows I'm right. I glance down at her footwear. Sandals, but not the closed back strapped sandals that I have on. She is not wearing the kind that cling to your feet, and have strong traction, allowing a level of stability when traversing the ground. Her sandals are more like flip flops, thin, flimsy and completely unsuitable to the task. She seems to have the same thought, and takes them off, looping both of the plastic sections designed to separate her big toe from the rest of them through her fingers. She begins to shift her weight from foot to foot, as though the sand itself is not quite burning her, but is certainly uncomfortably hot.

"There's no point in waiting," she says, and sets out before me. The task is difficult. Even in between steps, the sand sometimes seems to shift its texture, from soft and fluffy to hard and packed. Occasionally I find myself stumbling, and have to stretch out my hand in order to catch myself and set myself upright again. In these moments, with my hands against the hot grains, I appreciate my companion's haste, the way she seems to be desperate to hop herself up the dune as quickly as possible, even though this haphazard approach means that sometimes one step forward literally results in two steps back, as soft sand shifts and slips beneath her.

I quickly overtake her, but pause and call back over my shoulder.

"Don't rush. I know it's hot, but it will be quicker if you pace yourself. Feel for the spots where the ground is steadier."

She looks up at me, and for the first time I really take in her face. It's strange. She's been an integral part of my journey so far. She clung to me during both of my stretches in the jeep, but she had been sitting behind me and I had been gazing out over the Sahara. In the shipping container, she sat on the other side, with the other women and children, and I was too caught up in my plotting to pay attention to the features of the migrants who were not directly involved in my plan. Even when she asked to split water with us after we left the container, I only really gave her a cursory glance. It's strange that this is the first time I'm taking in her face. It's strange that so far in our story, she has been referred to as the woman in the blue hat, and that so far- in my head- that blue hat has been her defining feature. Something that can be removed. Something that she likely wasn't even wearing a few days ago. Something that isn't really a part of her in any permanent, tangible way. Now, seeing her, I know I could have labelled her as the woman with the almond eyes, the woman with the symmetrical smile, the dimpled cheeks and slender jaw. The woman of between 20 and 25 years of age. All of these would have been better descriptions. In another world, a world in which I was not in every second doubting the likelihood or even possibility of my own immediate survival, I would probably be shy around her; I usually am when it comes to beautiful women.

A slight flicker in those almond eyes, their pupils charcoal black. An almost imperceptible shifting - sideways, upwards, down, minutely, as though she too is letting her gaze flicker over my features, taking me in for the first time, reappraising her understanding of me. Who have I been to her so far on the journey? The boy with the bad haircut? She's probably spent most of the trip looking at the back of my head...

"My name is Kehinde," she says absurdly. Because, what better time to introduce yourself than whilst sliding down the side of a sand dune, in the process of walking away from the vehicle which was supposed to take you to safety, but obviously she too is tired of using half-baked labels. Not that a name is much better. Most of the time a name is just as arbitrary as that blue hat, but just much more permanent. A random chain of syllables which tells you nothing about the person behind them. But in this case, that's not quite true, is it? I'm not Yoruba, I don't speak Yoruba, but I do know the meaning of that name, Kehinde. I had a friend, Taiwo, a few years ago, and his younger twin was called Kehinde. They definitely told me that in Yoruba, Kehinde means the second born of twins, the one who comes after Taiwo. Even though Taiwo is born first, they believe that Kehinde is the older twin, who sends Taiwo out into the world first, to determine if it is time to be born.

'Where is her twin?' I wonder. Already in Europe, waiting for her to join? Still in Nigeria, having been unable or unwilling to take the trip with her? In Jannah, the afterlife, soon to be reunited with her? It's not the time to ask.

"My name is Hakeem," I respond, stretching out my hand. She reaches out to hold it, and I pull her towards me, digging my feet into the sand and leaning my body forwards with my torso twisted, so as to not break our connected grip. We make our way to the top of the dune together.

"You know, we're probably more visible here than if we were to go down the other side," Kehinde says, "if we stay on top like this, we can be seen from both directions." I look down at the steep descent, thinking about how, in order to get back to the jeep in the evening, we would have to climb it again, whilst both hungrier and more dehydrated than we are currently.

"I agree," I say emphatically. "Let's stay up here."

I start to kick at the sand constituting the tip of the dune, which itself is pointed, trying to flatten off the surface somewhat, and give us a flat platform on which to sit. It is a strenuous job that requires some physical exertion, and I am eager to preserve the little energy I have, so the platform I end up forming is quite small, but large enough for both of us to sit, and even for one of us to lie down if necessary.

We debate whether or not to take this course of action, alternating between laying and sitting in order to ensure that at least one of us is fairly visible if any vehicle were to pass by. The alternative would be to imitate those migrants who, in the shipping container, sat back to back, using each other as backrests. Given that I'm quite small, I estimate our weights to be relatively similar, so this would be a viable option. Standing for extended periods of time, though it would make us a little bit more visible, doesn't appeal to either of us, especially given the need to conserve energy. And at the end of the day, if a jeep does pass by, we'll hear it coming and be able to stand up and wave our arms and jump up and down frantically in the moment.

We decide to sit side by side for now and shift to the back to back position once we become uncomfortable. I remove the bottle of water from my backpack and we both take a few gulps, savouring the hydration. I cross my legs and gaze out over the Sahara, pensive and brooding, impotent to do anything more than wait.

Mustafa's dubious plan is now in place. We have separated. We have spread ourselves over as large an area as possible. And now there is nothing to do but wait. If the plan had involved more steps, had been more involved, it could have continued to be a distraction from despair. I could have been like a man in a car crash who has no time to register fear or shock or despair before his death, because the entirety of his final movements are engaged with spinning the wheel, slamming the brakes, scanning the road before him, proactively trying to avoid the inevitable. Sitting on this dune, gazing out at the sea of sand, I feel more like the passenger of the car, completely powerless to act further and therefore free in those final moments to think, 'this is how I die'.

Either Kehinde's thoughts are not running quite as darkly as mine, or she is just as desperate to distract herself from them.

"Tell me about yourself, Hakeem," she says softly, and I do. I tell her about my childhood, about my father and his stories, about his death and our fall into destitution, about my sister Karima and my sister Fatima and the way they smile and the differences between them that I know are really differences in personalities and not just differences in age because when Karima was Fatima's age I remember how she acted, and she did not chase lizards and dig in the ground for worms. I tell her about my mother, though I omit my suspicions about her recent sources of money, and I do not tell her about my dreams, my hopes, my plans. It would be far too painful to tell her my plans for the future and would only remind me of how quickly that future seems to be slipping through my fingers as quickly as the sand slips through my sandals and her flip-flops.

"My mum used to tell me stories," she says. "A long time ago. I haven't seen her in... six or seven years."

Our eyes meet, and she sees my question in the way my eyebrows lift, my lips part, but not to ask the question, just as a natural expression of curiosity and concern. She answers the silent inquiry.

"She's alive," she says. "They're both alive. I just haven't seen them in... a long time. But I still remember her stories. How about this, Hakeem? To pass the time, why don't you tell me one of your father's stories? And I'll tell you one of my mother's ones."

"Ok," I respond. "There was once a rich man. He lived in a large house, and was so rich that he ate meat every day..."

Five minutes later, after much questioning, chuckles, and ominous thoughts about whether hyenas can thrive this far in the desert, Kehinde begins her own story.

"In the Yoruba religion, the whole universe was created by Olorun or Olufin. They are eternal and powerful beyond measure. They are neither male nor female. They created the universe and made day and night. So far, very similar to the God of both Christians and Muslims. But here is the difference. In Yoruba religion, we believe Olorun did not want to manage the world they had created, and so created Orishas, agents who would bridge the gap between the spiritual realm of Orun and the world that you and I know, the world of your sisters and mother, the world we see. These Orishas include Obatala, Eshu, Ogun, Sango, and many others. They are responsible for specific aspects of life, the Yoruba people turn to them for guidance and assistance. The Orishas act as middlemen between humans and Olorun, so our prayers and devotion can be made to the highest power. Have you ever disobeyed your parents?"

The question is sudden... It seems to be thrown into the story abruptly, breaking the narrative. It takes me a moment to register it, and I repeat the question again in my head before responding.

"Sometimes..." I say hesitantly.

Surely this question can't have been part of the original telling. If it was her mother telling her this story, she would have been well aware whether or not Kehinde was the type of child to disobey her.

"We all have," Kehinde responds, wistfully. "We all have, because the being that gives us life is not always able to control us. To be alive is to make choices, judgements, and sometimes those judgements drift away from those of our parents. The Orishas were no different. They had been appointed by Olorun to run the world, but felt that they knew better what the world was, given that Olorun lived so far away in this heavenly realm, and did not directly engage with creation; Olorun was no longer qualified to decide how it should be governed. The Orishas had their own ideas about how the world should be, and they began to make decisions independently from Olorun. But, when Olorun found out, Olorun was not pleased. Rivers dried up. Crops failed to grow where they once had grown. Heat became unbearable."

"This sounds familiar," I pitch in. "Is Olorun angry at the moment?"

"Perhaps," Kehinde responds. "But our story is set in the past. Humans prayed to the Orishas as always, knowing that they were the intermediaries between man and Olorun, not knowing that the Orishas had angered Olorun. The Orishas were unable to answer their prayers, and looked for a way to calm Olorun and make Olorun forgive them, but they were unable to reach him, growing tired before they were able to reach the heavenly realm of Orun.

The young, beautiful Orisha, Oshun, took on the task, turning herself into a beautiful peacock and flying out towards the heavenly realm. As she passed the sun, her feathers began to burn in the heat. She pushed through, on and on, eventually reaching Olorun. But by the time she had, her feathers had been burnt, and she resembled a vulture more than a peacock. Olorun, seeing the sacrifice she had made, became calm and forgave the Orishas. The rivers began to flow, and the crops began to grow, and the heat began to subside."

Hyenas. Vultures. Are these stories supposed to be distracting us, or reminding us of the scavengers which may soon come in search of our remains? I look out towards the sun- not quite towards it, as it's too bright for my eyes, but in its general direction- I imagine myself flying past it. Already, at this distance, its heat is oppressive. Oshun must have had a very strong will and very magical feathers. My stomach rumbles oppressively.

"A lovely story," I say, "If your mother was as good a storyteller as you, you were a very lucky child." By this point, we are sitting back to back and so, though I imagine her smiling at the compliment, I have no confirmation that she does.

For a while, we sit in silence, perhaps 40 minutes or so, taking periodic gulps of water and getting lost in our own thoughts. Before long, I find I want to distract myself again.

"So I told you all about me, who I am, and I told you that my father told me stories. And then we came to our deal: one of his stories for one of your mother's. But we never got round to you telling me about yourself. Who are you, Kehinde?"

Kehinde makes a long, breathy noise, either a deep inhalation of air or a hearty exhalation. Without the visual reference, without the image of her lips and throat moving, I'm unable to specify which. I feel as though she is on the verge of speech but, before she can respond, the sound of a horn comes to us over the sand. We're both on our feet in seconds, turning, looking at each other in question, in shock, in tentative, very tentative, hope. The car horn. Does this mean someone has found us?

Kehinde has removed her flip-flops in seconds, she flings her small bag over her shoulder. She starts to scramble back down the sand dune, the way we came. In her haste, she stumbles, falls, and rolls down sideways to the bottom, peppering herself in sand. I grab the water bottle and my own bag and make my way quickly after her, concerned. When I get to the bottom, she's lying on her back, covered from head to toe in golden granules, smiling, wrinkles at the corners of those almond eyes. She gets to her feet unscathed and starts off at a jog back towards the jeep, not even bothering to put on her flip flops, which still dangle from her hands, swinging like a cheap plastic pendulum.

CHAPTER 31

Dinner time. Time for conversation. My mum sits at the head of the table, which is rectangular in shape, my little sister, June, opposite her. They take up the two narrow edges of the perimeter. Me and my brother sit opposite each other at the two wider sides, my chair doesn't quite fit into the narrow ones, so this is my usual spot. No C-food stew today, but Mama's cooking is as good as ever. It's some kind of black-eyed bean paste served with lentils and a side of green salad and yogurt.

"So, how was school today?" Mum asks me.

I tell her about my maths lesson and how I'm struggling a bit with differential equations, especially the complex ones. I don't tell her about how I spent my lunch break in my form room, strapped into the VirtuWorld, trying to gain back some ground in my ratings after finding myself with less time to play, due to my time in the control room. But I assure her that I'll work on my maths, and I have every intention to. If my grades slip, that could spell danger, putting her permissiveness in jeopardy.

"We had an interesting history lesson," I say. "We looked at the conflict between China and Japan in the mid 2030s and how the international community came together to help prevent an escalation to war."

"Yes," pipes up my little brother Toby. "A very interesting topic. If you look at the Senkaku Islands dispute and the growth of denialism in Japan with regards to atrocities in the Second World War, you could see tensions bubbling up way before 2030."

This is typical of Toby. He's in the year below me at school. He hasn't studied this yet, he has no business knowing it. I wouldn't have known it a year ago. But he's read about it in some book. I'm not jealous of him; I'm happy for him and his intelligence. But his intervention has somewhat overshadowed my attempt to distract my mother from my failings in maths by showing off my aptitude for history. He seems to almost sense this, and tails off rather than going into detail about exactly which author gave him such insight into the relationship between East Asian superpowers.

"Where China?" gurgles my sister June. She's been in a particularly loud and rambunctious mood all evening, and keeps wiggling her shoulders in the way she always does when she's feeling particularly mischievous.

"Far away," my mum replies with a smile.

"Where Japan?" June continues.

"Near China," Toby says with a chuckle. I'll give him that one.

"Where Sekaku Islan'?" June exclaims urgently in her high-pitched childish voice, as though nothing could be more important than getting an answer to this question. It's my turn to smile at her, for giving me the opportunity to show I've been listening in class.

"Either China or Japan, June, depending on who you ask."

"Taiwan also claims them," says Toby.

"But China still claims Taiwan." I counter.

He winks at me surreptitiously from across the table, and I suspect that he set me up to make a smart response on purpose. I almost grin back, but force myself to keep a straight face as he responds "touché".

Mum seems delighted. "Some healthy debate between my little

Einsteins, eh?" She says. "How refreshing. And what's your latest book, Toby? Are you still getting through the alternative histories?"

"Not at the moment," Toby replies. "I've been reading some books about the science of sports actually. They talk a lot about famous athletes and the reason for their success, strength and reaction time and such, but also about balance and the idea of proprioception."

My ears perk up at this.

"What's proprioception?" my mum asks my brother. But this time it's me who cuts in and takes over the conversation.

"It's like a sixth sense," I say. "It's the way that we understand where our bodies are in relation to the world around us. It's the reason why we can reach out and touch something without having to look at it. And it's also why athletes have such fast reflexes and can stay balanced in difficult situations."

My brother nods in agreement, a look of slight curiosity flits across his faintly Caribbean features, and my mum looks both surprised and impressed, her head turning from him to me.

"Have you guys been synchronising your reading?" she asks earnestly. "Have you managed to get your brother to pick up some books, Toby?"

"No," I respond, rolling my eyes in an exaggerated way. "My boss- one of my bosses, actually- told me about it. She's a neuroscientist. She knows all about this stuff. The concept of proprioception is very important to her... our... work."

"How so?" Toby asks. "You don't really need much proprioception to play video games like you do in sports, you only need fast reactions and good reflexes. You can play lying down, sitting up. A bit like reading a book. You need your hands to turn the page and your eyes to move across it, but the rest of it happens in your head, no?"

"It's actually more than that," I reply. "The hand movements are more complex in the games than turning a page, but that's not my point. We're working on something different in the office, something that uses your whole body, or at least the parts of your brain that control your whole body. It's not too simple to explain, but proprioception is not only key to what we're trying to do, but also a barrier in some ways..."

"Poopoosession" giggles June, waving her fork around.

"Proprioception" my mother corrects her, wide-eyed in a mixture of shock and amusement.

"A barrier?" asks Toby curiously. "How can it be a barrier?"

"Because..." I say, and my voice tails off, trying to find a good analogy or metaphor for the point I'm making. I sit with my thoughts for a few moments and then continue.

"You remember the room we used to share? When we were younger?"

"Yes," Toby responds.

We shared that room until my accident. It was only after the accident that I moved downstairs to the study, Mum and Dad moved into the large room that I had shared with Toby, and their room became June's room. Until then her crib had been in theirs. Toby took the old study. In those days I didn't play video games nearly as much, but he was still always in his books, always sitting in his bed, reading. It feels like a lifetime ago.

"Okay," I continue. "So you had your bed and I had mine, right? Your bed was on the other side of the room. In the right-hand corner, directly to the right after you entered, up against the wall. Mine was further down into the room, also on the right."

Toby nods. I keep talking.

"I never slept in your bed and you never slept in mine. Imagine one day whilst we were sleeping, Mum or Dad had come in and, without waking us up, swapped us around. When you woke up, until you opened your eyes, you'd still imagine yourself to be in your regular position. Right? When we wake up, let's say we wake up and the lights are off. Right? So we can't see anything. Let's say we wake up and it's pitch black. The lights are off. So your proprioception is still telling you you're in your regular position in your regular bed. You might step out of the bed, walk a few metres to the left and reach out your hand expecting to find the door handle. But it won't be there. At some point you'll realise what has happened and your understanding of where you are will completely switch."

I pause, recalculating, then continue. "Well, no, scratch that actually. You wouldn't be able to walk out of the bed to your left because you'd hit the wall straight away. Right? My bed faced towards the door and yours didn't. Either way, you'd soon realise that you woke up in my bed. Once that had happened, you wouldn't be able to trick your brain into going back to where it saw itself moments before, but that's what we're trying to do at work. Trick the brain into ignoring everything it knows about where it really is, what's really in front of the body, behind the body, around the body, and get it to ignore all of that and use the parts of itself that would normally control that, that are very heavily linked to that understanding of self, to move something else thousands of miles away, something that isn't even your shape."

"Poopoosession!" squeals June, again.

"Proprioception!" my mother replies, more firmly now, no doubt imagining June shouting her rendition of the word out in public or company.

My brother leans back in his chair, thoughtful.

"Interesting," he says. "One flaw in your analogy, however. Your side of the room always smelled of sweaty armpits. I'd have known where I was the moment I woke up, from the stink."

We both burst out laughing and Mum looks between us in mock disapproval. Once I've finished clutching my sides, I take the opportunity presented by the pause in the discussion to help myself to a heaped spoon of black-eyed beans and yogurt. Politely, my mum waits till I've swallowed before coming into the conversation.

“And do you think the same applies to self-perception?” she asks.

“What do you mean?” I reply.

“Self-perception,” she says.

“What's the difference?” I say blankly.

“Come on, Elijah,” she says impatiently. “Proprioception and self-perception aren't the same, at least from the definition you've given me. Proprioception is about where you are physically, where you understand yourself to be in the physical world. Self-perception is more how you perceive yourself, who you think you are in a moral sense. Do you see yourself as a good person? Do you see yourself as a bad person? Do you see yourself as a talented person? Do you see yourself as a talentless person? Do you see yourself as worthless? Or do you see yourself as useful? If it's difficult to go back to believing you're somewhere you're not once you've had it revealed to you where you really are, could it also be difficult to go back to believing you're a good person when someone points out your faults? To maintain an image of yourself that might not be true?”

Delilah's, 'Are you an agent of the darkness or the light?' seems to echo in her question, and for some reason I bristle before shrugging in a non-committal way.

"It's all getting a little bit deep, isn't it?" I say. "In other news, I've been thinking about your proposal, Mum. And I've got an idea of which instrument I might want to play."

This is in fact true, and not just a shameless and transparent attempt to change the subject. I have been thinking about various instruments. Some of them were written off out of hand. A drum set requires pedals, so that was a no-no. Even non-drumset drums like bongos, congas and djembes usually nestle between your legs, so that the drumming surface is around waist height. Your legs provide them with stability, hold them in place, the same goes for the cello. The double bass, given its size, would require me to stand- nope. Piano is a viable option. It has pedals but they're not really essential to playing like they are on an organ. They can be used to add texture and colour to the notes, but you can do without them. But piano just seems like a very obvious choice.

"An accordion," I say to my mum, with a mysterious smile. "I think I'd like to play the accordion." I've thought about it and it makes the most sense. Mum plays guitar and when she plays she often sings along. She hasn't got the greatest voice, but her voice isn't terrible either, and the lyrics to the songs add so much depth and colour. If I learnt the trumpet or the flute or any woodwind instrument I wouldn't be able to sing and play together. If I learnt the piano it wouldn't be very portable, and portability is of extra importance where I'm concerned. Like the guitar, the accordion gives the best of both worlds.

"Wonderful!" Mum beams at me, and her pleasure at the fact that I have taken her advice on board and seem to be being proactive about enacting it seems to override any concern about the rapid change of topic. "Let's look into getting you an accordion, then."

"They can be quite expensive," I reply, "but let's go for a cheap one. I don't want you to fork out any money, I can pay for it from my salary, but I'm also saving up for something more important."

"Saving up?" She tilts her head in question. "What are you saving up for?"

"Something," I say mysteriously. "We'll find out if it ever comes to pass. It's all very theoretical and up in the air at the moment. But if it is possible, it will be expensive, so I don't want to spend too much of my earnings straight away."

I don't tell her what I'm saving up for because, if I did, she would feel it was her responsibility to pay for it. After all, it would be a solution for a problem she caused. She would insist. But I've already cost the family a lot. And now I'm making money myself which, admittedly, she is keeping hold of for me, as per Joe Gradle and Thomas Rutchers' contract. I don't need to put that pressure on her at the moment, not while there's still so much uncertainty. She chooses not to pry.

"Well, I'm sure you'll tell me when you're ready," she says. "And I'm glad you're showing some financial responsibility. Saving is an important life skill. We can take a look for something second hand online."

"Sounds like a plan," I reply, pushing away my empty plate.

CHAPTER 32

Kehinde holds up her skirt with one hand as she runs, leaving deeper imprints in the sand - more widely spaced - than those she had left whilst only walking earlier, themselves still traced out in the opposite direction. The new footprints are slightly different still, the imprints of bare feet rather than flip-flops, rarely with indentations for all five toes in total, but still with separate dots over the narrow ridge of their upper perimeter, like tiny, slightly disconnected petals. She is not only running, she's sprinting with urgency, I'm struggling to keep up with her. I run directly behind her, her figure obscuring my view.

As we approach the jeep from a distance, I see others in the periphery of my vision, also running from their posts. Why are we all running? What is the purpose of our haste? And then it clicks. There is no guarantee that whatever vehicle may or may not have come will be able to tow us out of the sand hollow. There is no guarantee that, even if we were to be towed, we would not get ourselves stuck again just as quickly. Some are perhaps hoping that there might be space in the other vehicle itself, but few will be naive enough to imagine space for 28. Maybe people are acting as though this is a race because in some way it is; because those who arrive first back at the jeep are those most likely to ingratiate themselves with the people who have stopped.

I allow myself to drift leftwards, giving myself an unobstructed view ahead. I squint towards the jeep itself, expecting to see another vehicle beside it, but even from this distance it's clear that all is not entirely as it seems. What I'm seeing is not another vehicle, but a line of distinct animal-like shapes silhouetted against the horizon. Even from this distance, it's clear they are not donkeys or horses. Their humps are more than visible, increasingly so as we approach them. Camels. Perhaps 10 or 12. Neatly lined in single file. I am sure that what I'm seeing are camels.

A caravan. Of course. My dad used to trade with them all the time. Desert dwellers who would come down from the Sahara to the Nigerian border to trade their wares. The caravans were made up of anything from tens to hundreds of camels. They could transport anything from spices to textiles. Salt was especially common. Dad used to say that they mined it from salt flats in the desert, pumping water from underground sources into the salt flat, which dissolves the salt, then pumping it into evaporation ponds, where the sun and wind evaporate the water and leave behind the salt crystals.

They would also bring in the sweeter dates from North Africa, the kind that are larger and juicier than those that grow in Sokoto and Kano, which are always very popular during Ramadan amongst those who can afford them. I still remember Dad admiring some of the rugs, mats and blankets he acquired from the desert dwellers, as he called them, the handicrafts of leather and pottery, the intricate jewellery. This is a caravan making a journey of trade, and it has stumbled across us, abandoned merchandise that we are.

As we approach, and the camels come into greater focus, I can see that they are tethered together by thick ropes, keeping them in line and preventing them from wandering off on their own. Their fur is a reddish-golden-brown, somewhat darker than the gold of the landscape that stretches out around us. They have legs that seem pencil-thin when viewed in proportion to the muscular bodies but, when appreciated in their own right, are evidently sturdy and strong, with knee joints that, in places, seem bent almost backwards, hyper-mobile, extending beyond the range of motion of human legs, or even the legs of most animals.

Their necks are longer than I remember. I have rarely ever seen camels, perhaps I've just forgotten how long their necks really are. They are not long and straight like the neck of a giraffe, but long and curved, emerging horizontally from the body and curving upwards until they are vertical, as though stretching out towards the sun like the stem of a flower. Their proud and ugly heads are perched atop these stems.

Padded mats sit atop the camels' humps and, flowing over each side of these mats in almost perfect symmetry, are the wares of trade, meticulously tied and counterbalanced in such a way that gravity does half of the job for them, with no further fastening necessary. On a few of the camels sit people rather than goods, men who seem similarly dressed to the deceased Tuareg. If I'm not mistaken, yes, on the fourth camel down the ordered line, the woman who had the children, along with her daughter. So she secured herself a place. And where is her son? Yes, sitting with one of the men in Tuareg garments, comfortably secure between his legs, holding onto his forearm for stability, not unlike Kehinde's previous arrangement with myself.

Who else is back at camp? Who else has arrived back in such haste? Those who we left to remain at the jeep are all still here. Paul seems to be talking with one of the newcomers, this one on foot, rather than mounted. The two brothers sit on the sand, looking as despondent as ever, perhaps realising that such a leg injury does not bode well for being allocated a seat on a camel which may be subject to a lot of competition. The pregnant woman is... where is she? Yes, so she's already mounted a camel too. Not surprising, I suppose. Mustafa hasn't yet returned, but I'm sure that's Hasan I see running in from the other side.

Over the next few minutes, more of us filter in. The religious man who became the driver. The bilingual man who took over

Hasan's role as translator after the Tuareg's shooting. He quickly shuffles over to join in the conversation between Paul and one of the drivers of the caravan. The man who punched Mustafa arrives minutes later. The man is frowning, glaring and rubbing his knuckles, as though hoping to wrestle himself out of the desperate situation.

By the time Princess arrives, carrying her bags and looking weary, most of the others are also back, including Mustafa, who, for some reason, seems to be keeping his distance from Hasan and I, who are standing in a group with Kehinde. Why is he being so distant, not coming over and discussing the latest developments? Does he think that some members of the group still hold him responsible for shooting the Tuareg? Does he feel that, if he ignores me, people are less likely to blame me? Who knows.

The bilingual has now taken over the conversation with the turbaned stranger, who seems to be the leader of the caravan. They are talking in subdued French, and pointing around the group at intermittent intervals. Given the speed of their discussion, I'm unable to make out anything of what they're saying, but eventually the religious ex-taxi driver opens his mouth to speak, raising his voice so as to draw the attention of the bilingual.

"We need you to translate for us. The horn has been honked. We've come back. We have eyes. We can see the situation. It doesn't look likely that everyone will be able to travel, if any of us. You can't be making dealings on our behalf when we don't know what's being said."

There's a murmur of agreement amongst the English speakers in the group. Eloka still hasn't returned. I glance around surreptitiously, trying to spot him. The bilingual turns to look at the Ghanaian as he speaks, then nods his approval. He turns back to the turbaned stranger and says something to him in

French, and the stranger nods in turn. The bilingual turns away from the turbaned man, so as to face the majority of the migrants.

"They are a caravan," he confirms, "a very small one, from northeast Niger. They're not Tuareg, but Tubu, a different tribe. They've been down to Nigeria to sell some of their wares and to buy a variety of other merchandise and food to sell and use at home. They're heading back to their village, and in a few weeks some of them will be making a similar trip to southern Libya. He said they can take a few of us, given that they sold more goods than they bought on this trip, but that it won't be many, especially given they have already agreed to take the pregnant woman, and the other woman with her children."

The man who punched Mustafa speaks, interrupting the bilingual's flow.

"And why they no dump their wares? We go live not important like that? Life mo important than what the camels dey carry now?"

The bilingual responds calmly. "I did ask them if that would be possible and they told me it wouldn't. They said that they are not wealthy businessmen, but villagers. A trip all the way to Nigeria on camels takes them weeks or even months. They only do it a few times a year and the goods they trade provide them with the money to feed their families. Dumping their merchandise would put the lives of their own community at risk. They say if they dumped all their merchandise every time they came across stranded migrants they would have died themselves long ago. They say the desert can be heartless."

The angry man responds in turn with a question, loud and clear.

"They no understand what I say, English?" The bilingual shakes his head and the angry man continues. "We get weapon. We get gun. The woman here. She hold gun. They not give us space on camel. We force them." The man gestures at Princess.

The Ghanaian taxi driver responds. "Are you foolish?" he asks. "We killed the Tuareg and look where we are. You want to threaten the people offering some of us help, now? Doom us all again."

The angry man replies with a contemptuous shout. "And say they leave with three, four, five of us, the rest go die soon."

Princess herself clutches her bag to her chest and raises her own voice.

"No," she says. "No. Christ does not approve of taking things by force."

The angry man looks at her with a sneer. He looks at her and starts to walk towards her. "Screw your God and screw your Christ!" he grunts. "What they do for us here?" The man stretches his hand as if to snatch the bag from her and she clutches it more tightly still. The Ghanaian ex-taxi man himself makes as though to intervene, but is too far from the pair of them to get there before an altercation breaks out. The angry man grabs the bag from Princess and yanks it from her hand, throwing her to the floor in the process. He plunges his hand inside, searching for the weapon greedily, and then suddenly falls forward, landing on his knees with a dazed expression.

Eloka looms behind him, taller than anyone else in the vicinity. The spade that had been so unsuccessful in freeing the jeep is clutched in the sausage-like fingers of his hands, his dreadlocks flow down the back of his scalp and loop over his shoulder in a path not unsimilar to the path taken by the single stream of blood that rolls down the head and shoulder of the man he has just struck. The angry man falls forward again, so that he's lying face down on the desert sand, entirely unconscious, his hand bent awkwardly backwards- still in the position of rummaging through the bag in which he sought the weapon.

Eloka kneels, removes the hand from the bag, and hands the bag back to Princess, who takes it without comment. Silence fills the immediate vicinity ominously. The turbaned stranger holds the reins of his camel and glances at the scene with an expression of mild surprise and cautiousness, but without the alarm that might be expected. He does not question the situation, but seems to take it in his stride. He does not know about the gun. Presumably he doesn't speak English, so must be wondering what on earth that was all about.

He says something to the bilingual and makes sure to say it loud enough that those who speak French can hear and understand. I think I hear some version of the word *partir*, which means to leave. The bilingual man confirms by translating for the English speaking migrants. "He says they're pressed for time, they have to leave. That they can leave us a bit of water but not much, and that they wish us luck. They say they'll take the two remaining women, and then the two smallest and lightest members of the rest of the group, so as to not wear out their camels."

I look at Hasan, and our mouths both form O shapes, as though we dare not believe our ears; that we can't believe the same handicap that relegated us to the boot is the thing that saves us. A moment later, I'm not thinking of myself and Hasan, but of Mustafa. Mustafa, who is over six feet tall. Mustafa, who certainly is not one of the lightest of the group. Mustafa, who was my... is my... was my childhood friend. Mustafa, who is looking at me now with a pained expression plastered on his features, who is finally making his way over towards me. His eyes are both starting to tear, and displaying a raw and savage purposefulness.

He comes towards me until we're face to face and plunges his hand in his pocket, taking it out to reveal a small bundle of banknotes. He pushes these into my hand.

"You heard what they said," he says, his voice starting to become unsteady. "They'll take the women and the children and then the two lightest, the least heavy. That's you and Hasan. Take this money. You will need it."

I back away physically, shaking my hands in protest. "No," I say, my voice tinged with an edge of panic. "No, you'll need it. Another vehicle will come, a car. You'll need your money when you're rescued."

Mustafa shouts at me. He doesn't just raise his voice, but shouts as loudly as had the man that punched him. "You listen to me," he says. "There is no other rescue. I'm surprised these camels even showed. This is the end. There is no hope. If you don't take this money, it will be buried in the sand and will do nothing for anybody. You take this and you use it to get to Europe and when you are there, you remember that I gave it to you and you do not forget my family." He pauses, I can almost see my reflection in his nascent tears. He continues. "You send money to your mother and your sisters, but you send something to my family too. Promise me."

I don't respond. My heart is beating frantically. He grips me by my shirt and shakes me.

"Promise me!" He almost screams.

"I promise! I promise!" I exclaim, clutching at his hands as they fling me to and fro. By the time I unclutch them, he has released me, and the banknotes are in my own grip rather than his.

CHAPTER 33

The dentist waiting room. The smell of antiseptic. The pictures of perfect smiles and shining teeth on the walls make you feel more at ease. The receptionist behind the desk is always friendly and welcoming, ready to answer any questions you may have. Magazines and children's toys sit on a low table in the corner and there is always some toddler pushing beads along bent multi-coloured pieces of wire which travel in intricate spirals around a rudimentary toy. They always reminded me of roller coasters, and I have only ever seen them in dentists' waiting rooms. A burgundy carpet, plain blue wallpaper with the motto, 'a smile to remember,' stencilled on it in italic writing, the mother of the toddler is reading Gabble magazine from her chair, and a TV sits in the corner of the room, mounted to a bracket on the wall.

The volume is at a level that is not intrusive, but loud enough to listen in to if desired. Mum has decided to take the opportunity to nip into a nearby shop she quite likes, but rarely finds the time to visit. We're not in our local area, you see, but in a different part of London. My old dentist was much closer, but I had to change dentists after the accident because they didn't have a wheelchair recliner. This dentist does. The wheelchair recliner is a godsend, it means I don't have to be lifted up and down out of my chair every time I go for a checkup. The machine tilts my chair backwards so my mouth is facing the ceiling, and I can just open my gob, sit back and relax while they do their job. Well, not quite relax, no one is relaxed when another person is sticking cold metal objects around in their mouth and poking at their gums. But you get the idea.

I left my VirtuWorld goggles and gloves in the car. We arrived just on time and I didn't expect there to be a delay, so I thought it would be a quick in and out, but the dentist is behind schedule. I'm not going to play with the toy and, even if I did want to, the toddler has got in there before me. I'm also not that interested in Gabble magazine or any of the other gossip mags littered on the table, so my attention naturally drifts to the other distraction in the room, the television. I don't really watch much television, a bit of Fixflix here and there, but that's all. I always enjoyed games more than TV, even before my accident, though I didn't used to play them to almost the same extent. Television has always seemed very passive to me, something that doesn't require much interaction. It's never been my thing. But it's here and I'm here, and the remote, funnily enough, is on the chair directly to my left. So I grab it and start to flick through the channels.

Reality TV, adverts, bad comedy, news, a documentary about the history of astronom, that captures my eye for a minute, but the narrator's voice is really dull, so I keep flicking. I land on a channel which seems to be taking place in some kind of chamber, and I'm about to flick on to the next one when I pause, squinting at the screen. I'm sure I recognise the person speaking. Yes, definitely, I've seen her in the lobby of the Home Office building. Always very brief sightings where she walks through looking busy, accompanied by security. An older lady of about 50 to 60, with thinning blonde hair, deep wrinkles around the eyes and teeth that could compete with some of the posters stuck on the walls around me. I glance towards the bottom of the screen and see the words "Elsa Chamberlain, Home Secretary."

Interesting. Apparently this woman is my boss, and the chamber must be the Houses of Parliament. I grab the remote and turn up the volume a little. The woman reading Gabble magazine looks up curiously and our eyes meet for a second before hers flicker back down to the paper before her. I look up again at the screen and Elsa Chamberlain's voice speaks out at me in an affected drawl not dissimilar to that of Thomas Rutchers and Joe Gradle, though a few octaves higher.

"The Honourable Member for Salisbury misses the point entirely. Look at his party's record on the problem of immigration. Look at his party's record on dealing with the floods of dreadful specimens arriving at our shore. Yes, they have the rhetoric, the rhetoric of maintaining British integrity, the rhetoric of aiding with the European project, but they do not have the stomach to take things to where they need to go. Our party has effectively tripled deportations. We have expanded and improved on our program of utilising technology to secure our borders. Our party is the party of action, not the party of promises!"

The camera pans to a grey-haired man in an oversized gown with particularly large ears, sitting in a large green leather chair at the back of the chamber.

"Order! Order!" he shouts, as the grumbles and roars of what must be other MP's echo around the chamber. "I give the floor to the Honourable member for Croydon South."

A man on the other side of the chamber to Elsa stands up with a sheaf of paper in hand and starts to speak. He is younger than her, perhaps 35 or 40, and has an unflattering bowl haircut.

"The Honourable Home Secretary claims her party is the party of action, and that she is dealing with the issue of migration, but under her Government's tenure, the incidents caused by the pro-migrant rebel group 'Bye-bye Borders' have actually increased. She has been unable to find the ringleader of this group. Her Government has been unable to prosecute any but a few low-level foot soldiers. Bye-bye Borders have committed a number of sabotage actions this year alone. It is estimated that they have been successful in smuggling a significant number of undesirables into the country. The Honourable Home Secretary claims to be a member of the party of action, but her record has been one of inaction and incompetence. I put it to the House that the Home Secretary is not fit for her position!"

The man at the back of the chamber shouts again, "The Honourable Home Secretary and member for Surrey."

Elsa rises to her feet and stares at the man with the bowl haircut, her voice loud and clear.

"The Honourable Member for Croydon South clearly has no understanding of the complexities of the current situation. My party has been working tirelessly to combat the threats posed by Bye-bye Borders and other criminal organisations, and this is a long-term project. It cannot be solved overnight, and it requires a sustained effort. The Government is doing its best to protect the citizens of the United Kingdom, and we are making progress. I urge the Member for Croydon South to show a little faith and perhaps revisit some recent stories emerging about the affiliations some members of his own party have with pro-migrant groups. Indeed, was it not the Honourable Member for Liverpool who was found only last year to be meeting with asylum lawyers in a private capacity, attempting to discuss possibilities of revisiting asylum law and making it easier for undesirables to avoid immediate deportation to countries more suitable to assess their claims?"

Cries of, "POINT OF ORDER!" come from numerous locations on the other side of the room.

"The Honourable Member for Bolton West."

A woman stands, chubby, but not quite overweight, wearing spectacles and with hair in a tidy bun.

"I would request that the Most Honourable Home Secretary retract such unsubstantiated claims immediately. The so-called meetings between the Honourable Member for Liverpool and these lawyers were never shown to contain discussions of undermining this country's immigration laws and the

Honourable Member for Liverpool has denied any wrongdoing. I would suggest that members of the Government get their information from trusted sources, rather than base their policies and criticisms of members of the opposition on the nonsense written in the tabloids. I do hope the Chancellor isn't intending to structure his next budget on the contents of Gabble Magazine."

Almost automatically, my gaze flickers to the mother of the toddler, on her chair in the corner of the room, holding an edition of the Gabble magazine. As expected, she is frowning at the TV as though slightly offended, I repress a chuckle and then look back to the TV myself.

The man sitting at the back of the chamber pipes up again. "Order! Order! Quieten down! Would the Home Secretary like to retract her statement?"

Elsa smirks. I'm not quite sure I like my boss. "The Home Secretary would retract the part of the statement where she stated emphatically what was discussed between the pro-migrant immigration lawyers and the Honourable Member for Liverpool, and allow the members of the public watching to use their imaginations to fill in the gaps."

She's flanked by two other senior members of the Government. One is an Asian lady with a horsey face and long neck. She has a slightly crooked nose and large eyes, the other is a white man with a large forehead. He looks between the ages of 40 and 50, and is balding at a pace that makes his forehead look even larger. 'At this point, just shave the thing,' I think to myself. I know they're senior members of the Government because I've seen them on the front of the papers they leave in the common room at school, before, but I don't know their names.

The Asian woman is leering quite unpleasantly. She has a smile on her face that is not quite the same as the smirk that Elsa wears. Her smile is more a genuine smile of delight, a strange combination of happiness and contempt. The balding man with a large forehead looks slightly dazed and lost, as though he's just taken a generous portion of the tranquiliser-level painkillers I had to take regularly in the weeks following my accident. I wonder if he's high on drugs.

"The Honourable Member for Newcastle upon Tyne!"

A short man with shoulder-length braided hair. Strange for an MP. He has a slight tan to his skin that makes me wonder if there might not be some Rasta in him too.

"As an independent in this chamber, I have often voiced my concern with some of the rhetoric about so-called 'undesirables' and 'specimens' coming to the country. I do find that we must remember we are discussing human beings. But my question to the Home Secretary today is not about the migrants themselves per se, but those hired to manage the so called 'floods'. We must discuss the revelations that the Home Office has turned to recruiting children, who should be in school, to work in the Home Office, an issue which has been repeatedly raised in this chamber but which is yet to be adequately addressed by the Home Office. For what reason is this necessary? Do we not have enough patriots of age to defend our borders? Is it necessary for us to be indoctrinating our children into becoming weapons at such an early age?"

"The Honourable Home Secretary!"

Elsa stands again, three glimmering emeralds dangle from her ears and neck.

"The Honourable Member for Newcastle upon Tyne talks of a revelation, as though this whole thing were being kept as some great secret. Not at all the case! The so-called children in question are mostly teenagers in reality. And they generally either still attend school, or are provided with a premium private tutor education. What is school if not a way to teach the next generation about our values as a country, instilling within them a feeling of duty and commitment to this shared project we call the United Kingdom? Those accepted at an early age to work with the Home Office are patriots, and there is no age limit on patriotism!

If the Honourable Member for Newcastle upon Tyne wants to talk about indoctrination, perhaps he should address the indoctrination some of these loony leftists on social networks are driving into our kids' heads about how it's all our fault that the other side of the world is burning and how we should open up the floodgates, letting everyone in. I am proud of the Home Office's accelerated programme for young patriots, and the Honourable Member should be too. The United Kingdom needs more young people who are willing to put their country first."

The mother of the toddler looks up from her magazine and sighs, rolling her eyes. She has brown hair and an expression of wintery disapproval.

"They all say they're dealing with the problem," she says, not exactly to me, but probably to me, seeing as I'm the only person in the room apart from her toddler. The only other option is that she's talking to herself. "They all say they're dealing with the problem, but every time, every time I leave the bloody house, I see more of these non-indigenous so-called Brits. Skittles has it right, you know Skittles? Skittles Robinson?" A question, so she is speaking to me. She continues without awaiting my response. "I watch his talk show. We need a real deterrent. Deportation is only a deterrent if you get caught, if you don't get off the boat and find somewhere to hide. Gunships, weapons. That's the only way to stop them, make them too scared to come."

Her toddler is now looking up at her, having lost interest in the wooden bead toy. "Gumship," he gurgles, and the way he tries to imitate the word without quite getting it correct reminds me of my sister June. The woman looks at me, eyes wide and lips taught at the corners which, combined with a shrug of the shoulders and an outward opening of the hands, says ‘am I not correct?’ I see something flicker in her expression, as though she's trying to assess me in the same way I assessed the MP with the shoulder-length braided hair. As if she is suddenly unsure as to whether, or as to what extent, I am an ‘indigenous Brit.’ If it was my brother here instead of me, there'd be less of a question mark.

I'm sure if I told the woman before me that I'm actually one of the kids being referred to on TV, she'd have something to say about it either way. Maybe she'd call me a patriot. Maybe she'd look at me in respect rather than suspicion. But I'm not sure if I want her respect. I'm not even really sure if I'm proud of my ‘patriotism’, of my new job. I haven't really allowed myself to interrogate the question. I'm pondering all of this, eyes still locked with her own, when the dentist pokes his head around the door and calls my name.

"Elijah," he says, friendly, warmly. "Elijah, I'm awfully sorry for the delay. If you'd like to make your way through, we're ready for you now.

CHAPTER 34

A mild breeze tickles me, but cannot block the sun. Mustafa is already making his way back through the throng, already moving to the other side of the jeep away from me, leaving before I can hand him back the money he has given me. I make to follow him, to reason with him, to make him understand that he might still be rescued. But a voice rings out behind me, in French. I don't catch everything, but that word, *partir*, leave, is cushioned somewhere in the syllables.

Hasan grabs my arm. "They want to leave quicktime, dawg," he tells me.

Mustafa continues to walk, until he is at the very outer edge of the group's perimeter, as far from me as possible. Only then does he turn and look back at me. I know that were I to follow him, he would wander further, out towards the dunes. My hands close around the notes, in the same gesture of acceptance that I remember my mother using when I gave her the money for Fatima's medicine. I smile at Mustafa and nod, as I see him smile back through his tears.

I turn to Hasan. "We are definitely the smallest, right?" I say.

"We're the smallest men, yeah," he responds. "You still a boy, right? How old you is?"

"Sixteen," I respond.

Hasan's eyebrows raise, and he tilts his head and smiles, moving his pupils over to the side for a fraction of a second then shifting them back, as if to punctuate the 'I told you so' or 'I knew it' in his expression. "You are young, I'm a midget, we're the smallest. Don't look so down, dawg. Back one hour, I thought we were dead. Looks like we're good, now."

I gesture behind me at the others.

"They're not," I say.

Hasan's face becomes stony, but then he shrugs. "They're not," he agrees. "Dangerous journey. And it ain't over yet."

The leader of the caravan approaches us with what looks like his son. He is about 40 years of age. His beard is patchy and flaked with silver. A small tuft of hair sits beneath his ear but then melts into bare skin, before the beard re-emerges at the corner of the jaw and continues to his chin. His moustache stands alone, more uniformly black than the beard. His cheeks are sunken, the nostrils of his nose deeply defined, with grooves above the cartilage deep enough for light to puddle within them. Like Hasan, his eyes have yellows, not whites, in their corners, thin worms of red play over the white like bloody lightning. He wears Tuareg clothes; a white turban, a large, dark brown robe that reaches his ankles, and a pair of sandals. He speaks to a younger man in a language that I do not understand. (Not the language of the Tuareg, not quite as guttural. What was it the driver had called him? Tubu?). He then speaks again in French. He introduces himself as Hamid, and his son as Jibril.

Jibril is his father, minus 25 years. He looks to be about my age, and has slightly fuller features than his dad, with less sunken cheeks, and no cherry-coloured lightning dappling the corners of his eyes. Nonetheless, the resemblance is so striking that no one could mistake the nature of their relationship. Jibril is also wearing a turban, but, rather than a robe he has gone with tattered, hole-ridden jeans and a button-up purple shirt, missing at least two-thirds of its buttons, and cut off at the elbows. He smiles, points at me, and then Hasan, and says, "*Parlez anglais ou français*? Speak English or French?"

"English," I say. "*Petit français.*"

"*Tous les deux*," responds Hasan.

The boy's face seems to light up with excitement. He points at me.

"Afterwards," he says, in a thick accent, "You, me, English..." his face takes a confused expression, and he bites his lip, eyes darting quickly from side to side, as though searching for something in his mind. He turns to Hasan. "*Enseigner?*" he asks.

"Teaching," Hasan responds.

The boy smiles brightly again. The shift in his expression is almost comical. He looks back towards me. "Afterwards, you, me, English, teaching. I English talk want," he says.

"Oui," I say, giving him a nod. "D'accord."

The young boy's smile stays plastered to his face for another moment before he rearranges it back into the same confused expression and turns to Hasan.

"*Venez ici?*" he says questioningly. Hasan starts to step forward but the boy shakes his head. « *Non, qu'est-ce que 'venez ici' en anglais ?* »

« Come here, » Hasan says.

The boy turns back to me. "Come here," he says, and he turns back to Hasan. "*Suis-moi?*"

"Follow me," Hasan responds. The boy turns back to me.

"Follow me," he says.

I'm not quite sure why the boy is gravitating towards me rather than Hasan, given that Hasan would be a much more effective English teacher than me, with a decent grasp of both languages. Maybe it's because I'm around his age. But I don't question him, I follow him as he guides me towards one of the camels. His father takes Hasan over to another one.

The camel has a strong musky smell that fills the air. Its snout is elongated, its nostrils are slit-like, designed to close themselves from the dust and sand of the desert. Its rubbery lips seem almost to be puckered, exposing its protrudent bottom teeth. The ears are small and triangular, but its eyes are large and expressive, with long, thick eyelashes.

I can hear its breathing, deep and guttural. It is attached to the camel in front of it by a harness that envelops its face, looping once around the back of those triangular ears, once underneath the chin, if it can be called a chin. It does not protrude in the way that a chin should, and once around the snout itself, at the very base of the snout, behind the corners of the mouth. On its back is a multicoloured saddle, with three thin protrusions at its front, middle and back, providing a seat of sorts above its hump.

Underneath this saddle, balancing on each side of the camel, are bags full of tradable goods, stored in sacks of thin rope, through the grooves of which can be seen a plastic wrap full of traditional tea leaves, patterned cloths and silk, painted ceramics, and an array of spices and dried herbs. On the way down to Nigeria, to meet traders such as my father, these camels would often simply be loaded with large slabs of salt, as thick as paving stones. I remember well.

Jibril grabs the rope connected to the camel's harness and gently pulls downwards, so that the camel's neck moves, swinging downwards in an arc towards the floor. Once the head is low enough, the camel's heavy breathing turns into a grunt of what could be acquiescence or displeasure, and it folds its knobbly front legs, lowering itself to the ground. Jibril tugs at the rope again, until the camel's hind legs fold under it.

Jibril takes me by the shoulders and steers me towards the side of the camel, gesturing for me to mount in such a way that I sit between the middle and back protrusion of the harness. I swing my leg over. Even with its legs folded underneath it and its body flat against the ground, the camel is quite large, and Jibril needs to give me a leg up for me to swing my right leg over and settle myself in the harness. Jibril then takes my left hand and places it on the middle protrusion, gesturing for me to grip it tightly. He takes my right hand and places it on the front protrusion, which I grip in turn. Jibril takes my right elbow and pushes it upwards so that my arm is locked in a straight position. He loosens it again and then pushes it upwards again.

"*Reste comme ça quand il lève,*" he says. "*Tension, c'est important.*"

I think I understand what he's saying. Keep the tension in my arm when the camel gets up. I nod my consent.

"Very good," says Jibril with a smile. He lets go of my arm and makes his way to the front of the camel, gripping the harness rope again and pulling upwards.

The camel gives a long, low groan. The first thing to rise is its neck, and the bells that adorn it tinkle. If a camel wandered off, they would make it easier to find. It raises itself forward on its front knees with another gravelly grunt, and I find myself tilting backwards, gripping tightly onto both the middle and front harness protrusions, as I worry about falling backwards. Moments later, the camel thrusts itself upwards on its hind legs, keeping its front legs bent at the knees, and I'm suddenly tilting forwards. The tension in my arm is what prevents me from falling flat onto the camel's neck. Finally, it lifts its front legs, so that it no longer rests on its knees but on its feet, and I am not leaning backwards nor forwards, but perfectly vertical, at an impressive height, comparable to the height from which I looked down at the desert floor when sitting in the back of the jeep.

"*Bravo!*" exclaims Jibril.

I hear more grunts as Hasan mounts his own camel somewhere

behind me. A few camels in front, a third man is assisting Kehinde, and Princess has already mounted her own. I can feel the protrusion at the back digging into my tailbone ever so slightly, but at this point it's only mildly uncomfortable. It cannot compete with the other troubles of my body. My hunger, the thirst from rationing off my water hour by hour, the sensation of the sweltering sun.

The leader of the caravan, having obviously succeeded in helping Hasan mount, walks forward to talk with his son in the unfamiliar language. I see Princess try to turn in her saddle to look behind her. I try to do the same, but it's very difficult to do so whilst maintaining balance.

Princess shouts, "Mr. Imam, Muslim preacher, Mr. driver, come here!"

She has obviously not learnt his name. She isn't able to turn to the point where she can make any eye contact, so she shouts as loudly as possible, not knowing his exact location. Her shouts draw the attention of Jibril and his father, though they likely don't understand the meaning, given that they hear the words out of context, in a language they do not speak. After a few moments, the bearded Muslim man who had become our driver appears. I see him appear in my field of vision, walking towards Princess. She opens her handbag and pulls out the gun, throwing it down to him.

"In case of bandits," she says, "We may not share the same faith, but I think I can trust you. I hope the grace of God sees you and the others through this."

The man looks at the weapon gravely, nods and takes his own backpack from his shoulders, sliding the weapon within.

"May Allah guide us to our destination," he says, neck craned upwards towards the singing healer on her camel. He walks back towards the larger group and, as he does so, Hamid's eyes follow him, realisation dawning within them. He looks back at Princess and then back towards the man, seemingly remembering the incident with the bag and the spade. As he walks back towards the group, I force myself to crane my neck, pushing and pulling on the protrusions to retain balance with my body twisted. I manage to stretch myself to the point at which about half of the group is visible. I cannot see Mustafa anywhere, but it is not Mustafa that the man is approaching. He walks towards Eloka, who had knocked out the angry man during the fight for the gun earlier. He grasps his hands and embraces him, reaching into his pocket and pulling out a fresh bag of dates. He hands them to the tall, dreadlocked migrant, before shaking his hand again. But there is no space for Eloka on the camels; heavy, huge Eloka with his bulking frame, and so dates are the only thanks he receives.

Hamid calls out to his son in the Tubu language, and the son moves forward to one of the camels in front, detaching some large bottles of water from one of the camel's sides and bringing them back towards the group of migrants. My own camel gives an unexpected shift, and I wobble, not quite at risk of falling, but close enough to make me remember my lost sunglasses, and how exactly I lost them. I twist my body forward again, understanding that Mustafa does not want to be seen, that he has said his goodbye to me, and given me his parting gift, and accepted his fate. Minutes later, we set off to the north, bumping and swaying on our desert steeds.

CHAPTER 35

Combat Mutants 3: Return to the Qing Dynasty. Ming Lui. The Mantis. It took me a while to get it. It's been years since I've played that game. It was a game I played when I was a casual gamer, gaming on occasion, when my friends invited me for a match. I don't think I ever actually played as the Mantis, but I must have fought against the character once or twice. I had to do a quick Google search to remember their backstory in the game. Various fighting styles in the martial arts, named after animals, styles of Kung Fu, Karate, Taekwondo - etc, etc - warriors who find themselves exposed to radiation following a nuclear spill.

The mutations they undergo give them some of the physical characteristics of the very animals their fighting styles are based on. Ying Li, master of the tiger-claw school Fu Jow Pai, grows real claws and striped orange fur. Ming Bai, a practitioner of Shaolin snake-fist boxing, grows scales and has the tendency to swallow his opponents whole after defeating them, digesting them over the course of days. Like most mutant games, it isn't very realistic, but super fun.

Ming Lui, of course, was an expert in the praying mantis martial art style. The praying mantis is a long and narrow predatory insect. The fighting style involves whip-like circular motions that deflect direct attacks, followed up with precise jabs at the vital spots of the opponent: the nose, the throat, the eyes. After the nuclear spill, Ming Lui developed a face like that of a praying mantis, with huge bulging eyes protruding at the top right and left corners of a very angular triangle-shaped face and thin, ribbed antenna extending vertically from the top of his head.

His arms and legs became coated in a green leaf-like armour which enveloped them and ended in sharp, serrated edges that extended along the wrists and the underside of the forearm, up the bicep, towards the armpit.

Becky has done a great job in emulating this look. She wears traditional Kung Fu clothing, which includes a black tunic with a Mandarin-style collar, black trousers, and black slippers. She has somehow managed to hide her burgeoning figure and make it appear more masculine, given that the character she is emulating is a man. The black tunic is cut off at the elbow, allowing the plastic green armour enveloping her forearm to peek through, the serrated spikes clearly visible. The most impressive part of the transformation is how she has replicated the praying mantis face.

The two globulous eyes have been created with her hair, which is up in two large buns at the upper corners of her head. These 'eyes' are temporarily dyed a very pale green, with two small brown dots sprayed on for pupils. She has gelled, bobble-tied and sculpted two antennae out of the remaining strands. When she wears her headset, they poke out on either side of the elastic strap that runs along the top of her head, and the 'eyes' sit above either side of the other strap, which circles the perimeter of her head.

A green piece of fabric is looped under her chin currently, as she is not wearing the headset, and pins into each of the two buns of hair, giving her face the shape of a downward facing arrowhead or triangle. The fabric is the same colour as her face, a light leafy green dappled with symmetrical splatterings of slightly lighter and slightly darker hues. At the base of her jaw, along the contours of her chin, a red line has been painted - giving the impression of a slightly open mouth. The effect of this facial illusion is most effective when she closes both her mouth and her eyes, of course, as when they are open their authenticity highlights the inauthenticity of their counterparts. But she seems to know this, occasionally looking in my direction with lips and eyelids firmly shut, tilting her head from side to side in playfulness- given the counter-productiveness a wink or a smile would bring to the goal of obscuring her features.

This is the fourth time I have figured out one of her outfits. I have won the challenge. She is now officially impressed. She has told me as much. I am feeling very happy. And when she looks at me and wiggles her praying mantis head from side to side, I feel like wiggling my head right back. But I remember her eyes are closed and she can't see my reaction anyway, and then I feel like it would be stupid to do so.

Lunchtime is approaching quickly and it's not just us at the reconnaissance desk today. A few other members of the extended team are in the office. Gregory is here, plugged in to his own Falcon. Well, it's a misnomer to say 'his own' Falcon. Despite my initial experience with Becky, where we both flew our respective Falcons together over the waters between Italy and Libya, in reality, in one day any one of us might flip through 10, 15, or even 20 Falcons, and we rarely fly side by side. There's a system of artificial intelligence which identifies objects of interest spotted by Falcons in autopilot travelling all over the skies covering the Mediterranean and Aegean Seas. These points of interest are flagged to our systems, and we flip between Falcons to assess them with a more critical eye, to see what we're really dealing with; a floating dinghy full of migrants rapidly approaching waters they 'have no business being in,' a cruise ship, a floating piece of debris, or even a military vessel.

On any given day we all have a particular region that we are in charge of patrolling. There are other teams across Europe doing similar work, and we do communicate with them too to ensure as much universal coverage as possible. But Gregory believes that our technology is superior, our AI systems better equipped at aptly and accurately identifying potential zones of interest, and our Falcons themselves the best reconnaissance tools currently available - discreet, unidentifiable from a distance, and viciously effective. I thought his use of the word 'viciously' was a little strange when he framed it like that, but I guess I do understand what he means.

As well as Gregory, Thomas and Farhad are both at the desk, currently. Thomas is a tall red-haired man in his twenties, stick thin and covered in freckles. He keeps himself to himself but he's generally polite. Despite being at the same desk as him, we haven't really exchanged more than pleasantries. Our schedules very rarely overlap, as he generally tries to avoid working Fridays and weekends. Farhad seems fairly cool, he's half-British Indian, and you can see some of the same features in his face as in my chauffeur Jeffrey's - prominent cheekbones, thick eyebrows, large almond eyes. Becky's desk is next to mine, however, and as lunchtime is practically upon us, she turns her head to me again, this time with her eyes wide open.

"So, Elijah," she says, "since you've impressed me so much, I thought we could have lunch together in one of the rotation pods. Praying mantises are ever so messy eaters, and I don't want to embarrass myself. But I'm sure you won't make fun of me."

I try to suppress my smile and give off an air of aloofness. The rotation pods are simple pods where the bed sheets are changed after every visitor by the cleaners. They are much smaller than the pods dedicated to one individual, usually a relatively established senior employee like Jill or Jim, who for some reason or the other find themselves staying overnight regularly. The rotation pods have no personal effects inside, and are for occasional use by an ever-shifting rotation of different individuals. They don't usually fill up, but it's considered good practice to book one in advance if you know you'll be having to stay the night. At this time of day they're always empty, a perfect place for a quiet lunch and an alternative to munching at the desk, or heading down the elevator to the cafeteria on the second floor.

"Messy eater?" I ask, rubbing my fingernails with my thumb and looking at them disinterestedly but feeling reckless. "That's an understatement. I heard that female praying mantises bite off their partners' heads after copulation."

I feel a slight impact on, followed by a very mild pain in, my left arm- and realise that Becky has hit me with the lower side of her forearm, with the serrated edge of her plastic pincers. Not at all a hard strike, more a playful slap, but those edges really are sharp.

"Elijah! I'm sorry? Elijah! You silly boy!" she says playfully. "I would never do such a thing. If you didn't know, Ming Lui is a male character, and combat mutants is a PG game after all. Where do you get your ideas from?" I don't move my head, but I shift my eyes to the left and see her smirking. I can't help smirking back. A playful smirk, not a Joe Gradle smirk or the smirk of the Home Secretary. I spotted her in the main building reception atrium this morning, wearing the same emerald earrings and necklace she had been wearing in Parliament, accompanied by a bodyguard, walking somewhere purposefully.

"I know the character's male by the way," I say belatedly. "Don't let a throwaway comment make you believe otherwise. I don't want you to change your mind about my success in our challenge. I hope I've still impressed you."

Her eyes are open now, and she definitely winks. "You impressed me the first time you flew a Falcon, Elijah. The challenge was just a bit of fun. You have your food? Ready?"

"Sure thing," I respond and grab my sandwich from my bag along with a bottle of lemonade and a packet of crisps, placing them on my lap.

We excuse ourselves from the desk and make our way over to the right-hand side of the room, walking towards the rotation pods at the very edge of its perimeter. Becky gestures towards one of the doors and I shrug, nodding, rolling my way towards it. Unlike the fancy security doors to the floor, with their sliding glass, this pod has a simple, regular door with a knob on it. It can be locked from the inside. Becky swings the door open and I roll inside. She follows me through, letting go of the door for it to swing shut behind her, but it doesn't seem to close the whole way, stopping a good three or four inches short. I look down towards the base of the door and see a small child's shoe poking through, having evidently blocked it from closing. It swings open again to reveal Tim Weibers, a takeaway box full of noodles in one hand.

"Private lunch for two, is it?" He raises his eyebrow and his tone drips with amusement. "Mind if I join you guys for a bite?"

I hear Becky sigh behind me, but I don't want to be rude.

"Hey Tim, we have some reconnaissance stuff to discuss. Work stuff for our desk, but..." His face starts to fall into a hurt frown and I quickly follow up my words. I had been intending to say, 'but we can catch up another time.' Instead, I find myself saying, "But you can come in for a few minutes, it'll be good to catch up. How's things in combat and control?"

Tim's smile reappears and he steps into the pod. Even though he's only 12, given that I'm in a chair and he's standing, his eye line is slightly higher than mine. Yes. In the world of the wheelchair, you have to look up to younger children.

"Crazy, man." Tim replies. "Things are crazy in the combat and control team. Had one Arab today. Group of about... 30. Storming the tunnels. Had to use a real bullet on him. Not a rubber one. He was just taking the rubber ones like they were insect bites. Had covered his head with some sort of bucket with holes cut into it. Might have been wearing something under his clothes. Anyway, this Arab starts bleeding everywhere after I shoot him in the hip. I mean everywhere. It's only when you see the real thing that you see the graphics in these games aren't always 100% there yet. You know? I mean, let's take Final Facedown III for example."

Tim looks at Becky. "Me and Elijah have gone toe to toe in Final Facedown III before, you see. That's how we met, actually. Before we met officially. With me serving him a bullet in the neck." Tim turns back to me and winks, I force a smile in reply.

He continues, "But take Final Facedown III. There's blood. And it looks like blood. And it could fool someone who's never seen a real person get shot. But the amount of blood is different. Right? And the sheen to it, the real stuff, slightly darker. Anyway, so I shoot this Arab and his wife's already in the back of the van, right? I think it was his wife. She was distraught when he went down. So she jumps out of the van and starts giving it the whole, 'oh my God', talking in one of these jibber-jabber languages. Couldn't catch a word but you could kind of tell what she was saying by the way she was moaning. And they're causing this big obstruction on the road, now. An obstruction on the road is no good. Slows down the vans behind, which makes it easier for more of these undesirables to break into them."

Tim pauses to take a large forkful of noodles and savours the bite, smacking his lips in pleasure before continuing.

"So now I'm thinking, how do I get this Arab off the road? I ordered his wife and one of the others to drag him off. But they don't seem to understand me. They're just shouting back in their gibberish. Even when I point the thing at them. Fire off a few rubber bullets at their feet. It's becoming a whole situation. Right? And who knows if Rush is monitoring my screen, seeing how I deal with this. So I end up dragging him off myself. Onto the pavement. And his wife is thumping away at the Enforcer. Trying to unclasp its fingers from him. Thinking I'm going to finish the job or something.

I smack her out of the way, now she's unconscious on the road, have to drag her too, after. The rest of their group is running away, now they've realised exactly what happened. Ricardo, Jackson, maybe Rush, the rest of the team are zooming about with their own Enforcers. Trying to deal with this havoc. I tell you what, Elijah. You missed out, not choosing combat and control. Never a boring day."

"Sounds riveting," Becky says, sarcastically. "Absolutely riveting."

"No need to sound so sceptical!" Tim responds. "I'm sure you had a lovely day... flying."

He flops his childish frame onto the bed and lies back, stretching out his arms in a position that says, 'I am getting comfortable ... even if I'm making you uncomfortable ... this is Tim time.' He continues munching away at his noodles, abandoning his fork and fishing out strands with his fingers, dangling them above his mouth and dropping them in. Maybe he thinks that using the fork would be more risky from this horizontal position, with more chance of noodles falling onto his chest or slipping onto his chin just before arriving at their intended destination.

Becky decides to draw a line in the sand and put her foot down. "It was lovely hearing about your day, Tim, but time to get lost, please. Elijah and I have some work we need to discuss that concerns the - oh so unexciting - idea of flying. We can move to the pod next door if you feel like a lunchtime nap and want to stay where you are, or you could leave us here to talk. You'll have plenty of time for catch-ups later."

Here, Tim gives a mock wail of despair and raises his hand above him in a fist, but tilted slightly forward as though it were clutching onto some invisible dagger. He plunges this invisible dagger into his heart and gives a, relatively quiet, pretend cry of anguish.

"You are killing me, Becky! Don't bite my head off! You're killing me here! All I wanted was a lunch date with two of my favourites!"

He hops up off the bed with a mischievous smile, the kind of smile that only a 12-year-old could give, but laced with the cynicism of a 12-year-old who has seen and perhaps done things most 12-year-olds, or adults for that matter, have not.

"I'm only joking," he continues. "I didn't mean to intrude." The words 'didn't', 'mean' and 'intrude' all lift in pitch at the end, giving the sentence a slightly whiny and falsely shocked tone that seems somewhat contrived. At the door, he turns and winks at me. "Good to see you again, Elijah. I'm sure we'll be great friends." He lifts up his fingers in a mock gun gesture and points them towards me.

"Pow."

CHAPTER 36

I remember when I first met Mustafa. This is not a passive statement. I do not mean that I have the memory ready to be conjured. I mean that now I am remembering vividly, eyes closed, as my parted legs swing and sway beneath me in rhythm with the camel. I see it clear as day. I am in school. My father is alive. I have not yet had to leave the institution. But I am lonely, so to speak, in my own way. My current friends are not true friends, though I do not know this yet. I spend much time with a boy called Usman. He is larger than me, but I am small for my age, which is 11. 11 and a half, officially, if you were wondering.

I usually sit with Usman and Atiku during class, where we gather outside, covered by a canopy of straw, ninety of us, before our single teacher, watching as he draws words upon a blackboard he has erected before us on the grass. He is called Mr. Abdel, and he takes no nonsense from us, no Sir! He understands, we understand, that school is a privilege. Many of us are the chosen ones in our families, the child who has been selected to continue with their studies in a family where funds do not allow for each and every child to be given that privilege. Troublemakers do not last long with Mr. Abdel, for trouble is contagious. Naughtiness can be caught. He is a strict disciplinarian, and children have before been asked to leave and not return.

There is a girl in my class, Farha, for whom I have a certain weakness. But given that there are 90 of us, and that she is popular with the other children, she sits with different people every day. When I wish to distract myself from the blackboard by gazing at the curls of her hair, it can require some scanning. My neck twists to the left, my eyes drifting over the assembled faces and landing not on Farha, but on a new and unfamiliar face. A young boy whose cheeky smile and aura of general mischief tell me he has not yet been acquainted comprehensively with Mr. Abdel, his latent but sensible firmness and his occasional fury. He is not looking at me when my eye falls upon him, he is not. This I distinctly remember, or rather I see it in my mind's eye currently. He is not looking at me, just as I could not look at him as I departed; could not see him amongst the smaller crowd. Not quite ninety. Not even twenty eight. A group reduced to 20. 20 souls, stranded amongst the dunes. He does not see me look at him for the first time and I do not see him look upon me for the last time, either. For he must have been looking. He was too invested in my departure not to have watched me ride away, made sure I took the opportunity for life, even if he was watching from a distance.

Something, perhaps a stray fly buzzing, perhaps a gust of wind, perhaps the fingers of fate, something turns his head to the right. A moment later, our eyes meet. We hold each other's gaze. Perhaps because we are children, there is no awkwardness in this, in simply sharing a line of sight, drinking in each other's eyes. He nods. I smile. Now it is lunchtime, and the meagre school fees cover some semblance of lunch, some small but not insignificant sustenance, a mound of ebba with watery soup. Usman, Atiku and I sit together, having just gone to collect our portions. Usman is about to take his customary extra pinch of ebba from my plate. After all, he is, “a full four centimetres taller” and always says, "my body is larger and therefore I need a little more, just like a bigger boot needs a bigger foot to fill it, you are a very good friend for understanding." I always let him take it, I would be lonely without my friends.

Before the fingers descend, however, the new boy plonks himself down before us, a smile plastered on his dark and chubby cheeks.

"City life," he says, "You guys are going to teach me all about city life. I come from village."

He doesn't at this point say his name, as though it is unimportant, as though he does not need to introduce himself, as though the connected gaze we shared this morning was greeting enough, or introduction enough, and now we are already friends. He doesn't say his name just now. He does say it later, but I have no need to tell you what it is. You already know. You have met him. You have spent time with him. You have seen his kindness. You have seen his selfless love for others. You have borne witness to his last days upon this earth.

"City boy, is that what I am?" I respond to him, smiling. "And you are the one who does not know of Mr. Abdel. You don't want to start causing trouble with him." The boy's smile widens and his eyes flick between me, Usman and Atika, maintaining contact with us all. New potential friends. But then the same eyes flicker downwards, following Usman's fingers in their trajectory towards my plate, his smile is replaced by the furrowed brow and taut lips of the questioner.

"Hey," he says, emphatically, his tone rising, "why you dey chop your brother's food? What if he's still hungry?"

Usman's eyebrows raise, and he blinks softly, aware that he is being challenged. He gives the same explanation as always. He is four centimetres taller than me. Actually, given his recent growth spurt, probably closer to six centimetres taller. He needs more food than I do.

The new boy, still nameless, nods sagely.

"Interesting," he says. "Stand up, I'd like to see your height."

Usman's jaw twists slightly. His teeth, four of which have fallen out quite recently, their adult-sized replacements pushing through, seem to grind. But he has given his explanation, and a reasonable request to prove it true has followed, so he obliges. The new boy stands as well, the first time I saw him, this morning, he had been seated. I did not notice him approaching us moments ago, not until he plopped himself down before us. Only now that I see him standing do I appreciate that he is tall. Taller than Usman. At least six centimetres taller than Usman. He smiles, sits down, before Usman has the chance to, and takes a large pinch of Ebba from Usman's plate, which is resting on the ground, placing it directly in his mouth. Usman sits down tentatively, now definitely frowning, but trapped by his own logic.

The unnamed boy speaks again. "I have a different idea," he says. "In the country, we grew our own food. And we often went hungry. But... also, we sometimes had enough to eat. Maybe eating more food makes you grow. Maybe your friend is shorter than you because you've been eating his food. Maybe, if you left it on his plate, he would have the growth spurt."

The new boy takes an even larger pinch of food from his own plate and dumps it on mine, winking at me in the process.

"Eat properly, and don't let your friend steal your food. Maybe one day you'll catch up to my height."

I never have of course.

Another memory. I'm 14 now. My father is dead. Mustafa had to leave the school before I did. Mustafa is from one of these families, the kind that has multiple children and cannot afford for all of them to engage in the luxury of schooling. His younger brother is smarter than him academically, and so his younger brother continues in the school whilst he and I, my father having passed, try to find some form of work, but there is no work to be had. Not for two 14-year-old boys with few skills. And so, we wander through the streets, trying to find the courage to reduce ourselves to begging.

One day a young boy who we knew from school, Jamal, appears across the road. We recognise him, and he recognises us, and he beckons us. Jamal was always a bit of a hustler. He used to steal his father's kola nuts and bring them into school to try to swap them for more valuable items with other students. Not that any of the students had much to give. But I do remember that when we started one academic year, Jamal had been one of the students without a backpack, one of the students who would push his notepad and his textbook up the back of his shirt and then tuck his shirt in to hold it in place, tightening his belt. This was something that the very poor students did. By the end of the year, Jamal had traded his kola nuts in for other items, and had traded himself all the way from kola nuts to a backpack. The backpack had originally belonged to Toyin, whose parents quickly replaced it when she lied and told them it was lost. If they ever came to pick her up from school, she would make sure she was nowhere near Jamal when they arrived.

And now Jamal has the look in his eyes that always used to precede one of his deals. Intrigued, we cross the road to greet him. Jamal gets straight to business.

"I have two bicycles. Brakes don't work well. A little rusty and a few other issues. But they get you around. Me, I can't ride bicycle. I have weak legs. But I don't want to sell them for small money. There's a farm just outside the city and I know they are looking for people to go carry some of their vegetables into the market. Can you two ride them?"

Mustafa nods, by this point of course I know his name. He says there used to be one bicycle in his village that a few of the children would share. I shake my head, but Mustafa puts his hand on my arm to stop me.

"I can teach him how to ride the second one," he says, gesturing towards me with his head.

Jamal looks pensive for a moment and then nods. "I want 20%," he says boldly.

"No, no, no," Mustafa responds. "You give us a price, a fair price for the bikes, and we pay it off with our work. And then they are ours and we can continue using them. I'm sure you can always find more bikes."

Jamal goes quiet for a second but then nods. "The price will be a little above what would be fair if you were buying it straight away." We all nod in agreement, shaking hands on the deal as though we were adults.

Mustafa follows through on his promise, teaching me how to cycle, taking me through the side streets of Sokoto where there are no cars to run me over; holding onto my handlebars to start with in order to stabilise me; being patient as I wobble forward; encouraging me to go faster, telling me that stability comes with speed, that hesitancy is what results in loss of balance. I learn.

We go to this farm and the farmer agrees to pay us a small amount to cycle with some of his products and deliver them to his niece in the Sokoto marketplace. The cycle down to the farmer is mostly downhill, so we freewheel our bikes on our way there, not bothering to pedal, letting gravity propel us through the dusty roads. The trip back is uphill and some of the other cyclists helping to transport these goods show us a trick. They grip onto the sides of passing vehicles, letting the vehicle pull the bike uphill. The drivers rarely complain and, when they do, it is easy enough to let go of the car and grab onto another.

For a few weeks we are working, we are making a small amount of money to supplement the survival of our families. But, as you already know, it is not to last. A car swerves suddenly one day, blocking the route of the vehicle to which Mustafa is clinging. The driver slams the brakes immediately, but Mustafa himself, with no working brakes to slam on the bicycle, continues his momentum forward, tumbling over the handlebars and into the corner of the vehicle. His bike rolls onwards and smashes into the vehicle too, before tumbling back down the steep hill we are climbing. By the time it stops, it is no longer rideable, with a mangled wheel, twisted handlebars and a chain that has snapped in two.

Thankfully, Mustafa emerges from the accident with only a black eye and a broken tooth. He buys himself another chance at life. Another few years of life until... no, too difficult to think about. I am in the past, not in the present.

Jamal, of course, is not well pleased. We haven't yet managed to raise the full amount we promised him for the bikes, but I still have my bike and tell him I will pay the difference. The problem is that two weeks later, the left pedal and pedal arm fall off. I take it to a street mechanic who tells me that the teeth on the crankshaft are worn, and it needs a new one. He doesn't have the right size crankshaft and he doesn't think the bike is even worth saving for the money it would cost to buy one new. The bike is written off. The mechanic tells me that the teeth had been wearing for a while and this is something which had been a problem since before I bought the bike, "a ticking time bomb," is his choice of phrase. Once I relay this information to Jamal, he agrees to only charge for Mustafa's broken bike. We pay off the remaining balance and return to hopeless destitution.

Bump, sway, the camel moves beneath me. I open up my eyes, returning to the present. The camel directly in front of me, connected to my own by a rope, is riderless. It is weighed down by a heavy cargo of goods, and its short tail swooshes as it trots. The camel in front of it bears Princess. Jibril is walking at the front of the caravan, guiding it with quick and assured steps. The Tubu nomads seem to rotate roles, some of them walking in front, holding the rope, carving out the path for the caravan to follow, whilst others sit atop the bulky animals. They swap at semi-regular intervals, allowing themselves a sip of water and powering on. When they swap, the ease with which they dismount and mount the camels is astounding. Their stamina is admirable, but not infinite. An hour or so passes before we stop for the night.

The location that we stop in is a flat sandy area, close to a local well. The surrounding landscape is dominated by sand dunes, but this area itself has level ground. The sun is setting in the west. Though the sky is a deep shade of blue, a warm glow is cast across the desert. Jibril and his companions walk down the row of camels, yanking at the ropes until their heads lower and they bend down on their knees again, allowing us to dismount. The Tubu set up their tents. We help them take the wooden poles and material from the back of one of the camels, hammer the poles in the ground, and wrap the tent around them. Ropes and pegs secure its corners to the sand, the pegs are long and pointed, tapering towards the end, in order to provide stability, given that sand is not as firm as soil. We drive them into the ground with heavy mallets.

I know I should be happy, perhaps ecstatic. Hours earlier, I believed myself to be facing certain death, but the rescue is bittersweet, and I sit alone and brood, before the sound of footsteps makes me lift my head. Kehinde walks towards me. A smile adorns the space between her cheeks and yet her eyes betray that she too tastes the sourness of our salvation.

"We were interrupted," she says. "I didn't get the opportunity to answer your question. You asked me who exactly I was, to give you my story. Let's go and make some friends amongst our rescuers. Maybe try and learn some French. Eat something. Drink something. And I will tell you my story tomorrow, or the day after, or even next week. And I will be alive to tell it. And you will be alive to hear it. Our journey is not over."

CHAPTER 37

"You're very well adjusted for a gamer," Becky tells me, perched upon the bed that Tim Weibers has recently vacated, settling into her lunch. "Very well adjusted. I used to do tournaments, you know? That's how the Home Office found me. Big video game competitions, where I would be one of the only girls. A lot of the boys weren't so well adjusted. After all, you have to have a certain personality to spend 15 hours a day playing in the VirtuWorld, and some of them put in shifts that long, I'm sure of it. Yes, there was some natural talent, but you didn't get to that level without some level of obsession. Some obsessive personalities. Well, you don't seem to have one."

I smile wistfully at her, and respond.

"I don't think it was my personality that drew me to the VirtuWorld. I didn't stumble into it either. I rolled into it. If it wasn't for the chair, I don't think I would have played as much as I did, as I do. And I wouldn't have gotten this good."

"Hmm..." Becky looks thoughtful. "But the chair hasn't changed you. Has it? Obviously, I didn't know you before the chair..." She shakes her hands slightly and opens her eyes wide on these two words: the chair. "But... this might sound weird, but I hope it didn't change you. I like who you are today."

She flashes her teeth, pearly-whites nestled between her green lipstick, which melts into makeup on her skin.

The butterflies that start to flutter their wings within my stomach are somewhat neutralised by my surprise at the naivety of her statement, and I only manage a weak smile back as I mutter,

“Everything changes you, Becky, some things more than others."

Becky goes quiet, noticing the falter in my smile. She lets the silence stretch until it's almost uncomfortable, and I start to regret my knee-jerk defensiveness, realising she was giving me a compliment and that I took it as a slight.

"I'm sorry," I say." I didn't mean to..."

"No," she interjects. "You don't have to explain. Of course it changed you. It was a silly thing for me to say."

"Me too," I say.

"What you said wasn't silly," she responds.

"No, I don't mean that," I say.

"You too, what then?" she asks.

"Me too... I like who you are today," I say, looking at my knees.

The silence re-emerges, and the silence is not tempered by the sound of Becky chewing, or myself rustling through the packet of crisps nestled in the crook between my legs. Both of us sit still, awkwardly. The muffled sounds of the control room do filter through the glass door of the rotation pod, but nothing is distinguishable. The underlying hum of noise is not a hum from which any concrete meaning can be drawn, and so the soundscape is as good as silent.

Becky sneezes.

"Bless you." I say.

"Thank you," she replies.

We go quiet again. 20 seconds or so pass, and then Becky takes the initiative and opens her mouth again to speak.

“What would you think about maybe...”

She gets no further. The door to the pod springs open and Gregory stumbles in, holding our respective headsets and gloves in both his hands, and afflicted by a furrowed brow. "Emergency," he pants. "A Level 9. Becky, lunch break is over. I need you in the skies." Gregory's eyes flicker towards me and for a second I can almost see the question mark written across the lines on his forehead. His eyes flick to Becky once again as if asking for confirmation. He looks at me once more.

"You're ready, right? You think you can handle a real mission in the field? This is a level 9. Won't be pretty."

"I can handle it," I say confidently. "Why wouldn't I be able to?"

Gregory bites his bottom lip and then nods, throwing me my headset and gloves. "No time to roll back to the desk, and no point really. Just log in here and get a hold of a Falcon. We want you around coordinates 34.659, 12.711. Once you've connected to a Falcon around there, you'll see what we're dealing with. Elijah, I need you focused and ready. I don't want any squeamishness. You've come into this job on an accelerated program and there's no point trying to rose-tint your view of what will be needed. Joe will be dialling in and we can coordinate over audio. I'm heading to my desk. See you shortly."

Gregory removes himself from the room and I look over at Becky, who has a focused look on her face and is pulling on her gloves. I do the same, getting gloved up and pulling on my headset. "Open Falcon Finder." we both say, almost in unison, and before me I see a large interactive map. The map stretches from Iceland, at the top left of my field of vision, all the way down to Iraq, at the bottom right, and a number of red dots indicate the location of hundreds of Falcons, mostly centred in hot spots between Morocco and Spain, Libya, Tunisia and Italy, Egypt, Turkey and Greece.

"What were the coordinates again?" I shout in Becky's direction, but Gregory's voice answers me through my headset.

"I've dialled you in. 34.659, 12.711,"

"Thanks Gregory." I reply, repeating the coordinates. The map zooms in to a location just north of Tripoli and east of the Tunisian Kerkennah Islands. I use a pointed finger to move a small, winged icon around in the air before me, before landing on one of the red dots and bending the finger.

"Falcon selected," comes a smooth, feminine voice. "Falcon 12C46F. Commandeer Falcon?"

"Yes, commandeer Falcon," I confirm. The map shimmers out of existence and is replaced by the real time perspective of the electronic bird. I quickly slot my hands into position and begin the process of controlling its movements, as I am aware that the autopilot which has controlled it thus far will be shutting itself off. Okay, so what exactly is a Level 9? What am I looking for? Straight ahead of me, of course, is only sky. But below me, well, they call it a bird's eye view for a reason. I look down. Boats, almost all of them inflatable dinghies. Not just one or two, but dozens. Hundreds, perhaps. Spaced out enough so as not to jeopardise the safety of each other, but nonetheless, far more than would be expected.

"Trying to overwhelm us," Gregory speaks through the intercom again. "It's a regular tactic. Normal at the Great Walls of Ceuta and Melilla. Jim probably told you about it. They'll all try to hit the wall at once in order to overwhelm the defences. Well, it seems as though they've realised something similar can be done at sea. There's only so much reconnaissance we can do. Only so much that the Libyan coast guard can do. Only so much the OctoBots can do to drag boats back. They're relying on our good nature. Assuming we won't get our hands dirty. But we have a job to do. Okay, for now, Elijah, get higher. Scan. Keep us informed as to where the greatest concentration of boats is. Becky, with me, down low. Numbers are too much. There's too many of them for us to play nice. We've got to scare them. Get them to turn back."

A slight sound of static, and then a familiar voice joins the conversation. The low and very formal voice of Joe Gradle. "Sink a few of them."

"What???" I find myself asking loudly, before almost clamping my hand over my mouth. I don't, of course. My hands are occupied. But I do wonder as to whether my expression of incredulity would be taken badly. Of course, I'm in the pod rather than the control room, and Becky's also got her headset on, so no one would see me if I did.

"Sink. A. Few." repeats Joe Gradle. Putting emphasis on every word. "They're choosing to put themselves in danger. Make the danger real. Deterrence. Once they see a few boats sinking, hopefully the others will be smart enough to turn back. Start with beaks and wings. That should be enough. If necessary, commandeer some of the newer offensive Falcons."

"They're deployed near Turkey at the moment," Gregory responds, "or most of them are. It'll take a while for them to fly all the way to these coordinates. We won't have access immediately."

"What the hell are they doing near Turkey?" asks Joe. "They should be dispersed throughout the skies."

"They're still experimental," replies Gregory heatedly. "You only commissioned 10. We did ask for more. Turkey was a hot-spot yesterday."

"Well, as I say, beaks for now. Beaks and wings," Joe responds, "OctoBots are en route. Elijah, where's the flow of boats thickest?"

Having been paying more attention to the conversation than the flotilla of dinghies and rickety boats below me, I don't have an answer immediately prepared, but I raise my Falcon higher at Joe Gradle's question, trying to forget his suggestion to sink boats full of people as a deterrent, and not quite managing.

“Towards Malta,” I say. “There’s quite a lot of them in a single area more towards the islands.”

“Okay,” says Gregory seriously. “Becky. Farhad, Tom, I need you on it. Peck at the rubber dinghies with the beaks as we’ve practised. Avoid wooden boats for now, if there are any, or fibreglass. I doubt there’ll be steel but it’s possible. Aim for rubber dinghies, those that are large and visible to other boats, not the solitary ones. Peck in a few places, but don’t let them sink too quickly. Don’t decimate them. A slow, drawn-out sink lasts longer, is visible for longer, and will act as more of a deterrent."

"Falcon, split screen," I murmur, aware that I am supposed to be observing the general formation of boats from up high and not examining details, but unable to help myself. The familiar line separating the Falcon's current normal perspective and a zoomed-in optional perspective draws itself across the screen. I squint, and the left-hand side of my field of vision zooms in towards the ocean, towards the boats. Men, women, children, babies, grandparents, all are present. Some wear life jackets, some do not. The boats are packed tightly, many of the people having to sit on the edges, their feet dangling in the water. One little brown girl, her hair cut short, is crying fearfully. I cannot hear her, of course, I am literally hundreds of metres above her, and the zoom does not quite allow for enough detail for me to be able to distinguish individual tears, but I see enough to know that she is crying, and not much older than my sister June.

"Elijah, have any of them got close to Malta yet?" Gregory says. I don't respond.

"Elijah," Joe Gradle's voice brings me back. "I need you to get back to the present. I know this is a tough mission, and I'm sorry for it. But we have to do this. We are the guardians at the gate. These people are not welcome. Deterring them from crossing is key. Think of it this way: Sinking a few boats now will save lives in the future if it stops those who it causes to turn around from trying to re-enter Europe later. Get your head in the game. Earn your salary. Gregory is asking you a question."

"Malta, any of them close?" Gregory reiterates.

I focus on the right-hand side of my field of vision, glancing towards the island of Malta. None of the boats are quite within its vicinity yet.

"No, none of them are too close yet," I reply, awkwardly. "But they're headed that way."

"They will be soon enough then," responds Gregory, "unless we do something about it. I'm approaching their northernmost vessels now."

I glance down, looking for the other team members' Falcons, but the issue is that the regular perspective is too far away to make out individual birds, and the zoomed-in perspective is currently too close to give a decent chance of looking in the right direction. I widen my eyes, the opposite of squinting. Sure enough, this reverses the zoom in the left side of my field of vision to a point where I can comfortably look for Gregory's, Becky's and the others' Falcons.

A few moments later, I perceive it, a shifting in the sky. A dive. The movement of wings. I squint again, following the bird in its descent to see it drive its beak into one of the boats, rise, loop over itself and come down again intentionally. I imagine the people on board begin to scream as the air that provides their buoyancy trickles out with a rasp. As the boat begins to sink, from underneath the waves, emerging on each side to envelop it, perhaps to pull it downwards, I see tentacles. Giant tentacles.

Printed in Great Britain
by Amazon

38177648R00165